CW00864990

Romantic Reveries

The Revolt Against Reason in Christianity, Government, and Human Nature

W. F. Moquin

Copyright © 2019 W. F. Moquin.

All rights reserved. No part of this book may be used or reproduced by any means, graphic, electronic, or mechanical, including photocopying, recording, taping or by any information storage retrieval system without the written permission of the author except in the case of brief quotations embodied in critical articles and reviews.

This book is a work of non-fiction. Unless otherwise noted, the author and the publisher make no explicit guarantees as to the accuracy of the information contained in this book and in some cases, names of people and places have been altered to protect their privacy.

WestBow Press books may be ordered through booksellers or by contacting:

WestBow Press
A Division of Thomas Nelson & Zondervan
1663 Liberty Drive
Bloomington, IN 47403
www.westbowpress.com
1 (866) 928-1240

Because of the dynamic nature of the Internet, any web addresses or links contained in this book may have changed since publication and may no longer be valid. The views expressed in this work are solely those of the author and do not necessarily reflect the views of the publisher, and the publisher hereby disclaims any responsibility for them.

Any people depicted in stock imagery provided by Getty Images are models, and such images are being used for illustrative purposes only.
Certain stock imagery © Getty Images.

ISBN: 978-1-9736-6622-6 (sc)
ISBN: 978-1-9736-6623-3 (hc)
ISBN: 978-1-9736-6621-9 (e)

Library of Congress Control Number: 2019907998

Print information available on the last page.

WestBow Press rev. date: 7/05/2019

A Preface on Biases

Daniel Patrick Moynihan once said that everyone is entitled to his own opinions, but no one is entitled to his own facts. This book is filled with my own opinions, but they are all based on someone else's facts. The reason so many authors are mentioned is to prove I don't just make things up. The biases will be evident, so I may as well spell them out now. I stand within Christianity, although often on unsteady feet. As to politics, I have no party loyalty, because I believe that inventing government was humanity's greatest mistake – necessary as it was. That I am more biased against one American political party than another is because I regard one of them more dangerous to the future liberty and prosperity of the United States than the other. Had all of this been written a hundred years ago, my opinion on the political parties would have been reversed. As to human nature, my basis of analysis is the Hebrew Bible, augmented by the New Testament.

This book was obviously written, but it would be more accurate to say it was accumulated. It was a process of more than 20 years. That will be evident from dates that appear throughout. The project was finally finished in early 2019, and there are a lot of repeated statements simply because when I left the manuscript for a long period of time I forgot what had already been written.

I am not under any illusion that this is a scholarly work. It is simply the result of reading and rereading history for 70 years. The study of economics came later in life, sometime in the early 1980s. Theology, which I have largely abandoned, was and on and off study. Readers who know history will find little that is new. Those who live within Christianity, or who are opposed to it, will find some controversial ideas. As to economics, I have been affiliated with the Austrian School for some time. For those not familiar with its take on economics, the school was inadvertently founded in Vienna by Carl Menger in the early 1870s. I say "inadvertently" because his writings attracted followers who brought his views into the 20th century and expanded on his work. It is the Austrian School that has shaped my views on government. Anyone interested in learning about it can contact the Mises Institute in Auburn, Alabama at mises.org.

I am in debt to so many people for helping me learn. A couple of them are mentioned in the text – Mortimer Adler especially. By some quirk of fate he enabled me to meet Mark Selko, who lives in Beverly Hills. It was Mark who put me on to what I describe as the way the world works. Neither of them, for all the debt I owe them, would be in agreement with the results printed in this volume. Although one of them would agree more.

Part 1: Isn't It Romantic?

Chapter 1 A Necessary Foundation

> "The heart has its reasons, which Reason knoweth not." (Blaise Pascal)

> "The romantics admired not reason and intellect but deep emotion, subjective sensibility, and imagination. They exalted the heroic and the mystical rather than tolerance and rationality." (Walter Isaacson, in *Benjamin Franklin,* p. 478)

> "Emotion is the antithesis of logic. If somebody gets the promise of an easy happy ending, they'll buy it over reality any day." P. J. Tracy in *The Guilty Dead*)

To make sense of the title, a short explanation is needed. Some years ago, while doing research, I read a book on romanticism. It included material on *The Romantic Movement,* the title of a 1994 book by Maurice Cranston, but it included much more. When capitalized, Romanticism normally refers to a movement in the arts – painting, sculpture, poetry, and novels. Cranston's book, to be sure covers broader aspects and traces the movement in several nations. But the earlier volume, whose author I've forgotten, maintained that the uncapitalized romanticism has for centuries, had a significant impact on human activities throughout history.

A more recent work, *The Roots of Romanticism,* by the late Isaiah Berlin cleared away a lot of the fog that hovered over the subject. He did a brilliant job of defining the essential qualities of the Enlightenment and the character of the Romantic rebellion against it. For the Enlightenment thinkers there was an objective natural order of things that we can all perceive. They noted that Isaac Newton had brought order to the field of physics. Berlin then adds: "Surely, if this kind of order could be instituted in the world of physics, the same method would produce equally splendid and lasting results in the worlds of morals, politics, aesthetics, and in the rest of the chaotic world of human opinion." (p. 24). From this notion came the 19th century conviction of perpetual progress, an idea that came to a sudden halt in World War I. To me it was in itself a romantic notion, because it envisioned possibilities that could not be achieved. Why not? Because there was in Europe, the United States and elsewhere a much too optimistic view of human nature.

I regard the Enlightenment as one of the two strands of thought that defined the disasters of the 20th century. The other strand emerged from the peculiar and diffuse qualities of Romanticism that evolved in the German states during the 18th century. Isaiah Berlin did not attempt to define Romanticism. Considering all of its vagaries, it probably cannot be done. In his book *The Birth of the Modern* (1991), Paul Johnson notes that attempts were made in the early 19th century to come up with a definition. After coming up with more than 150, the attempt was given up.

But there were basic elements that give it coherence. First of all is the denial that there is a nature of things. "There was no structure of things because that would hem us in, that would suffocate us. There must be a field for action. The potential is more real than the actual." (p. 114)

The word "action" in the preceding quotation encapsulates so much of what the romantics believed. There is more to the universe, to nature, and to human nature that can be grasped by reason alone, than can be ordered, regulated, mandated, or even described. In nature itself there is great turbulence. In human nature there is will, passion, desire, appetite, the ability to imagine and create the new and unprecedented. This is the "field for action." This is the Kantian doctrine of free will – that human beings are not and must not be constrained or determined from the outside in their decision making.

We can, then, create the world we want, from works of art, literature, and music, all the way to the kind of society we want, heedless of any so-called external laws that only serve to circumscribe action. From this, it is not too far a step to the notion current among many that everything is socially constructed and can, therefore, be deconstructed. There is no essence of things; there is simply the existence we have and that we can change by effort of will through action. Existentialism, too, played a role here.

If all of this seems bizarre, it is probably because every thinking individual today would see that there is some validity in both viewpoints. There is an objective world, however well we can perceive it; there are laws of nature, and there are rational ways of living that most people accept. Conversely, within every human being there are will, emotion, desire, appetites, and passions that have played significant roles in every era of the past. What occurred when Romanticism appeared was the separation of these two compatible views into warring factions.

Granted, much of the above is simplified. The Age of Reason is relatively easy to get hold of; Romanticism, which originated in Germany in the 1770s, is not. Thus the bare bones of the matter above. To get the whole picture, one really should get Berlin's book or turn to chapter three of Jerome Blum's *In The Beginning: The Advent of the Modern Age* (1994). But the point is this: the modern era, from the late 18th century to the present, has been dominated in nearly every field of endeavor, by an uneasy and flawed weaving together of these two great strands of thought, Reason and Romanticism.

What fascinates me is what happens when romanticism overflows its banks in to the political and social realms, as it did first in the French Revolution, in fascist Italy, in Nazi Germany, and most certainly in the Soviet Union, and then beyond. In these instances, it often envisioned what are in effect unrealizable goals, programs, and demands – in sum, utopian dreams. It is necessary to realize that nationalism, as it grew from the late 18th century onwards, is an ideology opposed to what was then commonly called cosmopolitanism, or what we might call one-worldism. In Ivan Turgenev's short novel, *Rudin,* one of the characters, remarks that "Cosmopolitanism is rubbish, and the cosmopolitan is a nonentity, worse that a nonentity; outside of national roots there is neither art, nor truth, nor life, nothing." (Chapter 12) Here in a single sentence, we have one of the main roots of the anti-Semitism that flourished in Europe for centuries. The other root is Christendom's centuries-long denunciation of the Jews. This, in my mind, is the worst of Christendom's many crimes.

The British historian Tim Blanning addresses the same notion in his comprehensive *The Pursuit of Glory: Europe 1648-1815* (2007). In the introduction he states that "[It] makes more sense to conceptualize cultural developments not as a linear progression from faith to reason but as a dialectical encounter between a culture of feeling and a culture of reason." (P. xxvii) Later in the book he devotes a whole chapter to the subject, and the chapter is well worth reading.

In the mind of the German philosopher Johann Gottfried Fichte and others, the nation was defined by its ethnicity and its language (as it would be for Adolf Hitler). The 19th and 20th century in Europe provided vivid examples of what happens when this kind of nationalism is carried to its logical extreme. Most notorious were the pogroms carried out against the Jews in Russia and other Eastern European countries. (In Europe the Jews, regarded as a stateless people, were viewed as the prime examples of cosmopolitanism.) When the Austro-Hungarian Empire was broken up after World War I, nationalism took hold in the newly independent states, resulting in the persecution of ethnic minorities. Nazi Germany was the most extreme example. But, decades before Hitler, there was the Dreyfus Affair in France. That many-year episode brought anti-Semitism out in force.

Occasionally there was success in milder forms of nationalism in Europe – the unification of Italy and Germany, for example. Usually there is failure, accompanied by disastrous consequences: the Russian Revolution, Nazi Germany; Mussolini's fascism, Mao's China, and the mess the British and the French made in dividing up the Middle East after World War I. (An excellent book on that sad subject was published in 2012: *A Line in the Sand: The Anglo-French Struggle for the Middle East, 1914-1948* by James Barr. It is an excellent counterpart to David Fromkin's *A Peace to End All Peace* of 1989.) The problem with the British and French in the Middle East was the failure to do what made sense instead of using power to do what they wanted, regardless of consequences. Sadly, the consequences are with us today in endless strife.

Part of the point I make below, in the section devoted to government, is that the French Revolution was mostly a Romantic revolution, while the earlier American Revolution was largely an Enlightenment revolution. Here, revolution does not just mean the war for independence but the whole course of events leading up to the war and well beyond it. John Adams wrote of this in 1818 for the *Niles Weekly Register*: "The Revolution was in the minds and hearts of the people, a change in their religious sentiments of their duties and obligations….This radical change in the principles, opinions, sentiments, and affections of the people was the real American Revolution."

These assertions are not so simple, however. Utopias, from Plato until Marx, were rationally devised in part, based on the natural order of things – an Enlightenment view. But then the determination to create by efforts of will what proves to be basically implausible comes into play – the Romantic endeavor. The French Revolution began as an Enlightenment effort to restructure French society according to rules of reason. Within a few years it degenerated into a Romantic effusion of disordered passions, of will against will, a mad power struggle that ended in autocracy.

The previous paragraph implies the frustrating aspect of reason versus romanticism: thinking, will power, and emotions coexist within every individual and within every society.

A brief note on Utopia. The word is derived from the Greek. The *topia* part is from *topos,* meaning place, as in topography. The U can be looked at in two ways. Ou, or no, gives a negative view, while Eu makes it positive. Thomas More's *Utopia* is a positive interpretation, while Aldous Huxley's *Brave New World* is negative.

What Mussolini did in Italy and Hitler in Germany were Romantic dreams that ended in nightmares, the excesses of the will to power. The consequences of this blending of Reason and Romanticism for Western Civilization have been enormous. We are still living with the unintended results of all these failed endeavors, and will be for some time. The problem with the past is that it is never really over.

Tipping points. There have been times in the past when the course of events takes a sharp turn, and the consequences are often not recognized until much later. Consider Alexander the Great's conquest of the Middle East, Persia, and Egypt. The result was the spread of Greek culture throughout the region, with a major focus on Alexandria, where some outstanding scholarship took place. One specific result was the translation of the Hebrew Bible into Greek, a volume known as the Septuagint. This translation would have a significant impact during the spread of Christianity in the earliest years, because many non-Jews had become acquainted with Judaism. This fact made them more open to the message of St. Paul.

Another tipping point was the assassination of Julius Caesar in 44 BCE. The result of the conflicts that followed brought his adopted son Octavian to the role of emperor as Augustus. The empire, which lasted in the West until the 5th century, was the high point of civilization up to that time. Its fall led to localism and nearly endless wars for the next thousand years. The achievements of the empire culturally were lost until the Renaissance, and its road-building and water supply techniques were not recovered until the 19th century.

The Reformation of the 16th century ended the domination of the Latin Church in the West. Started by Martin Luther and augmented by Ulrich Zwingli and John Calvin in Switzerland and John Knox in Scotland, Protestantism came to dominate much of northern Europe. In England, as is well known, King Henry VIII broke with the Vatican because the pope would not allow him to divorce Catherine of Aragon. He made himself the head of what he called the English Catholic Church. But by the time of his daughter Elizabeth's reign, the nation had become Protestant by law.

Twenty-five years before the Reformation began, Columbus sailed across the Atlantic to reach what we now call the Far East. Instead, he discovered the Western Hemisphere. Needless to say, the world has never been the same since.

In Europe and North America there was a spirit of optimism in the late 19th and early 20th centuries.

Perpetual progress was the mindset of the time. Then came what historian Barbara Tuchman called the guns of August, the start of World War I in 1914. The most prominent result of this calamity was World War II, and Europe – along with the rest of the world, has never been the same. The German Empire, the Russian Empire, the Austro-Hungarian Empire, and the Ottoman Empire all collapsed; and thanks to the German military in 1917, the short-lived Russian Republic was overthrown by the Bolsheviks. The consequences of the Great War of 1914-18 are still with us in the Middle East.

The Great Depression started following the stock market collapse of October 1929. President Herbert Hoover was unable to deal with it and lost the election of 1932 to Franklin D. Roosevelt. The New Deal policies of the Roosevelt administration changed the course of American politics. Both political parties operate on the playing field he created. More than ending the Depression was at stake. What followed in succeeding decades was the complete involvement of the federal government in the economy. How that will play out is still uncertain.

During the years that I was writing this book, Rodney Stark published his *The Victory of Reason: How Christianity Led to Freedom, Capitalism, and Western Success* (2005). It is a very effective refutation of Romanticism, although the word itself does not appear in the book – at least it's not in the index. He maintains that "Faith in reason is the most significant feature of Western civilization." Mr. Stark also debunks certain historical myths. My favorite is the suggestion that the Dark Ages were not really all that dark.

I end this section with a statement by John Gray,

emeritus professor at the London School of Economics, excerpted from the *Times Literary Supplement* (London) of January 2, 2012, as quoted in the *Wall Street Journal* of January 19, 2012. "Old-fashioned despots may modernize in piecemeal fashion if doing so seems necessary to maintain their power, but they do not aim at remaking society in a new model, still less at fashioning a new type of humanity. Communist regimes engaged in mass killing in order to achieve these transformations, and paradoxically it is this essentially totalitarian ambition that has appealed to liberals....Liberals have seen the Communist experiment as a hyperbolic expression of their own project of improvement."

Chapter 2 Unintended Consequences: Getting to Where I Am

I saw in print once that Pablo Picasso said: "I do not paint what I see; I paint what I know is there." In that spirit, I will try to write about what I know is there, neither hampered nor deceived by the labels attached that confound the conventional wisdom. Unlike many of my friends and relatives, I was not brought up to think a certain way about anything. I was not raised to be a Democrat, Republican, Communist or Socialist, so I've had to muddle through on my own. Fortunately. I will certainly be judged wrong by many who read this, if ever there are any.

***

Praise Without Blame: An Acknowledgement

Some of the individuals who have been of great assistance to me through the years are mentioned in the text, as are the many authors from whose works I have freely stolen. The individuals I've known personally were not people who walked across the national or international stage to any wide acclaim, with one exception.

Mortimer J. Adler died on June 28, 2001, at the age of 98.5 exactly. His death closed a very significant chapter in my life, since I had worked for him and with him for 30 years, while he was chairman of the board of editors at Encyclopaedia Britannica. He gave me a career without intending to. When I started work in his office late in 1964, I did not expect that he would become my mentor any more than he sought to undertake that task. The influence he exercised was due to proximity, through conversations, through attending his lectures, and from reading his books. Mortimer was a man of incredible brilliance, with knowledge of a wide range of subjects. He taught me how to think clearly and how to use words. He did not teach me what to think about; that was already in hand – or rather, in mind. Looking back, I suspect he never quite knew what to make of me, because our backgrounds were so different; be he trusted me to do the assigned work, and I don't think I ever failed him in that. He was always a good and generous friend; and the debt I owe him cannot be repaid.

Perhaps by explaining myself, I am rendering payment in part. I suspect, however, that he would not want such a reimbursement; because where I have ended up is quite far from where he did. He was an Aristotelian and a Thomist. I was never ideological, not even in my Lutheran heritage. Thus, while I owe him so much, he cannot be blamed for the conclusions I have come to. Were he still here, we would doubtless have some amazing discussions.

In the first paragraph of the *Metaphysics*, Aristotle states that all men desire to know. Today we would say, "All people desire to know." Stated either way, it is manifestly wrong. How so careful an observer of life, of human nature, could have made this error puzzles me. Even at his time it should have been obvious that the bulk of humanity is satisfied in knowing very little, and that mostly to do with how to make a living or how to get out of doing so. Even those who have genuine leisure to pursue learning rarely do it, except within a very narrow frame. Aristotle rightly understood that schooling preceded education and that it was the responsibility of those who had been well schooled to educate themselves during adulthood. We may assume that he spoke of the desire to know as pertaining to the elites of his day, those who had the responsibility of governing the city-state.

There is a peculiar 38th chapter in the book of *Ecclesiasticus,* a book accepted by some as belonging to the Hebrew Bible. The author states: "The wisdom of the scribe depends on the opportunity of leisure; and he who has little business may become wise. How can he who handles the plow, and who glories in the shaft of the goad, who drives oxen and is occupied with their work, and whose talk is about bulls? …So too is every craftsman and master workman who labors by night as well as by day…. So too is the smith sitting by the anvil, intent upon his handiwork in iron….So too is the potter sitting at his work and turning the wheel with his feet…All these rely upon their hands, and each is skillful in his own work. Without them a city cannot be established, and men can neither sojourn nor live there. Yet they are not sought out for the council of the people, and they do not attain eminence in the public assembly….But they keep stable the fabric of the world, and their prayer is in the practice of their trade. (Revised Standard Version). The New English Bible ends he passage with slightly different wording: "But they maintain the fabric of this world, and their prayers are about their daily work."

The previous two paragraphs seem only tenuously related. How to relate them? For one thing, Aristotle would never have praised the common work of the world so effusively. (The verses quoted may well be the only passage in ancient literature to do so.) The notion that ordinary tradesmen and artisans, even slaves, could maintain "the fabric of this world" would have been absurd to him, as it would have been to Plato, and as it has been to most elites for most of human history. One can read contempt for regular work in the novels of the 19th century, in Dickens, in Trollope, in George Eliot, in Balzac, and many others. Arnold Bennett is the chief exception to this rule. It is also present in nonfiction writers of the time, among them Karl Marx and other socialists. Such was Lenin's contempt for the average worker, especially for the farmer, that he rewrote Marx; he proclaimed the need for a "vanguard of the proletariat" to lead the revolution and to bring about the better world. How many of today's politicians similarly regard themselves as the vanguard of democracy, in the hope that voters will be sufficiently fooled into thinking there's a better world waiting on the other side of the next election?

Lest one think I am being too selective in criticizing the Communist butchers, think back to the Middle Ages. How much real respect did Christendom have for the ordinary laypeople? Precious little, if my reading of history is adequate. The same may be said for all religions that I've ever read about. Those at the top reap the rewards of the work done by those at the bottom. Thus it has ever been. Knowledge, which is said to be power, was the province of the few at the expense of the many. That has changed little. The many still seem to shy away from too much learning. In many ways they cannot be blamed. To make one's living adequately, to seek to better one's condition, within the limits of a short lifetime is about all most people can do. This was especially true when a lifetime meant only 30 or 40 years.

Whether the ancient contempt for those who do the basic work of the world persists is hard to say. But the evidence of it abounds when one considers the huge incomes paid to movie stars, rock bands, and professional athletes versus even the best-paid workers in any field, apart from high-tech companies. Perhaps those who work on Wall Street are also exceptions. It is also worth noting that in the United States government workers generally get higher salaries than workers in the private sector, while it is the income in the private sector that pays for the nonproductive work of government officials.

If Aristotle is mistaken in his claim about knowledge, the author of *Ecclesiasticus* is also in error. His verdict on the workers of the world, those who make the world go round, is sound. And it is the only ancient passage I am aware of that contains such fulsome praise for ordinary work. But he, being devoted to wisdom, must exclude them from the governance of the city. (This is no plea for democracy, believe me.) His flaw is in believing that there are any citizens possessed of sufficient wisdom to run a society. To run a government, perhaps, a society, no. The 20th century provided a brilliant display of how "the best and brightest" frequently create disaster, and they show no willingness to stop their efforts.

What does all this have to do with anything? It has

to do with knowing, with what a mind is capable of and what it cannot do, and with how I came to realize what knowing was really all about. It has to do with Aristotle because it has more to do with the years I spent working for, and sometimes with, Mortimer Adler, one of the leading Aristotelians of the 20th century. When I arrived in his office, I had already proved myself as a decent student, but I was faced everyday with how much there was to know and how little knowledge I had acquired. I was about to make good on a pledge I made to myself on college graduation day. But as the decades have passed, I have become quite skeptical about human mental abilities. I appreciate physicist Richard Feynman's probably jocular definition of science: "Science is the ignorance of experts."

More than thinking was really involved in the learning process. The proper use of language mattered. Sloppy vocabulary leads to sloppy thinking. I had mostly learned this from a former professor of systematic theology, Joseph Sittler, years before, but it had not taken root. Say precisely what you mean, use words the meaning of which we can all agree on and make sure that we all understand them in the same way. The Humpty Dumpty approach to dialog makes no sense: a word means anything I want it to mean. No, I had to learn precision. Every discipline has its own vocabulary. When it becomes jargon, it becomes obfuscation. Mr. Adler had the ability to explain in the clearest and most precise manner the ideas in all of the noted philosophers, and some of the theologians as well. I was so fortunate to be in a job that actually paid me to read and learn. But I had no idea how my views would develop and change over the years. Fortunately, I had never been an ideologue, firmly committed to unshakable positions – apart from my Christian beliefs. Even these had been growing and maturing over the years, until I found it easy to unload theological study altogether. By this I mean setting aside man-made doctrines which serve as dividers, not unifiers, for the many denominations.

Politically, I was as knowledgeable as Will Rogers, who found his information in the daily newspapers. In economics I was a complete ignoramus. This latter condition I shared with the bulk of mankind and certainly with the great majority of my fellow citizens. Every once in a while I would pick up a book that would get me thinking about politics or economics. Why talk now about politics and economics, when philosophy seemed my destiny? Because we are all in the middle of politics and economics all our lives; and philosophy was by no means my destiny. It was to become a tool, as my study of history was, on the way to wisdom and understanding, if I was lucky.

Part 2: The Christianity versus Christendom Problem

Before getting into this chapter I must briefly clarify my conclusions. All of humanity is religious. Christianity is not a religion, but Christendom is. Christianity puts an end to the "burden of religion." But there is a thing called the Christian religion, but I prefer the term Christendom. Now for a few quotations.

First a few words from Montaigne: "O senseless man, who cannot make a worm and yet will make gods by the dozen."

And from Dietrich Bonhoeffer: "The Christian is not *homo religiosus*, but simply a man, as Jesus was a man – in contrast, shall we say, to John the Baptist. I don't mean the shallow and banal this-worldliness of the enlightened, but the profound this-worldliness, characterized by discipline and the constant knowledge of death and resurrection." (In a letter from prison to Eberhard Bethge, July 21, 1944)

> "Religion and piety are found among all nations. But the prophets were those who in the name of God stood up against that

which most people to this day call religion." (In *God in Search of Man* by Abraham Joshua Heschel, pp. 230-231)

And from a book published in 2010: "Only now are the long centuries of 'Christiandom' apparently coming to an end, and the consequences of this new stage in Christian life have yet fully to be assessed."(Diarmaid MaCulloch, *Christianity: The First Three Thousand Years,* p. 188).

"Is he an atheist?"

"Not in the least; he believed in himself." (Jules Verne, in Paris in the Twentieth Century).

From the prophet Amos: "I hate, I despise your feasts, and I take no delight in your solemn assemblies. Even though you offer me your burnt offerings and cereal offerings, I will not accept them, and the peace offerings of your fatted beasts I will not look upon. Take away the noise of your songs; to the melody of your harps I will not listen. But let justice roll down like waters, and righteousness like an ever-flowing stream." (5: 21-24, Revised Standard Version). These verses from the earliest of the so-called writing prophets should have marked the beginning of the end of institutional religion. Sadly, they didn't.

> "In the 20th century, State worship has become the aggressive and sometimes successful rival of the Christian worship of God." (Ralph H. Gabriel in *The Course of American Democratic Thought,* 1939. p. 38)

> "Edward Gibbon's *Decline and Fall of the Roman Empire* was much concerned with the cause and effect of historical events and the individuals who created them…. Gibbon strove for the truth in order to better understand events, regardless of the cost…. The early church, which he so much admired, was replaced by a new church introducing superstition, polytheism, paganism, venality, and simony. (Alan Strauss-Schom in *The Shadow Emperor: A Biography of Napoleon III,* 2018, p. 423)

> From the prophet Jeremiah. "For in the day that I brought them out of the land of Egypt, I did not speak to your fathers or command them concerning burnt offerings and sacrifices. But this command I gave them, 'Obey my voice, and I will be your God, and you shall be my people; and walk in all the way that I command you, that it may be well with you.' (7:22-23, Revised Standard Version)

I think it is chapter 12 of Dostoevsky's The Brothers Karamazov in which there is a confrontation between the Grand Inquisitor and a silent Jesus. The Inquisitor knows that Christendom has a great racket going – imprisoning, torturing, and killing people who deviated from sound doctrine. This chapter is my favorite for distinguishing between Christianity and Christendom. In spite of reading and rereading history for decades, it took me a while to make this sharp distinction. It would help if all Christians could do so.

Before going on, I'll make a brief summary of what Christianity entails. To do so it is necessary to make an arbitrary distinction between doctrines and messages. I define doctrines as formulated teachings by denominations that are meant to be believed. In other words, doctrines are man-made. Messages, on the other hand, are the main content of the Bible. There are three basic ones: the fact of a fallen human nature – a humanity alienated from its Creator; the meaning of the life, death, and resurrection of Jesus; and what being a Christian entails. This last one includes what the church is and what its mission is. Historically, it has been doctrines that have separated segments of Christianity from each other. It is one of the reasons Protestantism went into a decline in the late 19th century – too many denominations to choose from – which one was right? Now, to continue.

It was when living in La Grange, Illinois, that I first learned that "church" had a plural. During my first nine years in Chicago, my family belonged to two congregations. In those early years, awareness of my surroundings was admittedly quite limited. After we moved to the western suburb, I began to see more of what was around me. It dawned on me, as I walked to grade school that I was passing churches: Presbyterian and Methodist, to be exact. And one could hardly miss the

Congregational Church on La Grange Road, at the edge of the shopping area. Later, on the way to high school, I could see Emmanuel Episcopal and the First Church of Christ Scientist not far away. The latter is no longer there; the property was sold and the building torn down, to be replaced by a house.

When we were settled, neighbors invited us to join St. John's Lutheran, a Missouri Synod congregation. My mother decided it would be better for us to go with the Swedes instead of the Germans, so we started going to Grace Lutheran, a congregation of the Augustana Synod. It was a much longer walk that to St. John's, but it was the turning point in my life. So I started Sunday school there in the fall of 1940.

As I was growing up and attending my home parish as well as others on occasion, questions arose. Why so many churches? What were the differences? It was not long before I knew that most of the congregations I visited were somewhat similar to my own, except for one. That, naturally, was the Roman Catholic parish, St. Francis Xavier, located a short block from Grace Lutheran. In those pre-Vatican II days, the Catholics represented a sort of opposition. For the Bible Church people and other Fundamentalists I met, they were the enemy. I naturally sought out the differences and found many. Discussing these differences with members of other churches proved fruitless, since everyone will stick up for what he knows best. We teenagers didn't know very much.

In college my world expanded considerably. Denominational differences were still of interest, but now I was learning about entirely different religions: Judaism, Buddhism, Hinduism, Islam, and others. We studied them in class. Now a real dilemma arose. Without ever doubting the Christian faith at all, I had to deal with comparative religions. By what standard could one assess them? What did the term True Religion mean when applied to any of them? Was Christianity truer, or was it the only true one? How could one make such a claim? If they were all more or less on the same level, did it matter with which one a person was affiliated? Wasn't it just a matter of where one was born and the religion he grew up with? Surely there could be no objective standard of truth in these matters. Just as one defended the honor of one's denomination, so members of other religions would zealously defend their beliefs.

The problem for me was The New Testament's claim to exclusivity, a claim that many Christian "leaders" seem to have forgotten. How to overcome that claim, or how to live with it? It took several years to arrive at an answer, an answer that will perhaps be misunderstood, perhaps not appreciated even if understood. It is also a faith-based answer, thus open to criticism from many sides. Perhaps I am gullible and doctrinaire, but one has to stand somewhere and for something.

At this point I want to make three debatable assertions, which is where I ended up.

1. Jesus was not a religious person.
2. The Bible is not a religious book.
3. Jesus was put to death by the combined authorities of religion and government. (My overall thesis in all of this exercise is that the two obstacles to human well being are religion and government. This is not a popular view, nor is it a normal human way

of thinking about two of the most dominant forces in every society.)

The barest fragment of an answer to my dilemma came from reading a book of sermons by Paul Tillich. Its title was *The Shaking of the Foundations,* and the sermon was called "The Burden of Religion." I read this in the mid-1950s. His dichotomy between the obedience of faith and the observance of rituals stuck as a seed in my mind and would germinate later. The later began when I started reading Karl Barth. This was at the suggestion of the Rev. William Buege of Christ Church in Minneapolis, the most consistently outstanding preacher I have ever listened to. I started with *The Epistle to the Romans,* the book that had shaken the 19th-century theological foundations of Western Christendom just after World War I. I was hooked. I tackled the *Church Dogmatics* but must admit to not having read all 13 volumes. On religion he made much the same point as Tillich, but he was even more emphatic. He even pulled Christianity out from under the umbrella of religion altogether. Might he be right?

It was natural to read Dietrich Bonhoeffer in those seminary and post-seminary years. His fame was worldwide as a budding theologian who had been executed by the Germans in April 1945, so close to the end of the war in Europe. His *Letters and Papers from Prison* were famous even outside theological circles. Two phrases he used stuck in my mind: religionless Christianity; and Man come of age. These two phrases proved very potent for me, although the churches in the West have never to my knowledge taken up the challenge they pose. The challenge would be a threat to all denominations. (I'm quite aware that Bonhoeffer meant something quite different from what I make of his "religionless Christianity.")

The challenge for me was to take what I had gleaned from Tillich, Barth, and Bonhoeffer and relate them to the message of the New Testament. If Christianity was only one religion among many, the one into which I happened to be born, I was at a dead end. But what if it were not a religion at all? What if, in its earliest centuries, it had gotten enmeshed in all the trappings of religion, slowly and unintentionally at first, but enmeshed nevertheless? What if the message had been twisted into sets of rules, doctrines, formulas, vestments, incense pots, and liturgies and then reformulated to be poured into the old wine casks of religion. It was a natural process. The whole ancient world was, as Tillich called it, a theonomous one, a set of god-ridden cultures saturated everywhere with priests and their demands. What more natural than that this new Jewish movement be transformed into something it was never meant to be? And that it finally be taken over by the state and turned into the official religion?

The conclusion I reached was this: Christianity was religionized, theologized, philosophized, and politicized and loaded with ancient superstitions over a period of four centuries, much to its detriment. The outcome was a monstrosity called Christendom, or if you prefer, the Christian religion.

To arrive at a conclusion meant looking at the New Testament, and looking, and looking. Was there anything in it that would lend itself, without too much stretching, to the views those theologians had expressed? There was, and to avoid making a mystery, the result is this:

1. Religion says: Become a convert and follow the rules.
2. Christianity says: Become restored to full humanity through the life, death, and resurrection of the only true human being who has ever lived.

These are opposites. But by what means can one come to such conclusions? One might say simply, by reading the Bible; but that is hardly an answer. How many millions of people have been reading it for centuries and coming up with such varieties of interpretations?

A general survey of the literature of the great religions does demonstrate one fact: the Bible gives the most accurate portrayal of human nature to be found. One would have thought that the ancient Hebrews would have been more fastidious and self-serving in writing their scriptures. But no; all the flaws, the deceits, lies, crimes, idolatries, and apostasies are there for all the world to read. Nor does the New Testament present a glorified picture of humanity. If you need to be convinced, read the second half of Romans 1. This is not to say that other writings ignored the flaws of human nature, but the Hebrew Bible proclaimed the faults of a specific people within specific circumstances.

Now, two seemingly conflicting statements must be made about the Bible. For most Christians and for Orthodox Jews it is divinely inspired. This I believe to be true. I will go as far as to assert that it is the inspired, inerrant, and infallible word of God. But it is not the literal word of God. To get bogged down in controversies over literal meanings of words or the historicity of certain events is pointless, if only because many of the original words are of uncertain translation. Demanding adherence to specious literal interpretations is a waste of time. Such doings try to make the Bible something it is not. They are also a needless attempt to protect the words at the expense of the Word. Making such claims for the Bible is a pathetic attempt to find a fall-back position of certainty. Christians need no such thing. Jesus is self-authenticating, so is the Bible. So, while I cannot take it literally in every case, I take it seriously.

We proceed by faith in everything, including our view of the written texts and our own view of ourselves. The Word of God, if it is true, needs no protection from anyone, certainly not highly fragile minds incapable of comprehending the immensity of it. As Word of God, the Bible is not subject to scientific scrutiny. It is subject only to faith as it presents the object of faith: the acts of God in history. All the specious arguments of atheists can make no headway against faith, largely because their own arguments are based on their own peculiar faith. (I am not here denying the merits of literary or historical criticism; they are valuable tools for studying and analyzing the texts.)

But it must also be asserted that the writers of the books of the Bible were subject to all the limitations imposed upon them by their time. Those who wrote the Hebrew Bible and the New Testament did not say to themselves, "We are writing the Bible, so we had better be very careful, because hundreds of years from now people will be reading it; and many of them will take every word literally" The compilers of the original narratives in the Hebrew Bible certainly had some sense of what they were doing, but they were creating specific documents for a specific nation and time; and many of the events they described took place long before there could be written accounts.

The writers were not psychics, nor were they mindless scribblers taking dictation from the Holy Spirit. St. Paul said as much, when he stated that: We have this treasure in earthen vessels. These earthen vessels comprehend every way of expressing the New Testament message, including the thought forms, the language, and the worldview, of the 1st century. He is saying, in effect, that the Jesus event is something unique in history. It is so distinctive that no categories of human thought ever contrived will suffice to explain it, certainly not the worldly philosophies of the time, whether from Plato or Aristotle. Nevertheless, all that Paul or any other apostle had was the vocabulary, the imagery that they knew in a Roman Empire saturated with Greek thought and terminology. Jesus himself said much the same thing when he spoke of not putting new wine into old wineskins.

If Karl Barth is correct, and I believe he is, God is the absolutely unknowable One, the One who cannot be reached or known by any human endeavor. Only His acts within the historical process can be apprehended, and then only in a limited way. (The great 12th theologian, philosopher, and physician Moses Maimonides made much the same argument in the opening chapters of his *A Guide for the Perplexed.*) Did God send Cyrus the Mede to destroy Babylon and restore Judah to its homeland? The Bible says so, but secular historians would just record the events as they happened and take no notice of a divine agency. There is passage in John's gospel in which Jesus is praying: "Now is my soul troubled. And what shall I say? 'Father, save me from this hour'? No, for this purpose

I have come to this hour. Father, glorify thy name." Then a voice came from heaven, I have glorified it, and I will glorify it again." The crowd standing by heard it and said that it had thundered. Others said, "An angel has spoken to him." (John 12:27-29, Revised Standard Version). Faith apprehends what unfaith cannot. But unfaith responds by saying: There was nothing to apprehend. So the score is tied.

Furthermore, the writers of the Bible had to use human language to describe the absolutely indescribable. Often their language was very colorful, as it is in the Book of Revelation. Much of the writing is in poetry: not just the Psalms and Proverbs, but much of the Prophets as well. Colorful, extravagant, pedantic, hyperbolic, hopeful, and always faithful. As St. Paul himself admitted that eye has not seen nor ear heard, nor has it entered into the mind of man what God has prepared for those who love Him. Paul Tillich dealt with this issue by using the term "symbolic language." Readers of the Bible should understand that prophecy and prediction are quite different.

Fundamentalists and other "Bible believers" have no appreciation for the varieties of ancient literature. Consider Homer's *Iliad* or the writings of Hesiod: *Theogony* and *Works and Days*. The ancient Greeks would have taken these as fairly literal accounts of events long past. The same is true of the *Epic of Creation* in ancient Mesopotamia. Today we can look at these amazing works and say they are myth. Buts myth is often based on fact. There was a Trojan war. Can we put some of the writings of the Hebrew Bible in the same category? Must we take the first 11 chapters of Genesis as narrative history? However we read those chapters, the point of each event is the same: God has acted in meaningful ways.

Paul and the other early Christians were confronted with something that had never happened before, something indeed quite new under the sun, something that was totally unexpected and a totally unrepeatable event. The writers of the New Testament did their best, progressively, to understand and interpret this genuinely unique event. I say progressively, because there is an obvious development in the writings, especially the Pauline ones, from the earliest letters to the later ones. The same is true of the gospels. The last of these to be written in its present form was St. John's, a writer who is quite clear in his message. It is, in fact, a work of genius and effectively provides a commentary on the first three gospels.

But suppose that Jesus had appeared as the Messiah that Israel had awaited. Had that been true, Jesus and legions of angels would have reconstituted Israel and made it the world's great nation, and the Roman Empire would have disappeared, leaving Gibbon nothing to write about. The specific and literal promises of the Hebrew Bible would have been fulfilled. The final judgment would have probably already taken place. Where would we all be? No answer is possible.

That did not happen. But Jesus did appear in a religion-saturated world. Nevertheless, I contend that Jesus was not a religious person. What He was and did were not about religion. They were about the end of religion. "End" here has two specific meanings. One is the goal to which religion points but can never reach. The other is simply putting an end to religion as a necessary ingredient of human nature. Christians are part of a new creation; the old creation was imbued with religion, but the new will have none of it. Consider a passage in Matthew 15:21-28. Jesus and his disciples are up north, in "the district of Tyre and Sidon" This is in what is now Lebanon. "A Canaanite woman from that region came out and cried, 'Have mercy on me, O Lord, Son of David; my daughter is severely possessed by a demon. But he did not answer her a word. And his disciples came and begged him, saying, 'Send her away, for she is crying after us.' He answered (perhaps with a twinkle in his eye?), 'I was sent only to the lost sheep of the house of Israel' But she came and knelt before him, saying, 'Lord, help me.' And he answered, 'It is not fair to take the children's bread and throw it to the dogs.' She said, 'Yes, lord, yet even the dogs eat the crumbs that fall from their masters' table.' Then Jesus answered her, 'O woman, great is your faith! Be it done for you as you desire.' And her daughter was healed instantly." (Revised Standard Version)

There could hardly be a stronger indication that He was not just for Israel. Luke's gospel is insistent on this subject. The Fourth Gospel is much plainer on it. And St. Paul, who headed the Gentile mission, was plainest of all. By the time he wrote the letter to the Romans, he had developed as full an understanding as he could of what the "Jesus event" was about. And what it was about was the restoration of true humanity to a race that had lost all touch with its Creator. It was not about the literal fulfillment of the Hebrew Scriptures' promises to Israel.

There have been attempts to interpret the Jesus event as some kind of unexpected interruption of the still incomplete story of Israel, especially among fundamentalists who teach Millennial doctrines. I would have thought that John Calvin's refutation of this notion in his *Institutes of the Christian Religion* would have ended the argument, but apparently it has not done so. This doctrine, called dispensationalism, has reared its head again and is gaining new adherents among fundamentalists. The *Left Behind* series of novels has certainly attracted a large readership. Bad ideas never seem to disappear.

I think it can be claimed that even the history of Israel was not about religion, although – in the spirit of the times – it was certainly wrapped in all the proper accoutrements: rituals, priesthood, incense, sacrifices, Temple worship, and the rest. Beginning in Exodus we see the institution of a highly organized state religion, comparable in many ways to the other state religions of the ancient world. In Jerusalem this religion was centralized in the Temple built by Solomon and later rebuilt after the Babylonian captivity and restored by Herod. But in following the Hebrew Bible through to the end, we also see the gradual collapse of the priest-dominated religion in favor of a personal relationship with God. We are left with: "What does the Lord require of you but to do justice, love mercy, and walk humbly with your God." (Micah 6:8 in Revised Standard Version) This is a truly magnificent transformation.

It is quite true that the basic documents of the Hebrew Bible comprise the Torah, the books of the laws of Moses. These presuppose obedience on the part of the Israelites. Obedience would seem strongly to suggest religion. Not necessarily so, however. Israel was confronted with the Law. Fulfilling the Law would have meant keeping faith with the Creator. For the Law is more than just a set of commands. It is not just a threat; it is also a promise. It presents a portrait of what a genuine human being is like in his dealings with his Creator and his fellow humans. Is this impossible? Apparently it was and still is. We deal with laws all the time and apparently find not too much difficulty in obeying most of them. It's a matter of will, along with our knowledge of penalties. There seems to be an inherent disposition in human nature to play fast and loose with the laws of God, as though there were no penalties. But these laws are as indestructible as the other laws of nature. Break them and be broken by them. It is one's humanity that is broken by disobedience.

What happened to Israel? Because of disobedience, both the northern and southern kingdoms were conquered – first by Assyria, then by Babylon – and sent into exile. After citizens of the southern kingdom were allowed to return home and rebuild their temple, they created for themselves a tight, exclusive religion that was in no position any more to be a light to the Gentiles. Obedience to law, the Torah, was everything. If there was to be a light for all the nations, it would have to come from outside, while seeming to belong only to the inside.

Why disobedience exists is explained by that amazing little episode in Genesis 3, called the story of the Fall. Take it literally or take it as a bit of ancient wisdom literature, the point is still the same. When humanity willfully separated itself from God, all contact with the Creator was lost. Humanity had no knowledge of its origins or its purpose. Out of the failed desire to acquire this knowledge has come religion, an entirely man-made speculation.

Religion is synonymous with humanity's complete unawareness of the Creator as well as a futile attempt to reach Him. Religion is the first fruit of the original sin. Hence, religion is embedded in human nature as its fundamental flaw. Every human being is religious, even the atheist and the agnostic; because everyone has what Paul Tillich called "ultimate concern," even if the concern turns out to be quite less than ultimate. The following sentences are from his *Systematic Theology,* volume two, page nine: "Although man is actually separated from the infinite, he could not be aware of it if he did not participate in it potentially. This is expressed in the state of being ultimately concerned, a state which is universally human, whatever the level of the concern may be."

Without knowledge of the Creator, humanity can only make of itself what it will. All of its ethics, it morality, its right and wrong, its good and evil are human judgments and adjustments based on centuries of experience, trial and error, and forlorn hope. Civilization, the attempt to live together peaceably, is the human counterfeit of the City of God. Such are all its failed utopias now and forever, even promoted by those Christians, trying so hard to be relevant, who are foolish enough to believe that a Kingdom of God can somehow be erected on this planet by adhering to one political agenda or another. They should pay attention to Luther's explanation of the petition in the Lord's Prayer that asks: Thy Kingdom come.

So when we come to the Jesus event, we are dealing with the restoration of human nature to its origins, to its Creator. We are not dealing with the founding of a new religious system, not even with the best of all possible religious systems. We are dealing with the permanent antidote to the plight of religion, that pandemic human flaw, which is basic to all our other errors.

In his Letter to the Romans, Paul describes the Godless state of humanity and the turnaround that was effected by the ministry, death, and resurrection of Jesus. He does not do this in religious terms but in terms of the human condition. From chapter 5: "While we were helpless, while we were yet sinners, while we were enemies, we were reconciled to God by the death of his Son." In the same chapter he picks up the theme of the Fall: "Then as one man's trespass led to condemnation for all, so one man's act of righteousness leads to acquittal and life for all." (Revised Standard Version).This is the fundamental historical fact, anterior to all possibility of faith. It is not faith that makes it so; it is faith which accepts the news.

Once this reconciliation has been effected, what are people to do, keep on in the same direction? No, there must be a complete turnaround. St. John takes up this subject in his third chapter, the famous colloquy about being born again. This could easily be regarded as metaphor. It is not useful to be a Biblical literalist generally, but there are some times when it is called for, and this is one of them. When Jesus says one must be born again, he means it quite literally. One must become, in Paul's language, a new creation. Being born again: notice the passive verb. One does not bear oneself again; it is an action of the Creator. One is born again against the background of the reconciliation of which Paul speaks. All of us were born into this world. Now one can be born again into the Creator's world and recognize it for what it is.

Once one is born, one is expected to live, otherwise one dies. Once one is born again, the challenge is to live the new life. What has religion to do with this? Nothing. Why does it seem to have so much to do with it? Because from very early this whole astounding Jesus event was turned into a belief system instead of a life system. And it did happen quite early, as soon as the second century and even while the early Christians were being persecuted for their faith.

Having used the word "faith," I must assert that in spite of a certain unfortunate sentence in the Book of Jude, it means complete trust in the Word of God, the Word who is first of all a Person and secondarily the writings about Him. It means "working out your own salvation with fear and trembling," because we never know, we only trust. But our trust is not in ourselves or in a system, or in our "theology," or in our personal interpretations of biblical passages no matter what guarantees these may seem to offer. Blaise Pascal called it the Wager; and Kierkegaard called it a leap into the unknown. But if this is not the direction taken, all we have to work with are the standards we've always had; and they will lead us nowhere. The one and only thing Christians have to stand on is the certitude that God's Word is true, always and forever. The word of God is true, though every man be false, as St. Paul said.

Having said this, we must then take a real leap of faith and regard ourselves as God regards us. This is perhaps the most difficult task of all: to see ourselves as God sees us – called to be saints, transferred from the kingdom of darkness into the kingdom of the Son of His love, a new creation, the people of God, the Body of Christ, and all the other terms the New Testament uses. It is for this that we belong to communities with other Christians. Believing and doing are the hardest things in the world, impossible, one might say. (On the difficulties, see Luke 18:18-24) But there is a Spirit that enlivens and teaches and protects these communities.

Yes, we have in our communities so many of the trappings of religion. Perhaps there is no alternative. We are in this world, and it is a world of religion. And as Paul said, we have this treasure in earthen vessels: our buildings, the stained glass windows, the music, the hymnals, the offerings, the sacraments, and even our Bibles. But to place any reliance on these vessels, liturgies, music, buildings, stained glass windows, vestments, and all else is a serious error. They are the earthen vessels, the old wineskins. We go to churches as we go to gas stations: to get refueled. They are halfway houses that we inhabit briefly before heading back into all the rest of our activities.

The Bible, as I mentioned earlier, does not provide roadmaps; it does not instruct us about all the activities we are to pursue. But it is as new creations that we pursue them. It is from that perspective we approach everything. This is not easy, but wandering aside is easy. Jesus was quite plain on this matter on more than one occasion: the road is narrow and quite hard to travel. John Bunyan showed how hard in his *Pilgrim's Progress*. Thus it takes real effort, but it is a Spirit-guided effort for those who are willing to make the journey. It takes more effort than anything else any human being can do, because in the process we are being re-created. This process we cannot see or feel. This, too, is in faith. Our lives are hid with Christ in God, hid even from us. St. John, in his first Letter says: It does not yet appear what we shall be, but we know that when He appears we shall be like Him, for we shall see Him as He is. (I John 3:2, Revised Standard Version) That's the goal, the end of the line.

None of this means that our lives are to be given over to religious exercises. As a new creation, one lives in the world by finding one's own particular calling, or vocation, and following it. All vocations are secular; for Christians, there can be no religious ones. We look to the Bible to learn who we are and who we shall be, but we make our own judgments about how we shall fulfill our individual potential. From the Adam and Eve story we can glean this: humanity has a God-given responsibility to use its mental abilities to learn how to live in this world.

I have neither the time nor the interest to go into the whole tawdry and often-scandalous history of Christendom as it has played itself out for so many centuries. To read it is to become revolted. It's a wonder any of our denominations have survived. Nor is it any wonder that so many people have been repulsed by what they saw and have turned away. What decent human being would not? Would Voltaire have declared war on the church he grew up in, had its crimes not been so overwhelming? Yet, within this rotten husk of the Christian religion, Christianity has survived, still survives and flourishes. One wonders whether to look with delight or with trepidation on the slow death of the Christian religion in Europe. A question remains: Does Christianity have a message for today's societies, given the past of the Christian religion.

Before ending this section, I will make two points. In an effort to try to understand and explain the absolutely unique Jesus event, early theologians turned to the popular philosophies of the day, usually Platonism or

Neo-Platonism. This was a serious error, as was the medieval error of trying to use the admittedly profound system of Aristotle. This philosophizing was a mistake because it ended up creating a larger framework within which the Gospel message could be put. Unfortunately, God cannot be explained by anything greater. If the Hebrew Scriptures were unable to foresee the fulfillment of God's promises accurately, how can the speculative wisdom of a few bright men in Greece be expected to provide a fitting superstructure or framework for it? The Jesus event is the largest possible framework in the universe. It is absurd and unfortunate that the attempt to wrap it in philosophical swaddling clothes was ever made, no matter how well meaning.

The second error was certainly more serious: the blending of Christianity with the state. This occurred early in the 4th Century, during the reign of Constantine, and it has plagued Christianity ever since. The early Christians were admired by outsiders who looked at them and remarked: See how they love one another. By the 4th Century those same outsiders would have said: See how they hate, persecute, and kill one another over doctrinal differences. This entanglement with the state has always been, and continues to be, pernicious. It makes denominations just one more power in the political arena, and a weak contender it has become in the past 1700 years. For an excellent insight into this matter, look at the earlier mentioned book, *Earthly Powers*, by Michael Burleigh.

First, there can be no such thing as a state church, no matter who is using the term. Second, no denomination is a church. Denominations are simply useful institutional arrangements devised for convenience. The churches, as a plural word, are local. As a singular word, the church is comprised of the whole people of God in all times and places. God alone knows His church, and it has no knowable history.

Having made these two assertions, how can one help but regard modern Ecumenism as anything but humorous, and sometimes also pernicious? Is it any more than the pursuit of power by political-religious hacks, who love wearing their ecclesiastical finery in public? There is nothing wrong in denominations seeking understanding among themselves, as the Faith and Order and Life and Work movements did after World War I. But to sacrifice the message and the mission so we "can all get along" is destructive. There is, however, a genuine ecumenism. It is the work of the Holy Spirit in preserving, directing, instructing, guiding, and protecting the church in its God-created unity and diversity. The whole Church is always one, without human effort.

How did the denominations get into the mess they are in today? I've already alluded to their ties to the state. (When I use the word "state," it will almost invariably mean government.) This long and sordid history has been told by so many historians, there is no need to review it here. There is a clue to explaining the errors denominations have fallen into in Paul's Second Letter to Timothy, the fourth chapter: "For the time is coming when people will not put up with sound doctrine, but having itching ears, they will accumulate for themselves teachers to suit their own desires, and will turn away from listening to the truth and wander away to myths." (Revised Standard Version).

Today the denominations in the West exist in a political

environment largely shaped by Marxist socialism and its various loathsome offsprings, including American Liberalism. The utopian programs have come to dominate most political thought. Because so many facets of the socialist agenda seem to coincide with what Christians are supposed to want for society at large, church leaders have readily taken positions on these matters. These individuals uncritically accept political programs and promote them, forgetting (if they ever knew) that the mission of the church never was to reform society. One can understand the appeal, although the results are plainly visible.

Because so many socioeconomic movements have the appearance of merit, they are willingly embraced. This is true of denominational leaders who adhere to the Left of the political spectrum, the mainline denominations and its National Council of Churches; as well it is true of the Evangelicals associated with the Christian Coalition. To make the assumption that the gospel can become a means to our ends is entirely unwarranted and deserves the contempt with which society so often rewards it.

The denominations are caught in an historical bind of their own making. It's called religion as an extension of politics. Having for centuries enjoyed the perquisites of power and wealth, they are now powerless. Having set aside their fundamental responsibilities to find ways to remain "relevant," they are now earning the disrespect they merit. All of Europe is rapidly sliding into atheism and nihilism, and the United States is having a good go at the same process. Such is the result of centuries of spreading the Christian "religion."

During the 19th century the Protestant denominations

in the United States found themselves increasingly marginalized. The more austere versions of Calvinism had already been thrust aside in favor of a more upbeat, progressive message. The most liberal Protestant leaders developed a "religion of humanity," which abandoned traditional Christian doctrines. Some Christians became cheerleaders for the "democratic faith."

They viewed the United States, in Lincoln's words, as the last best hope of earth, the goal toward which Christianity had always been tending. Even Evangelicals in the 20th century have not been immune to this merging of American nationalism and Christianity. The following quotation is from the opening statement by the Rev. Harold J. Ockenga of Park Street Congregational Church in Boston, delivered at the founding session of the National Association of Evangelicals in 1942: "In America....we should have, first of all, capitalism as the economic form, second, democracy as the political form, third, Christianity as our religious form." Admittedly, this is from the Right of the political spectrum, but it coincides well with attitudes that became common following the Civil War.

Protestantism, and Catholicism as well, were under fire in the 19th century. Remember, Darwin's *Origin of Species* was published in 1859. We are familiar with the ongoing strife this has caused, as the churches sought to beat back another advance in science (perhaps a very questionable advance). Secondly, outright atheism made its presence felt in one of the most popular platform lecturers in the late 1800s, Robert G. Ingersoll. This rather fascinating character told his audiences that humanity and society can save themselves without the aid of religion (by which he meant Christianity).

It is hardly coincidental that atheism is being popularly revived in the early 21st century. Books by Richard Dawkins (*The God Delusion*), Sam Harris (*The End of Faith*), Christopher Hitchens (*God is Not Great*), Victor J. Stenger (*God: The Failed Hypothesis*), and Daniel C. Dennett (*Breaking the Spell: Religion as a Natural Phenomenon*) all became best sellers in 2005-7. That all of them fail to comprehend the problem of religion is quite understandable.

There is a more dangerous kind of atheism, based on Psalm 14: "The fool says in his heart, there is no God." The heart here means will power, the seat of the passions, appetites, and desires. It is the will that can convince even those who believe in God that they can live as they want to, as long as they do their "religious" thing occasionally. Thus, there can be atheists who believe in God, absurd as it seems.

Another very popular 19th century lecturer was a Baptist pastor from Philadelphia named Russell Conwell. He kept to his Christianity, even in a modified Puritan form, when he delivered his lecture, *Acres of Diamonds,* at least 6,000 times. Its theme was simple: get rich. He aligned Christianity with the post-Civil War Gospel of Wealth in the Gilded Age, which seemed to promise an endless era of prosperity.

Speaking of that era, Mark Twain and Charles Dudley Warner co-wrote a novel, *The Gilded Age,* as a scathing attack of the *mores* of the period. To get a notion of the mindset of the rich and powerful of that time, one can easily get hold of Andrew Carnegie's 1889 essay, "Wealth," as it was published in the *North American Review.* A Google search led me right to it. The recent biography, *Mellon,* a life of Andrew Mellon by David Cannadine, offers a mass of information about the attitudes and actions of the new industrial and financial elites, those whom Theodore Roosevelt castigated as "malefactors of great wealth."

As the Protestant denominations thrashed around, trying to find a message and a purpose, they only became more irrelevant. True, some of them created a Social Gospel in an attempt to find relevance as they aided the poor, and even this noble endeavor was often misguided. As the denominations sought to express themselves during the Progressive Movement in politics, they became what they are today, the mainline denominations. One critical writer has said that mainline churches soon become sideline churches. It may be too early to tell, or too late to do anything about it. (Coincidentally, as I write this paragraph in the spring of 2007, the centennial of Walter Rauschenbusch's book, *Christianity and the Social Crisis,* was noted in the *Wall Street Journal* under an article entitled "Christianity without Salvation." Enough said? There were two other publishing anniversaries in 2007 that were far more meaningful to me: the 50th anniversary of both Ayn Rand's *Atlas Shrugged* and Jack Kerouac's *On the Road.*)

Not all denominations under the Protestant umbrella fell into this trend. The basically foreign-language churches that had not been a significant part of colonial America escaped, for a time, the demons that were besetting those churches that had been dominant in the original 13 colonies. The Lutherans were among those that had not then caught the vices of the new age, but they have steadily been making up for lost time. Of the Orthodox churches in the United States I can say almost nothing. They do, by virtue of holding onto their languages, seem to have escaped the worst of current political contamination; but considering their origins, they have little to boast about. The Roman Catholics, during the 19th century, were in a building and consolidating process; and they were distrusted and opposed by the Protestants. Only in the late 20th century have they wandered into the fold of modern social policy, and then not everywhere. In some places, of course, their leaders have embraced Marxism openly, hence Liberation Theology.

Will the denominations, forms of the Christian religion, be called back to their message and mission; and if called, will they respond? Or will they wither away into irrelevance, places to which New Age people looking for something vacuously "spiritual" in their lives will have recourse now and then? Truth has become a very hard sell today, and a message as scandalous as Christianity offers can have little general appeal. Gospel means "good news," but it isn't necessarily good news to everyone.

The Evangelicals have been a big disappointment, too. It is sad to have to admit that, late in life, I find myself in more agreement with them than I do with my own denomination's positions. I have greatly enjoyed and appreciated hearing Charles Stanley on television on Sunday morning, for instance. The Evangelicals do claim a strong biblical base, after all. Should they not realize that it is not their mission to save America? That the United States is not now, nor ever has been, a Christian nation; that there is only one Christian nation – the Israel of God, the Body of Christ? Are Evangelicals afraid of losing out in the political arena? Are they terribly depressed as they see the "culture" descend into the sewer? So what? Get over it. Do what you can where you are, but don't presume to dictate how secular society should define itself. I do recall someone saying, "My kingdom is not of this world." *Not* is the operative word.

The Creator will dispose of the United States in His own good time. It won't be a pretty picture, but there is nothing we can do about it. There are long-term trends that cannot be reversed without a powerful effort. The likelihood that such an effort will be made is virtually nil. A free society cannot sustain itself over the long haul, and democracy always fails – as will be shown below. A verse from Revelation 22 comes to mind: Let the evildoer still do evil, and the filthy still be filthy, and the righteous still do right, and the holy still be holy.

I can congratulate the Evangelicals, and Fundamentalists, for not getting taken in by the ecumenical movement. But they must be *very* careful about failing to recognize that there are Christians in all denominations, people of genuine faith who are as distressed at what their denominations are about as they are. The current Episcopalian and Presbyterian dilemmas are an example. The United Methodist Church may be, as of early 2019, on the verge of splitting up over the ordination of gay clergy and same-sex marriage. True ecumenism is God's affair, because only He knows where his people are. And remember that denominational leadership is much like political leadership; it sometimes exists primarily to serve its own ends.

This leads me to a rather peculiar thought: no history of Christianity can ever be written. All the historians can deal with is the Christian religion.

Is there still a message? It's necessary to end this section on a negative note, although there will be serious disagreements. The Peace of Westphalia ended the Thirty Years War in 1648. Prior to the war all of Europe had been, if not Christianized, at least enveloped within Christendom. The war had many aspects and phases, but prominent among them were the hatreds between denominations – Catholics, Lutherans, and Reformed. The enlightened segments of Europe's populations decided that if what they had witnessed was Christianity, they wanted nothing to do with it. Thus was born the secular society in which we now all live. I suspect that in the Northern Hemisphere the likelihood of getting the message of Christianity across to the non-Christian populations is slim. Certainly the individual congregations have messages preached to them on a weekly basis. But can the message make its way outside the walls?

Chapter 3 Extra Added Attraction: Four Matters of Doctrinal Opinion

This section may easily be avoided. It is mostly about doctrines – church teachings – that have served to divide denominations from one another. I made an arbitrary distinction between doctrines and messages. There are three clear messages in the Bible. The sorry condition of human nature runs through the whole volume, from Genesis to Revelation. The other two are specific to the New Testament: the life of Jesus and its meaning, and what the church is. Doctrines are man-made exercises in thought. As such, I feel free to ignore them.

Sacraments. Now for a short excursion into theology that will probably not be of general interest nor find many adherents. The first topic is the Lord's Supper, the Sacrament of the Altar, or whatever else it may be called in some denominations. My views on it are of a fairly recent development, with roots that go back many years. While in college, riding around one Sunday afternoon, some friends and I stopped in a small Swedish Lutheran church in Aledo, Illinois. The pulpit stood a platform at the very front of the chancel, with the altar, or communion table, on floor level below it. This struck me as peculiar at the time, but I made nothing of it, since I had not yet begun my theological studies.

In my home parish, the altar stands at the rear of the chancel, up against the wall. (In the last couple of years 2014-2015) a free-standing communion table has been placed in the center of the chancel.) On occasion, in addition to attending my home parish, I would venture over to Christ Church in Oak Brook, Illinois, for the last morning service. There, the pulpit stands raised on the right side of the chancel, while there is a large table surrounded by chairs at about floor level in the center to the left of it from the perspective of the congregation. It was at this point I began to understand that what had always been an altar to me was really a communion table.

Further reflection led me to think about the sacrament itself. Outside of Eastern Orthodoxy, there are basically three views of the Lord's Supper. For Roman Catholicism it is the sacrifice of the mass, a sacrament in which the elements – bread and wine – care changed into the body and blood of Christ by a process called transubstantiation. Intellectually, this makes sense, or is at least comprehensible, providing one accepts the Aristotelian metaphysical reasoning behind it. There is a plausible biblical basis for this view in John 6, although I cannot accept it. The Fourth Gospel is the latest one, and the author may well have been influenced by the very popular mystery religions of his time.

Among the Baptist and other more fundamental denominations, the Lord's Supper is celebrated as a simple memorial, if it is celebrated at all. "Do this in remembrance of me." Nothing mystical happens to the bread and wine (or, more likely, grape juice). For the Anglicans, I can make no case; what they believe varies so widely that no one view asserts itself. The Anglo-Catholics among them probably adhere to the Roman view, or some modification of it.

The Lutheran doctrine puzzles me. Luther was, after all, a medieval monk. He wanted to rid himself of all that he found objectionable in Catholicism. As he explained the Sacrament in his Large Catechism, he seems quite right. He says that it, like baptism, "was instituted by Christ without man's counsel or deliberation." And, further, "all temporal things remain as God has created and ordered them, regardless of how we treat them." Yet he, too, insists on finding a "real presence" in the bread and wine. It is this I have a problem with.

In baptism, the water is unchanged. It does not become holy water. Why then in the Lord's Supper, must such a change be imposed on the elements? Which raises the question, what is the sacrament for? For me, it is an expression of the unity of the Body of Christ, the church – the unity of the members and their unity with their Lord, who promised to be always with them. Would it not be strange if transubstantiation were true – but in a completely different way? What if it were not the elements that were transformed, but the members of the congregation that they become increasingly incorporated into the Body of Christ? Because the church is the Body of Christ in the world: as St. Paul noted, "we do not know Christ any longer after the flesh." If this is true – and the theologians can argue it – how sad it is that the Lord's Supper has been used over the centuries to divide the church instead of uniting it.

In I Corinthians 11, St. Paul gives the earliest version

of the Last Supper. He stresses that it is a memorial, something no denomination I am aware of would deny. He then says that "as often as you eat his bread and drink this cup, you proclaim the Lord's death until he comes." The sacrament becomes then both a proclamation and a forward look, an anticipation. In verse 29 Paul makes the unusual declaration, "For anyone who eats and drinks without discerning the body eats and drinks judgment upon himself." Discerning what body? Certainly not the body of the man Jesus; much more likely the Body which is the church. For me, this is an indication that the Lord's Supper is not some kind of "medicine of immortality" for individuals, but a process of incorporation (from the Latin *corpus*, meaning body), a unifying event. To be and remain Christian, one needs all the help he can get; and he can get in it the Lord's Supper if he is willing to believe – the really hardest thing in the world to do.

Ethics. Second, can there be such a thing as Christian ethics? Decades ago I read, over a period of years, three books on the subject, all by European theologians. I got the feeling that something was wrong, that these authors were still steeped in the medieval mindset of class structure which Europe never seems to be able to unload: a place for everyone, and everyone in his place doing his duty as he or she sees it best. I realize this is a gross simplification, but I simply could not find in any of these volumes – one of which was by Dietrich Bonhoeffer and another by Regin Prenter – any basis for a Christian ethics. (I have forgotten the third author.) Some while afterward, in reading one of Karl Barth's volume of Church Dogmatics, it was a pleasure to find his assertion that there indeed was no such thing as Christian ethics.

So, on the face of it, there are two opposing views that apparently can't be reconciled.

As I understand it, ethics has to do with behavior, with the actions people take. In ancient Greece, this came under the heading of practical philosophy, prudential wisdom. It had to do with the choices we make based on what is in us, on our general and specific dispositions. Behavior is obviously based on what we think, the values we hold, the beliefs we have, and - too often – on our emotions and will power. If these underlie our behavior, they are not in themselves ethics but rather the foundation for same.

Consider for a moment Nicodemus, the Pharisee who came to visit Jesus under cover of darkness one evening, so he'd not be seen by other Pharisees. Here was a very pious Jew and very decent human being who lived as best he could, according to all the many precepts of Judaic law: there are many of those regulations, and they are quite precise. It was the view of him and his fellow believers that this was how to please God. Jesus countered this inbred and strongly held belief system with his statement of the need to be born again. In part, this meant a reorientation from focus on laws to a focus on the humanity around him – recall the priest and the Levite who walked by the man in the ditch without offering help lest they inadvertently become polluted and in need of days of purification. So it was left to the outcast, the despised Samaritan, to offer help.

The question that popped into my mind was: If Nicodemus was born again and became a follower of Christ (and he may well have), what actions could he take that a non-Christian could not also take? What could he do that a pious and compassionate Jew, Hindu, Buddhist, or even an atheist could not also do? That Christians are often accused of believing one thing and doing another is true; and the accusation is, sadly, frequently justified. Yet if they were completely consistent in their believing and doing, how would they differ in terms of the question above?

Christians are not now, if they ever were, recognizable just by looking at them. The Christian is always in the process of becoming: the technical term is sanctification. And this is something the individual himself is not necessarily aware of. In Colossians 3:3 Paul says "your life is hid with Christ in God." And in I John 3: 2 is the assertion that "it does not yet appear what we shall be, but we know that when he appears we shall be like him, for we shall see him as he is." There is a hidden quality in Christianity that goes beyond the world's inability to perceive; there is also an inability of believers to perceive themselves accurately. Who we are is first; what we do follows. Unfortunately, what we do so easily falls short of what we ought to do, because we walk by faith and not by sight and can rarely see the long-term outcome of our actions. And, more unfortunately, that obscene abomination called Christendom has recklessly disregarded all the laws of God over the centuries and put Christianity in bad odor. That is a burden Christianity can no longer afford to bear.

Culture. To read through the historical books of the Hebrew Bible to learn about Israel's past is useful undertaking. Christians and Jews ought to be well versed in the biblical messages. It's also fascinating to ponder what is not mentioned in those books, as well as in any history of Israel such as John Bright's History of

Israel (1960). How did the people live from day to day? What were their pastimes? I must confess to having no information on the subject.

Now, let us turn to ancient Greece, especially Athens. We have plenty of information about how the population lived, and we know what their pastimes were. The Olympic Games were first celebrated in 776 BCE and lasted until 393 CE, when they were abolished by the Roman emperor Theodosius I. These games were the most prominent of the Greek athletic contests, but they were not the only ones. Then we have the poetry and drama, in the surviving works of Aeschylus, Sophocles, and Euripides, and in the comedies of Aristophanes. The dramas and comedies were played out in festivals dedicated to the god Bacchus. There was music, although it has not come down to us. The great architecture and sculpture we have many examples of.

So the question comes to mind: Which of these societies would you prefer living in? In our secular society, the answer is obvious. But another question came to mind: What relation do Christians have to the secular culture – to the sporting events, rock concerts, movies, theater, ballet, and opera? I suspect it would take an orthodox rabbi to get an answer. I certainly don't have one, and it's not just because I like the Kentucky Derby.

The truth problem. In John 14:6 Jesus makes the remarkable statement: "I am the way, and the truth, and the life; no one comes to the Father, but by me." (Revised Standard Version). It is hard to disagree with David Hume's statement that all knowledge comes from observation and experience. What that means is that all knowledge, and what we call truth, inheres in human minds. It is subjective. This applies to the laws of science as well as to any understanding of human beings and their motives and actions. How valid are human assessments of truth? In this life, we can only conjecture. Even some of today's scientific certainties may eventually come undone, as they have in the past. What Jesus has done is to set himself up as a truth independent of all human-devised truth. How can he do this? Simply because he was the only true human being, the one who knew and performed the will of God perfectly.

Chapter 4 Addendum on the Good Life.

The "good life" poses a problem for which I have no solution. I bring it up because of a series of lectures Mortimer Adler gave back in the late 1960s and which the office staff attended. They were later published as a book entitled *The Time of Our Lives*. The subject was the good life and how to achieve it. Underlying the whole was moral philosophy based on Aristotle's *Ethics*, the ethics of common sense.

The book raised several problems for me in relation to my theological views. The good life is obviously a secular concept, an idea that has no necessary relation to Christianity, or indeed to any religious system. I was driven instantly to ponder the life in Christ, the obedience of faith. Was the good life opposed to the obedience of faith, or could there be some compatibility between them? Jesus did, after all, speak of the abundant life. Every rational individual wants a good life for himself and his family; and he works toward that end. This goal means the acquisition of sufficient material goods, although it can mean much more, especially as it relates to one's children. The good life I am speaking of here is something else – the sum of a whole life lived well.

Having a basis in Aristotle's *Ethics*, the good life was naturally rooted in that philosopher's discussion of the difficulty in choosing what is really good versus what is only apparently good. This is a more complex problem than first appears. Mortimer laid out this complexity as follows: "1. A given object is really good for us (it is naturally desired), but it does not appear good to us (it is not consciously desired); 2. It appears good to us (it is consciously desired or wanted), but it may or may not be really good for us (it may or may not be naturally desired or needed); and 3. It is both consciously wanted and naturally needed by us, and so it is an object that both appears good to us and is also really good for us." Such is the human condition.

The book deals with another problem: can the good life be planned? Mortimer admits the limitations of the guidance moral philosophy can give when he says that "each individual life is an uncharted sea, full of unforeseeable dangers and untoward complications." Goethe would have agreed. Robert Burns put it with more charm in "To a Mouse."

> The best-laid schemes o' mice an' men
> Gang aft a-gley
> An' leave us nought but grief an' pain,
> For promised joy.
>
> Still thou art blest compared wi' me!
> The present only toucheth thee:
> But och! I backward cast my e'e
> On prospects drear!
> And forward though I canna see,
> I guess an' fear.

We admit up front that no one plans to lead a bad life, not even criminals: what they do they consider good for themselves. (I exclude moral idiots from this discussion.) But can a life be planned? Throughout history the lives of most individuals have been planned for them by virtue of their low status in society. They were forced to live in ruts not of their own making. Many people still do, but in this country it is as much of their own making as not. Do individuals generally have enough intelligence and moral discernment to plan a life? From early years I certainly planned my life, and I carried out the plans. That did not stop me from making an unexpected course correction. Anecdotal, yet hardly unrepresentative in this era of frequent career changes. Uncertain times make for uncertain prospects. The fact that circumstances change constantly makes for a high degree of uncertainty, something most people are unprepared to cope with – hence all the reactionary and backward-looking institutions that desire to keep everything as it has always been. But it has not always been so.

But we are talking about the good life, not career choices. One's plans can change, but one can still achieve the good life, providing we do not make certain features obligatory, such as schooling, work, family, and location. What then is this core thing, the good life, when we divorce it from all the unnecessary accoutrements? We are driven back to the lifetime pattern of making right choices and all the difficulties inhering in that process.

It is easy to look at someone we admire or envy and think that this person has a good life. But what we usually mean is that the individual has a lot of stuff, especially wealth that we do not possess. Since we never walk in that individual's shoes, we really are in no position to assess his or her life as good. It's incumbent then to look to the self and make an assessment. Have I had a good life – we are not talking only about a morally excellent life, but a life with which we can express overall satisfaction and a minimum of regrets. Aristotle would insist on a morally purposeful life.

How can such a judgment be made until one reaches the end? Remember the words of the poet. Must not an assessment of the thoroughly secular good life be based on some kind of faith, a firm belief that this is what a good life really is? It is hardly possible for a young person to look ahead and see any guarantee of a good life down the line, considering and the bumps in the road and all potential detours.

If the good life is not defined by how much stuff and wealth one collects, how is the abundant life that Jesus spoke of defined? It certainly cannot be based on a shopping list of goods owned. If the good life is an inner quality with certain outward ramifications, so is the abundant life. Pardon me if I seem vague, but this is, as I said, a problem I've not solved.

If the good life is assessed as such toward the end of one's existence, what about the abundant life (whatever it is)? Does not the good life in a Christian sense lead toward an end, a goal, a summing up? If so, the bumps and detours do not matter much, because, as St. Paul said, "I have learned to be content in whatever conditions I find myself." And, "whether we live or whether we die, we are the Lord's." Did St. Paul have an abundant life? What about the martyrs? Did Mother Teresa have an abundant life; she obviously lived the life she wanted to. The issue of the good life probably never crossed her mind.

Which brings me to the most difficult part of this narration: combining the secular good life with the abundant life. Jesus also spoke about taking up one's cross and following Him. Precisely where is the abundance in that? When Dietrich Bonhoeffer wrote of "the costs of discipleship," he meant paying a price for one's stand in the Christian community, as he was forced to do. When I hear the word abundance, I think of a cornucopia, the proverbial horn of plenty. I don't think of suffering, martyrdom, or paying a price except perhaps in after-dinner heartburn.

I live in a moderately affluent western suburb of Chicago. Beverly Hills or Bel Air, it isn't, but it does well enough. The worldly goods of the secular good life are all around me. How many people here think they have a good life I have no way of knowing. But there are Christians here, and their lives are, to all appearances, quite like all the non-Christians, again speaking economically. Their inner life I do not know. There is not much suffering for one's faith and certainly no martyrdom here. Would these local Christians think they are living the abundant life in the sense Jesus meant it – if we really knew how he meant it? Can financial or career success achieved by Christians be equated with the abundant life? Some Christians have thought so: where do you think Max Weber's Protestant work ethic came from? Work hard, be committed, earn your way, receive your rewards, as an indication that you may be among the elect.

I must admit that this ramble may represent nothing more than my own version of "liberal guilt" for never having played a significant role in the life of the church or of having failed to benefit society in any great way. There is little chance of martyrdom in this household and no suffering except the aches and pains that come with age. All the earthly abundance I desire, I have; and it is really rather meager by most current American standards. What good one does is rarely apparent, while the evil, unintended or not, somehow remains to haunt the memory.

I think this has been a problem worth considering, because there are some New Testament episodes that make it almost irrelevant. The one that comes to mind occurs in the ninth chapter of Acts, after the conversion of Saul of Tarsus. Saul, now blind, awaits the restoration of sight from the laying on of hands by one Ananias of Damascus. Ananias, aware of Saul's hostility toward Christians, is fearful; but God assures him, saying, "Go, for he is a chosen instrument of mine to carry my name before the Gentiles and kings and the sons of Israel; *for I will show him how much he must suffer for the sake of my name.*"

Some few years ago, at Christ Church in Oak Brook, Illinois, I heard a sermon by Dr. Arthur DeKruyter based on the Annunciation to Mary. The tenor of it was this: when God chooses you, think what might be in store for you. Perhaps you will want to respond like Jonah and run away, if you could envision what the future might bring. Mary certainly suffered a great deal, when her son became an adult. John the Baptist came to an untimely end. So did most, if not all, of the apostles. Now, how is it possible to understand the abundant life and the good life? Are God's most specially chosen messengers meant to suffer, while the rest of us enjoy the affluence of 21st century America?

Perhaps the abundant life can be defined as the life in Christ, whatever the consequences.

Having now dealt with religion versus Christianity in its traditional form, it is time to turn to its most dangerous current manifestation: the secular powers. It is these that may well do away with our liberty and prosperity, and we will be the willing accomplices.

As a preliminary to the next section, here are a few words from Andrew Carnegie speaking to an English audience. "The great error in your country is that things are just upside down. You look to your officials to govern you instead of your governing them."

(Quoted in *How the Scots Invented the Modern World* by Arthur Herman, p. 343.) And, by the way, the book is very much worth reading.

Part 3: Government and Its Discontents: Our New-Age Religion

First a brief clarification. All human beings by nature engage in economic activity – they need food, clothing, and shelter. Government, on the other hand, is human invention. It originated in the ancient city-states as a means of protection from attack by outsiders and to control whatever crime may have existed within the community. Unfortunately, the arming of a segment of the population created a system of control over that population. This is the situation in which humanity has lived since at least the third millennium B.C. What mattered was government, the arena of society that always expands. The citizens existed to provide taxes and men for armies. Now, again, a few quotations. Note especially the last one, by C. S. Lewis; it is quite appropriate for the 21st century.

> "Cursed are those who trust in mere mortals and make mere flesh their strength." (Jeremiah 17:5)

"If you love bad news, devote your life to studying government." (Lew Rockwell, in *The Free Market,* July 1997.)

"[T]here is certainly something mad about all-consuming political passions." (Michael Burleigh in *Earthly Powers,* 2005, p. 88)

"Nothing is more misleading, then, than the conventional formulae of historians who represent the achievement of a powerful state as the culmination of cultural evolution: it is as often marked as its end. (Friedrich A. Hayek in *The Fatal Conceit*)

"When the traditional foundations of a culture crumble, as we are seeing them do today in the United States and in the western world, when government by law gives way to government by irresponsible force, the preoccupation with liberty as an end in itself is replaced by a new search for security, mental, social, economic, and even physical." (Ralph H. Gabriel in *The Course of American Democratic Thought* (1939), p. 22

"It's one lot of people making rules for another lot of people to live by, when they wouldn't accept them themselves." (Anne Perry in *Southampton Row,* p. 13)

Government mistakes – not inherent flaws in free markets – are the root of every economic crisis in modern times. (Steve Forbes in *Forbes* magazine May 31, 2019)

"It has been said that all government is evil. It would be more proper to say that the necessity of government is a misfortune."(James Madison)

"What are kingdoms but great robberies? For what are robberies themselves, but little kingdoms?" (St. Augustine in *The City of God*)

"I never thought the government would go so far afield. I never thought politicians would become so untrustworthy. I never thought courts would go so nuts to the left, and I misjudged the quality of the government that we have." (The Rev. Jerry Falwell, founder of the Moral Majority)

"The masses, it seems, have vague aspirations toward liberty and human brotherhood, which are easily played upon by power-hungry individuals and minorities. So that history consists of a series of swindles, in which the masses are first lured into revolt by the promise of Utopia, and then, when they have done their job, enslaved again by new masters." (George Orwell, in "Second Thoughts on James Burnham")

"In our time, political speech and writing are largely the defense of the indefensible." (George Orwell, "Politics and the English Language," 1946)

"[T]hose whose decisions will inevitably affect human life for generations are not expected to know anything in particular before setting to work, They do not have to be political scientists, economists, or even lawyers….[T]hey need only be expert fund-raisers, comport themselves well on television, and be indulgent of certain *myths*." (Sam Harris, *The End of Faith*, p. 39)

"Grant did not have to go any distance to find crookedness in government. He had only to look out his windows. Then, as now, the District of Columbia was a byword for corruption." (Geoffrey Perret in *Ulysses S. Grant: Soldier and President*, 1997, p. 435)

"Congress is our only native criminal class." (Mark Twain)

"He sometimes thought it a pity the United States hadn't the practice of parceling out peerages instead of taking the sometimes ruinous course of doling out high government offices to make good on campaign promises. So much better a baronet than a booby." (Martha Grimes in *The Stargazey*, p. 97)

"I keep thinking that even this spineless lot of halfwits who pretend to govern us can't humiliate themselves further, but they always find some excuse to retreat or surrender." (David Roberts, *The Quality of Mercy.*)

"Never complain that the people in power are stupid. It is their best trait." (P. J. O'Rourke, in *On the Wealth of Nations,* p. 96. This book, incidentally, is a very good introduction to Adam Smith's much longer work.)

"There is little doubt that the modern cult of power worship is bound up with the modern man's feeling that life here and now is the only life there is." (George Orwell, March 3, 1944, from *Collected Essays, Journalism, and Letters of George Orwell,* vol. 3, ed. Sonia Orwell and Ian Angus)

"It is quite easy to imagine a state in which the ruling class deceive their followers without deceiving themselves." (George Orwell, review of Bertrand Russell's Power, Jn. 1939, *op. cit,* Vol.2)

"The more I see of the representatives of the people, the more I love my dogs." (Alphonse de Lamartine, French foreign minister in the 1848 revolution. Quoted in *The Shadow*

Emperor, by Alan Strauss-Schom, 2018, p. 123)

"The modern state exists not to protect our rights but to do good to us or make us good – anyway to do something to us or make us something. Hence the new name "leaders" for those who were once "rulers." We are less their subjects than their wards, pupils, or domestic animals. There is nothing left of which we can say to them, "Mind your own business." Our whole lives are their business." (C. S. Lewis, "Is Progress Possible?: Willing Slaves of the Welfare State" from *God in the Dock,* p. 514, in *The Timeless Writings of C. S. Lewis.*)

Prologue

It was not government that cleared the fields and forests for American farmers.

It wasn't government that invented the steamship, the telegraph, light bulb, the telephone, automobile, phonograph, movies, airplanes, radio, television, computers, or smartphones.

It wasn't government that gave us McDonald's, Wendy's, Burger King, Kentucky Fried Chicken, Taco Bell, Domino's, Pizza Hut, Dairy Queen, or White Castle.

It wasn't government that devised the general theory of relativity or quantum mechanics.

It wasn't government that created Ford, General Motors, Chrysler, Toyota, Honda, or Nissan.

It wasn't government that presented us with Prudential, Met Life, CNN, or John Hancock.

It wasn't government that gave us A. G. Edwards, Merrill Lynch, Goldman Sachs, Lehman Brothers, Morgan Stanley Dean Witter, or Charles Schwab.

It wasn't government that built US Steel, Bethlehem Steel, Goodyear Tire and Rubber, Firestone, Alcoa, Standard Oil, Texaco, Mobil, Chevron, Exxon, or Nucor Steel.

It wasn't government that built the homes we live in or made the clothes we wear.

It wasn't government that provided the amazing variety of food in our supermarkets.

It wasn't government that gave us Apple Computer, Intel, Microsoft, Sun Microsystems, Dell Computer, Compaq Computer, Hewlett-Packard, Oracle, Cisco Systems, IBM, AT&T, Xerox, MCI Communications, Novell, or Lotus.

It wasn't government that gave us the *New York Times, The Washington Post,* the *Chicago Tribune,* the *St. Louis Post-Dispatch,* the *Los Angeles Times,* or any other newspaper. Nor did we get from our masters in Washington, DC, *Time, Life, Newsweek,* the *Saturday Evening Post, U. S. News and World Report, Sports Illustrated, Field and Stream, Good Housekeeping* or any other worthwhile magazine.

It wasn't government that built Warner Brothers, United Artists, Paramount, Twentieth-Century Fox, Disney, RKO, CBS, ABC, NBC, Fox, Comcast, Viacom, or MGM.

It wasn't government that built Las Vegas, Atlantic City, or Disney World.

It wasn't government that built New York City, Philadelphia, Pittsburgh, Cleveland, Chicago, Atlanta, Cincinnati, St. Louis, Kansas City, Dallas, Houston, Santa Fe, Phoenix, Miami, Los Angeles, Seattle, or Minneapolis-St. Paul.

One might say that government gave us the Internet, but it certainly was an inadvertent gift; and without Tim Berners-Lee we might not have it now.

Chapter 5 The Real Dismal Science

The theme of what follows is this: In contrast to Thomas Carlyle, politics, not economics, is the dismal science and the scourge of humanity. Economic activity derives from human nature. Government is a human invention, based on good intentions that went awry.

Is there a theme developing? Yes – it is well worth considering by today's Americans, especially the masses of America-haters who see only the warts in our history, the effort it took to build a free and prosperous society. It was not always a pretty picture. Slavery was always a curse, and the Native Americans suffered far more than was necessary. The rights of women were often limited. The captains of industry rarely treated their workers fairly or honorably. But an economy is always a work in progress, subject to the best and worst qualities of human nature. It's always easier to blame a system than human folly, although it is humans who create systems in the first place. What is missed by the vehement critics of the United States is this: every evil pointed out has been prevalent around the world for centuries: slavery, oppression of women, genocide, inequality of income and status, and more. Maybe it is time to accept the fact that it is human nature that is at fault.

The free-market economy has taken more than two centuries to develop. Even as this process was taking place, those involved were not specifically aware of what they were doing, any more than the people who lived in the Middle Ages knew they were living in the Middle Ages. No free economy that delivers wide-spread prosperity can ever be built by government planning. The planned society has certainly been tried often enough; the 20th century was rife with them. They all ended in disaster, as will our nation if the planners get their way. One would have thought that 6,000 years of historical failure could have provided enough clues about what works and what doesn't, but apparently not. A short and very readable treatise on this subject was written by Ludwig von Mises; entitled *Planned Chaos,* it is still in print.

Those who witnessed the early growth of a free market society, both in Europe and North America, were often distressed at the unfairness of so much of it. Yet the results have been spectacular, especially in the significant declines in poverty around the world in the last 50 years. The never-ending insistence by political types that they can make it better has been disproved so often that one wonders how anyone can fall for their malevolent prattle. One must realize that if a free society were left to its own devices, the government crowd could not be the society-saving, money-grubbing, power-hungry celebrities they so want to be. What follows is a discussion of the secular religion that emerged following the French Revolution (or more properly after the Thirty Years War), a religion that became more than a plague on all societies in the 20th century and continues to this day.

Chapter 6 Tom Paine's Dilemma

Tom Paine was a propagandist for the American Revolution. He later went on to make a name for himself in the French Revolution but fell out of favor in the United States. His book, *The Age of Reason,* did not win any favorable reviews among the Christian denominations. In 1776 he published *Common Sense,* one of the best known and most articulate defenses of the colonial cause against England. In this tract he stated that: "Government at best is a necessary evil, at its worst an intolerable one." That will be the thesis of what follows. This is dedicated to those who believe that governments do good things by expressing good intentions. This is the heart of political romanticism.

Why is there so much misery in this world? Why is there so much destitution, so many epidemics of disease without medicine, so much starvation, so many little deadly wars, so much inter-ethnic strife? Is it really possible to look back on the incredible amount of violence, war, and bloodshed practiced by governments from ancient empires into the 21st century and still claim that there is something seriously wrong with a free and prosperous society that needs radical surgery?

Without the Soviet government, about 40 million

people would not have been eliminated "for the good of the state." Without the National Socialist regime of Germany, there would not have been more than 15 people put to death "for the good of the state." Without Mengitsu's government in Ethiopia there would not have been mass starvation; the same can be said for Somalia. Without Pol Pot and his friends there would not have been genocide in Cambodia. Without Mao there would not have been more than 76 million people done away with, as the cost of building Communism in China. Without the Islamic terrorist government of the Sudan, would the people in Darfur really be worse off? Would Zimbabwe survive without the brilliance of Robert Mugabe? Would anyone care to discuss "fairness" in these glorious contexts?

(I wrote the previous paragraph sometime in the early 2000s. Now it is 2019, and we have Al Qaeda, ISIS, Iran, Hezbollah, and the overall mess that is the Middle East. Of course there is North Korea, probably the worst government, apart from the Islamic states. Venezuela put up with the imbecility of Hugo Chavez in Venezuela, only to be succeeded by and equally tyrannical dictator, Nicolás Maduro. His status as of early 2019 became uncertain when another president appeared to challenge him. Argentina was fortunate to rid itself of Peronism, at least temporarily.)

Need one be reminded of what England did to the Irish for hundreds of years? One wonders who the barbarians really were. Without government enforcement, could racism have endured so long in the United States? Without the federal and state governments there could have been no Jim Crow laws, no *Plessey v. Ferguson,* and far fewer lynchings. Now, to make up for past mistakes, these same governments have reversed course and implemented new racist laws under the guise of civil rights. Without governments it is unlikely that many people would have taken it upon themselves to fight either world war to bolster the egos of their beloved leaders.

There are two great obstacles to human well being: apart from human nature itself, they are government and religion. This is now and has always been the case. Yet, seemingly, we cannot do without either, nor can we get rid of either. The latter is part of human nature, while the former were devised by humanity for its own protection – the necessary evil.

To begin the journey down this path, it is first necessary to revert to the topic of the previous chapter: Religion. It is not out of place here if religion is properly defined, because in human societies religion and government can coalesce into one. Or government can simply replace what we normally understand as religion to become the focus of superstition. State-worship is not new. In the societies of ancient Egypt, Mesopotamia, Greece, the political and the religious were united. Rome was an exception.

In Martin Luther's *Large Catechism,* the Reformer treats the subject: "What is it to have a god?" His answer: "A god is that to which we look for all good and in which we find refuge in every time of need....That to which your heart clings and entrusts itself is, I say, really your god." Notice that "god" does not have a capital G here. Luther is saying that whatever people look to as explaining the meaning of their lives, whatever people regard as the source of the good things of life, whatever people regard as a guarantor of security, to this will they give their devotion. In Luther's terms, it is possible to be polytheistic, to be devoted to a number of gods just as the ancients were. In his explanation of the First Commandment, he lists a number of gods, and they are fairly common abstractions: wealth, power, wisdom, and property. If we view American society closely we can see others: celebritydom, spectator sports, shopping malls, rock concerts, movies, and television easily come to mind. Even family or career can become gods.

But Luther's point is a simple one: To elect for oneself a god within creation is to miss the one God and to put one's ultimate trust in one or more facets of an existence that will one day die. (This is called demonization, assigning absolute merit or value to something that cannot bear those qualities.) But if we comprehend the biblical message, humanity cannot but miss the One who is God. Being unable to perceive the Creator, human societies must devise gods for themselves. These gods of religion are needed as explanations, as comforters, as aids in time of trouble, and as servants in time of plenty.

Now, of all the things that Luther or anyone else might certify as a transient and false god, there is a single overarching one: government, the most pervasive institution in modern human societies. The future French premier, Georges Clemenceau stated this truth vividly in 1884: "Yes! We have guillotined the King, long live the State-King! We have dethroned the Pope, long live the State-Pope!.....All the crimes that have been accomplished in the world, the massacres, the wars, the breaches of sworn faith, the stakes, the punishment, the tortures, all have been justified in the interests of the state, the *raison d'état*." (Quoted in Jonathan Fenby, *France on the Brink*. p. 428)

All of which is to say: people, even atheists, will have faith in something. It may be something as impermanent as the self. It may be in things quite transient, the incessant pursuit of pleasures and pastimes that bring a temporary happiness. It may be in something apparently permanent, such as property. The joke of property is that it remains for someone else after we are gone: some gods are more durable than others. The pursuit of happiness may itself be the idol. It has been much overrated. There is the fairly well known story about Solon's visit to the court of King Croesus. The king was offended when the great lawgiver did not consider him the happiest of men, with all of his wealth and power. Solon insisted that the happy life was the sum of a whole life lived well. I personally wonder how one can be happy at that point, facing imminent death. The life of Croesus did not end happily. But I have wandered from my course, as my mind often does. Back to government. Three additional and, for me, irrefutable theses are necessary here:

1. Every human being, in all times and in all places, should have the rights mentioned in the Declaration of Independence: the rights to life, liberty, and the pursuit of happiness. The last of these three phrases means the right for everyone to seek self-fulfillment according to his own abilities and insights; the right to seek to improve his life as best he can with no one holding him back or throwing unnecessary obstacles in his path.

2. No government, anywhere or at any time has ever brought forth a society that was a benefit to all its citizens. All governments at all times (even today) are collections of oligarchies – the self-appointed or elected few ruling over the many. All governments exist primarily for

themselves, and they will pander to the citizenry only to the extent that it is necessary to maintain power. Heads of government always get along better with each other than they do with their own citizens, in case you haven't noticed. Thomas Jefferson asserted that all governments tend naturally toward tyranny.

3. Governments are inherently parasitic: they produce nothing, nor do they earn anything. All governments up to the founding of the United States existed by taking as much wealth from the producers in society and arrogating it to themselves to create classes of privilege and power. The five percent have always, prior to the American and French revolutions, lived at the expense of the ninety-five percent. In the 20th and 21st centuries this ancient trend has been gradually revived. The Soviet Union was the most elite society of modern times, much more so that the France of Louis XIV. The American Left has as its aim the creation of just such a society in this country, but its adherents will not say so openly. Success is plausible, since democracy as a system always fails. That subject will be covered below.

Did I say "irrefutable?" All history prior to 1776 as well as most of the 20th century was a refutation, but I stand by my words. The political class, the statists, those whom Thomas Sowell has called The Anointed, naturally will disagree – as will their gullible sycophants and willing accomplices.

Back to Tom Paine and the necessary evil. Picture yourself as a wealthy and sought-after celebrity. You can't go out in public without being hounded by hordes of shrieking fans or camera-laden paparazzi. Who wants to stay cooped up inside all the time? To go out, a celebrity needs protection. Some celebrities travel about with a large entourage of "friends" to fend off unwelcome admirers. Others just hire a bodyguard. Now, a bodyguard is expected to provide protection and no more. But what if said bodyguard decides to take control and dictate all aspects of the celebrity's life? After all, he has the muscle and the gun. What began as a necessary evil becomes an intolerable one. Somehow, our unfortunate celebrity finds a way of getting rid of this bodyguard and hires a new one. The same story repeats itself: from bodyguard to controller and extorter of wealth. How many times must this scenario repeat itself before our hapless celebrity tries another course of action – if there is such? Growing old helps; the stars of years gone by are of interest to very few. *Sunset Boulevard* provides a great example.

Does not another question quickly pop up: After thousands of years of oppression, how long will societies repeatedly reassert their fondness for their oppressors?

One looks around the world from one's living room and notes the most absurd events. A homicidal maniac governed Iraq until 2003, yet his people for some reason put up with it, while enduring misery. A collection of hate-filled clerics governs Iran, as the prosperity of that nation is rapidly eroded. The countries of sub-Saharan Africa endure the worst conditions imaginable at the hands of demented dictators, who collect foreign aid and stash it in their Swiss bank accounts. President Mugabe of Zimbabwe seems to take delight in ruining his own country. (He was deposed in 2017, but the future of Zimbabwe remains uncertain.) Fidel Castro certainly enjoyed destroying Cuba's economy and civil society, and his brother Raul carried on with the mission after Fidel's death.

The woeful tale of Yugoslavia is too familiar to need repeating. In the more "civilized" parts of the globe, Europeans put up with velvet fascism that stifles more prosperity than it could ever create – and this at the hands of mainly unelected officials. In Europe it is so obvious that the governing classes exist primarily for themselves that one wonders that the populations don't catch on. But, then, Europeans have never known the kind of freedom experienced by 19th-century Americans. In the United States the Constitution is being incrementally shredded, while the greater part of the fun-loving, good-hearted population goes on its merry way gazing occasionally at the fluctuations in the financial markets and pretending in election years that what happens in the federal and state capitals is of some significance. But these are just personal gripes. It's really not possible to generalize accurately about a large population.

How can one possibly be so negative about government now, in this glorious age of Democracy? Did not St. Paul himself say in that Epistle to the Romans: "Let every person be subject to the governing authorities. For there is no authority except from God, and those that exist have been instituted by God. Therefore he who resists the authorities resists what God has appointed, and those who resist will incur judgment. For rulers are not a terror to good conduct, but to bad." Yes, he did say it. But, of course, he never lived in the Soviet Union, nor was he incarcerated at Auschwitz. He was, in fact, imprisoned in Rome during the reign of Nero. One wonders if his sentiments had changed by that time. To be fair, he had no notion of the sovereignty of the people as it emerged in the United States after 1776. In his day, sovereignty resided in the emperor. But it is still necessary to deal with his assertions.

Was Paul right? In the light of historical experience, no. But his letter is in the Bible, and the Bible is true. Yes, but his assessment of government is not the only one in the Bible, and it is a minority view. Biblical literalists will not agree, but I am willing to say that he was speaking of something that was the overarching reality of his world, the government of the Roman Empire; and he was, after all, a Roman citizen. And he was saying it within the limits of what he knew and understood at the time, much as he expressed no negative view of slavery in the Letter to Philemon. No one today would accept his casual attitude on slavery or his apparently anti-feminist rhetoric, but in his time the attitudes were an integral part of the social and economic system. I think we can safely look with some skepticism at his view of government, realizing that to do so does not in the least undermine his message about what he knew best, the Jesus event and its significance. There have, after all, been far worse governments than that of Rome, as anyone who lived during the 20th century can testify.

There are other statements on government in the Bible beside Paul's. None of them needs to be normative for the way we think about the issue, but they indicate that there was no hard and fast position on the subject. The writers of the biblical texts did write within the contexts of their time, as well as within the context of their understanding of the acts of God in history. Consider a couple of examples.

Late in the period of the Judges, the people of Israel

came to Samuel and asked for a king "to govern us like all the nations." Samuel tried to discourage their demand, saying to them, "These will be the ways of the king who will reign over you: he will take your sons and appoint them to his chariots and to be his horsemen, and to run before his chariots; and he will appoint for himself commanders of thousands and commanders of fifties, and some to plow his ground and to reap his harvest, and to make his implements of war and the equipment of his chariots. He will take your daughters to be perfumers and cooks and bakers. He will take the best of your fields and vineyards and olive orchards and give them to his servants. He will take the tenth of your grain and of your vineyards and give it to his officers and to his servants.... He will take the tenth of your flocks, and you shall be his slaves. And in that day you will cry out because of your king, whom you have chosen for yourselves; but the Lord will not answer you in that day." But the people refused to listen to the voice of Samuel; and they said, "No, but we will have a king over us, that we may be like all the nations." They got their king, and all the prophecies of Samuel were fulfilled; and in time disaster overcame Israel. (I Samuel 8, Revised Standard Version). This does have the ring of truth, doesn't it?

From Psalm 2: "Why do the nations conspire, and the peoples plot in vain? The kings of the earth set themselves, and the rulers take counsel together against the Lord and his anointed, saying, 'Let us burst their bonds asunder, and cast their cords from us.' He who sits in the heavens laughs; the Lord has them in derision." (Revised Standard Version)

The Old Testament passages have as a fundamental

assumption the idea of theocracy, direct rule by God. This was obviously the original intention, as evidenced by the giving of the Law to Moses. With their insistence on having a king, just as other nations had, the people of Israel rejected theocracy. With a king, they would have a government legislating for them although the Law of God was still a fundamental fact of Israel's existence.

Theocracy is not possible on earth. (It has certainly been tried often enough and failed.) The Latin Church of the Middle Ages attempted to force its will on the populations of Western Europe, with every threat it had at its disposal, including torture and murder. In the present century we see Islamic mullahs imposing their fraudulent and demonic theocracies, whose only benefit is to themselves, while the citizens suffer. (Early in 2011 it appeared that many in those nations had run out of patience with their dictators. One could only hope the rebellions succeed, but by early 2013 they had not.) Any attempt to rule in the place of God is a fraud, because it is perpetrated by very fallible men, men who are so obviously overwhelmed with a lust for power and loot, as well as being convinced that they have all truth. Nor is a secular version of theocracy plausible anywhere today, although there certainly are a number of vicious and humanity-destroying facsimiles run by all-knowing elitists.

Human imitations of theocracy are bound to fail because God is the only source of good, the only One who knows what is really good for humanity. Humans can only presume to know good. Having no certain knowledge of the will of God, human authorities can only impose their versions of good on subject populations. When this happens, God is removed from the equation. This is not a matter of conjecture. Every single attempt at theocracy fails: the medieval church, the New England Puritans, the Cromwell experiment in England, the Muslim theocracies of today. People who know what is good for other people are the most dangerous individuals on earth. What is at issue, of course, is power.

Closely related to the concept of theocracy is the attempt, imagined or real, of some Christian institutions and leaders to impose on society values based on tenets of theology. This is an accusation often leveled at the Christian Coalition, an organization that has aligned itself with conservative politics in the United States. On the other side of the political spectrum is the National Council of Churches, quite devoted to the politics of the far Left. For Christian denominations to take strong political positions is an error because it is divisive and cannot earn respect or admiration from the secular society at large. This does not mean that Christians have no place in the "public square," but they participate there as individuals. The less some of their leaders say, the better.

Gatherings of church "leaders" making pronouncements on the ills of society are more often ludicrous than not, because they simply do not know what they are talking about in many cases – especially when they make economic analyses. (My own denomination has been engaged in a valiant campaign to preserve the family farm. Had the same "leaders" been around a century ago, they would doubtless have sought to preserve the horse and buggy trade. I wonder if they lament the passing of the typewriter.) The proposed solutions of many of the clergy are usually pallid rehashes of Marxism or at variance with developing trends in the economy. Remember that churches tend to be quite reactionary, tied to the status quo and unable to perceive forward movements in society. They are alarmed by what Joseph A. Schumpeter called the creative destruction that is a necessary aspect of any economic and technological progress. (By churches, in this context, I mean denominations.) Labor unions share this reactionary stance and are even more fearful of change than the priestly class.

Apparently the denominations cannot get beyond their historical ties with the state. That such ties still exist in Europe is undeniable, but they have no place in this country. That church "leaders' insist on adopting and promoting political agendas is intensely divisive, or should be, for their congregations. (But, of course, many such leaders do not have congregations; they are bishops or bureaucrats.) That church leaders look at some political agendas as automatically good, because they sound good, is appalling. The evils inherent in political desires to reengineer society should by this time be apparent, after a century of Stalinism, Hitlerism, fascism, and more recently, Islamofascism. But the dream apparently lives on. Can it be that some Christians are so stupid that they think it possible to build a kingdom of God here on earth? Can they not realize that the most horrific evil will always present itself as good? Such is the essence of the Anti-Christ, who appears as pure and righteous to all who behold him (or it, or them).

About 75 years ago Oswald Spengler weighed in on the clergy in politics. (He is famous for his *Decline of the West.*) Speaking of the French Revolution, Spengler said: "In such times we find a certain clerical scum that drags the faith and the dignity of the Church into the dirt of party politics, which allies itself with the powers of destruction and while mouthing the phrases of altruism and protection of the poor helps the underworld to destroy the social order – the order on which the Church irrevocably and fatally rests."

In the 20th century, the French novelist Georges Bernanos put this sentiment into a more contemporary context: "I believe that our children will see the main body of the troops of the Church on the side of the forces of death. I can see myself being executed by Bolshevik priests who carry the *Social Contract* in their pocket but have a cross dangling from their neck." The *Social Contract* is, of course, the famous work by Rousseau, and the context of which Bernanos speaks sounds suspiciously like Liberation Theology. It wasn't, however, since he made the remark in 1926; but it is pertinent to the subject. (Both quotations are from *Leftism Revisited* by Erik von Kuehnelt-Leddihn)

Perhaps if the clergy were not so narrowly trained, they might gain a wider perspective on how the world works – on economics, that is. On this, they are mostly quite ignorant. Schooling may not be a solution, though. Many students arriving at seminaries these days bring with them their political and social agendas and simply want to use positions in churches to advance them. It is like having a Fifth Column within the denominations, eating away at the message and mission of the New Testament, all the while preaching some wishy-washy, namby-pamby, watered-down message that can pass muster as being sweetly orthodox without being offensive.

For many of the clergy, their kingdom is definitely of this world, and their theology has become a political ideology.

Judaism has a similar problem. Why this is so has long puzzled me, and the conclusions I have reached about it may be off target. First, the facts. The most notorious event of the 20th century for Judaism was the Holocaust. The best estimate is six million Jews killed by the Nazis and their willing associates. Little known is the fact that Stalin had also terminated Jews in Russia before the Germans put the Final Solution into effect. It is Hitler who remains the political demon, and his savagery may well have driven Jews to the political Left. That most of the Jews in the United States and Israel adhere to Leftist politics is undeniable. (I did not make this up. Murray Rothbard told me.) David Ben Gurion, Israel's first prime minister, was a dedicated Socialist. Few seem to realize that Hitler was also of the Left – he was a Socialist. He and his chief followers often expressed their debt to Marx. (Anyone interested in learning of the grim realities experienced by German Jews from 1933 to 1939 should get hold of *The Third Reich in Power* by Richard J. Evans, published in 2005, or, more recently, *The War of the World* by Niall Ferguson, in 2006).

I think the Hitler excuse is too facile. The movement of large numbers of Jews toward Marxism and its imitators began long before Hitler was on the radar screen. (Remember that many of the early Bolsheviks were Jews. Trotsky is the best known. On the eve of the Nazi-Soviet pact in August 1939, the Soviet foreign minister, Maxim Litvinov, a Jew, was replaced by Molotov so as not to offend Hitler.) I have found a reason for this that is plausible to me, but it may, as noted, be quite off base. The fundamental documents of Judaism are the Law and the Prophets. The Law is certainly a collection of Do's and Don'ts, but the heart of it is the Ten Commandments. These depict what a human being ought to be in response to the Creator God. The Prophets contain ringing endorsements of social justice. Now, if it is possible to know what the Law is and what social justice is, does one need any more the Law-giver as a point of reference? Is it not possible to take the directives found in Law and Prophets and seek to apply them directly to secular society? Marxism promised to do precisely this, with what results we now know. (If you don't know, read *The Black Book of Communism*, one of the great books of our time.)

Furthermore, the Jews have been the most consistently persecuted people in history, and they will continue to be so if the Muslims get their way. Anti-Semitism has never disappeared from Europe, in spite of the Holocaust; and it is even showing up in the United States among those who support the rights of the Palestinians, without considering what Israel is as a nation. It is hardly any surprise that in their long history, the Jewish populations of Europe would hope and seek for justice for themselves. "At the end of days, the evil will be conquered by the One; in historic times, evils must be conquered one by one." (Abraham Joshua Heschel, *God in Search of Man*, p. 377)

That Communism has proved to be a murderous catastrophe does not dissuade the adherents of Liberal politics. The expressed hope on the part of many is that the same social justice goals can be achieved while avoiding such barbarism. Do they forget that the imposition of force is necessary to keep socialism functioning? The desire on the part of others is simply to gain and keep power. All of Europe is socialist today, but more after the pattern of the Third Reich than of the Soviet Union, in spite of the efforts of certain French intellectuals. It is hardly known that Hitler's economics ministry made the first plans for a European Union, in the early 1940s. I do not make this stuff up. You can find out for yourself by reading a revealing volume, *The Rotten Heart of Europe*, by Bernard Connolly. This fact has been supported by Robert Skidelski in the third volume of his biography of John Maynard Keynes. The reference is on page 195.

The persistent attempts to create perfect social justice never seem to cease in Europe. The late member of the British Parliament, Ivor Thomas, proved conclusively that this quest is a delusion in his *The Socialist Tragedy* (1949). He spoke from experience, having been a member of Clement Atlee's Labour government after 1945 – until he perceived what the "wave of the future" actually entailed. Nevertheless, the delusion persists. For many others, however, the Liberal cause is only about power and control. They suffer from no delusions about achieving social justice, nor would they ever want it. And, in spite of the collapse of Communism and the discrediting of socialism generally, the "intellectuals" never give up. A book by Jean-François Revel published in the United States in 2009 brilliantly documents their continued efforts to put a good face on Communism. The title is *Last Exit to Utopia*. These Liberals (Leftists) and their malevolence will be addressed in a chapter on the Intellectuals.

I should address the term Liberalism. The word itself is obviously derived from the Latin word for "free," *liber*. For more than a century after the American Revolution it referred to those who favored what Adam Smith called "a system of natural liberty." This meant economic as well as political freedom. It especially meant the free-market economy. Without economic freedom and all it entails, political freedom cannot mean much. In Europe today, the word liberalism is often still understood in this traditional sense. It is in the United States that the word has been completely bastardized. The Austrian-born economist Joseph Schumpeter correctly stated that "the enemies of liberty, as a supreme but unintended compliment, have thought it wise to appropriate the label." (It's in his *History of Economic Analysis*.)

American Liberalism today is completely aligned with its siblings on traditional Left, with Socialists old and new, with National Socialism, with fascism. It is one of the latest in centuries of manifestations of Statism, an ideology at least as old as Plato's *Republic*. Statism is the proper collective word for all of these shabby freedom-hating ideologies, what George Orwell in 1940 called "all the smelly little orthodoxies which are now contending for our souls." What they all have in common is the unspoken slogan: All power to the state. I have not the time to trace the development of this political force. Erik von Kuehnelt-Leddhin has brilliantly done it in *Leftism Revisited: From de Sade and Marx to Hitler and Pol Pot* (1990). A more recent work on the same subject is the delightfully well-documented *Liberal Fascism: The Secret History of the American Left from Mussolini to the Politics of Change* by Jonah Goldberg (2007).

As to the term Conservative, I really don't know what it can mean today. I am not one, in spite of what one may gather from this text. The whole playing field of politics was drastically altered after the Russian Revolution of 1917.

The shift toward Statism occurred in the United States during the 1930s, as a response to the Great Depression. Hosts of Socialists and fellow travelers descended upon Washington, DC, to help "fix" the problem. That they had no idea how to do it mattered not at all. And they could not have done it even if they knew. But the ideology was in the air. It had triumphed, in one form or another, in Russia, Italy, and Germany. In spite of the fact that nearly all (I'm tempted to say all) their programs failed and the Depression was not overcome, the way politics was done in the United States had changed. Conservatives, whatever they stand for, now play on a field that was created by Leftist Statism. All they can do is offer battle on this or that program. One of my favorite columnists, the late Samuel Francis, has called the Republicans the Stupid Party; and judging from their antics he cannot be far off the mark. That mistakenly assumes that one party is home to whatever a conservative movement is. Friedrich A. Hayek has made a good argument on this subject in his essay, "Why I Am not a Conservative" in *The Constitution of Liberty*. It might be beneficial for the country to have a Constitution Party.

Now, back to the Bible on government. Finally, what does the writer of Revelation have to say about the Roman government that St. Paul had so generously praised? This is from chapter 17. "Then one of the seven angels who had the seven bowls came and said to me, 'Come, I will show you the judgment of the great harlot who is seated upon many waters, with whom the kings of the earth have committed fornication'....And he carried me away in the Spirit into a wilderness, and I saw a woman sitting on a scarlet beast which was full of blasphemous names, and it had seven heads and ten horns....and on her head was written a name of mystery: 'Babylon the great, mother of harlots and of earth's abominations.' And I saw the woman drunk with the blood of the saints and the blood of the martyrs of Jesus." (Revised Standard Version)

The telling phrase in the previous quotation is "the blood of the martyrs of Jesus." Paul did not live to witness the persecution of Christians by Rome. True, he was executed by Roman authorities about AD 65. But this was a singular conviction and execution. Prior to this, the martyrs were few. St. Stephen was the most famous, and the yet unconverted Saul was an approving witness to it. The intermittent persecutions started in a small way with Nero and grew dramatically over the next two centuries, coming to an end with Diocletian's ferocious efforts about AD 303. The bishop of Ephesus who, in his exile on Patmos, wrote Revelation was responding to the persecutions instigated by the emperor Domitian in the last decade of the 1st century. How Paul would have written had he lived another 30 years is anyone's guess. St. Augustine's 5th-century response to the evils and follies of the Roman Empire, *The City of God,* was a descant on the Book of Revelation.

We can gather from the few citations above the certainty that there was no wholesale endorsement of the institution of government by the biblical writers, apart from Paul's faint praise. Nor was there any general denunciation of it as an institution, apart from Samuel's cautions to Israel. The denunciations by prophets such as Amos and by the author of Revelation were directed at governments that usurped the role of God on earth, a feature that was revived with ferocity in the 20th century.

Governments were also denounced for perpetrating specific evils, especially oppression. Daniel's rage against Antiochus IV Epiphanes was not directed at government as such but at this maniacal ruler's persecution of the Jews in the 2nd century BC. The Bible does not theorize about government in a philosophical way. This task was left to the Greek philosophers Plato and Aristotle.

All that the Bible says about government can be of little passing interest to the secular world. There, the critique must be framed in the whole course of history, not only in the course of history but against all the thinking about the subject during the past 5,000 years. Government, or the state, appears as a given from the beginning. Certainly it had an origin, but in the historical period for which we have written records it is already there. It is taken for granted. The powers that be in every place are already on the scene. The types of Plato's ideal Guardians, the bodyguards of the state, already live and have seized control. Who is there to question their authority, and to live to talk about it? The five percent have the power, and the 95 percent are forced to support them. (The percentage figures are approximations, but they seem to be close to past existing situations. In fact, five percent may be a little large; but we must include the military forces as part of government. Soldiers did not necessarily get rich, but they had the weapons, and they were often richly rewarded after a conquest.)

There is little doubt that the philosophers from Plato until at least Fichte and Hegel regarded government as humanity's supreme achievement. The most blatant example during the Renaissance was Machiavelli and in the modern period was Thomas Hobbes, author of

Leviathan. But even the writers who were forerunners of more open and democratic systems, such as Locke and Montesquieu, did not question the need for government. The idea that governments ought to be severely limited in their scope of activities is quite a modern invention, one that was only celebrated and spelled out with any honesty in the United States. Europeans cannot envision limited government.

By the time we get to Plato's *Republic* and Aristotle's *Politics* in the 5th and 4th centuries BC respectively, governments have been around for a very long time. They antedate Plato by many more centuries than have passed since the philosopher lived. Their origins are lost in the fog that shrouds the past. But of their origins it can be stated with certainty: governments were never designed. They arose through a process of trial and error. Every society, even the small tribal ones, had leadership. One function of leadership was the need to protect the tribe or city state from attack by other tribes. Tribal leaders were bodyguards. Their function was to allow the people to get on with their daily work.

At what point the leaders of society took on the function of directing the daily work is impossible to say, but by the time we get glimpses of ancient Egypt, Mesopotamia, and China, this is the case. (Historian William H. McNeill, in his *The Rise of the West,* makes a good case that the earliest governments in ancient Mesopotamia were probably simple democracies.) But as the societies increased in size, systems for central control and planning were very likely installed to assure the food supply. This latter consideration was especially true in Egypt, where the whole population was mobilized under government command and control to make sure there was enough food. As smaller units merged into larger ones, food supply became a permanently pressing need, because armies had to be fed and so did their animals. The early empires seemed to have existed for one purpose only, to make war. This purpose has never faded away.

Ancient governments were not all as inflexible and controlling as Egypt, China, or the Persian Empire. There were well-known exceptions in Athens and the Roman Republic. The partial democracy at Athens was always unstable and susceptible to demagogues. Finally it, with the rest of Greece, fell under the control of Philip of Macedon. In speaking of Greek democracy, Professor McNeill makes this fascinating comment: "The most fundamental peculiarity of European society – the absolute primacy of the territorial state over competing principles of social cohesion – has its origins in the Greek *polis,* where it was carried to an extreme which has seldom been approached since." In another context he refers to "the Greek notion of the supremacy of the state over all aspects of human activity..." (pp. 217, 302). Mussolini would have approved.

I hope I am not misinterpreting those sentences when I suggest that they mean: Everything is political. Every segment of every life is to be focused on the state. Benito Mussolini, the founder of Italian fascism and a devoted disciple of Karl Marx best expressed this notion: "everything within the State, nothing outside the State, nothing against the state." This quotation could well have been used by Hitler, Lenin, Stalin, Mao, Kim Il Sung, Fidel Castro, and certain late-20th and early 21st century American politicians. In Germany, propaganda minister

Joseph Goebbels mad a similar declaration on November 15, 1933: "The revolution we have made is a total one. It encompassed every area of public life and fundamentally restructured them all." (Quoted from Evans, *The Third Reich in Power,* p. 121) This concept is still quite alive in the world today. It still dominates Europe, as it always has. It seems to be the unspoken motto of Islamic states, and it has gained a large following in the highly bureaucratic and corrupt European Union.

The Roman Republic also had elements of popular democracy, notably in the election of Tribunes of the People. Democracy actually increased late in the Republic, as the suffrage expanded; but this did not hinder the ambitions of Pompey or Caesar. When Octavian, or Augustus, took control of the Republic he transformed it into an empire and ruled with a façade of democracy, and he did so by absorbing the tribunician power. Within 50 years of his death in AD 14, the autocracy was in place and would remain so until the end of the empire. Democracy departed the scene until the end of the 18th century, save for a few ill-conceived and always short-lived medieval and early modern experiments.

Most of the attempts to create a form of democracy or popular rule in the late Middle Ages and after had an economic basis. Such for instance were the two best known Peasants' Revolts: that of Wat Tyler in England in 1381 and of Thomas Müntzer in Germany in 1524-25. During the Civil War and the Cromwell era in England, the Levellers and Diggers made economic demands that bordered on Socialism, but the Lord Protector rebuffed them. An excellent account of the disturbances in England during the mid-17th century can be found in a small volume by Christopher Hill entitled *The World Turned Upside Down* (1972).

While no genuine democracy was achieved in Europe until the French Revolution, there were successful examples of partial economic freedom achieved in many of the cities on what was then a politically very divided continent. Believe it or not, economic freedom is what freedom is all about. It can exist under a monarch, a benevolent despot, or a republic. Note that I am not talking about democracy here: freedom and democracy are not synonymous: as democracy increases, freedom decreases. On the subject of economic freedom, one cannot do better than to read Tom Bethell's *The Noblest Triumph: Property and Prosperity Through the Ages.* A similar work is *Property and Freedom* by Richard Pipes.

The highly competitive, and often warring, city-states of Italy achieved significant measures of economic freedom when Italy was divided. The cities of northern Germany and the Low Countries also made great strides toward economic democracy (which must never be confused with Socialism) in the late Middle Ages and early modern era. Lack of centralized governing authority contributed to these achievements. The very fragmentation of authority in Europe made the localized growth of free economies possible. In England the government was centralized under a monarchy, but there were always countervailing powers in the nobility. The kings found it helpful to win the cities to their cause with liberal charters in return for financial aid. This was especially true for the City of London.

There is no need to track through the well-traveled highways and byways of historical exploration on the subject of government. Suffice it to say that for all of human history until the end of the 18th century, governments existed as controls on their own populations and did not recognize the rights of people against their governments. People were subjects, not citizens. England is the exception here. In the centuries following the Magna Carta of 1215, the rights of the people became an issue that fed into the thinking of the colonists in North America, when they broke from England in 1774-81.

Governments exist for their own sakes, and they will perpetuate themselves at any cost. There is certainly no doubt that governments had to pay some attention to the governed, as Machiavelli so well demonstrated in *The Prince*. But the incipient experiments in freedom never took permanent hold anywhere. Only when great force was brought into play did the ruling powers give way. This happened toward the end of the 18th century in North America and France, at a time when public opinion began to count for something. The outcomes were quite different. In North America, men who never wanted a popular democracy created a republic; in fact, they feared democracy with good reason.

In France a popular democracy was launched in 1789 in the name of three incompatible notions – liberty, equality, and fraternity. In four years it turned into a bloody Reign of Terror that killed its children. It also gave birth to all the political evils that have afflicted the world since then: Socialism, Communism, fascism, genocide, and more. (Even the "Heil Hitler" salute was first used at the time, with a different connotation, of course.) Virtually every aspect of modern totalitarian ideology and practice had its roots in the French Revolution, an event that spawned much evil and very little good. (I must admit that I may be alone in this interpretation of the French Revolution. In his *The Anatomy of Fascism,* Robert O. Paxton sees a much less direct connection between that event and Nazi Germany. But, for me, the similarities are stunning.)

Reverting now to the second thesis mentioned earlier: No government has ever created a society that is good for all of its citizens. This is not the place to get into a discussion of economics, but in fact the bulk of most people's time is spent on economic matters – working and providing food, clothing, and shelter for themselves and their families. Every society is first and foremost an economy, or collection of economies. Everyone is a consumer, and many are producers.

Ivor Thomas, in his book *The Socialist Tragedy,* devotes a chapter to human nature. He notes that: "The prime fact of human nature which the wise statesman must take into account is that men will exert themselves for their own benefit, or for that of their families, regarded as an extension of themselves, as they will exert themselves for no one else." Which is one way of saying that what is everybody's work easily becomes nobody's work; and what is everyone's property is no one's property. (Aristotle recognized this in his *Politics.* Not much attention was paid to this fact for many centuries, until an English economist, William Forster Lloyd, commented on it in 1832. In 1968, an American economist, Garrett Hardin, explained the flaws about "public property" in an essay, "The Tragedy of the Commons.")

Individuals will, by nature, seek some form of self-fulfillment (at least many of them will). Personal achievement can be a lifetime pursuit. In the professions learning never stops (or never ought to). Work is an ongoing process that fills most of one's time. People also enjoy many kinds of play and recreation. It is possible, in other words, to go through a whole lifetime paying scant attention to what the ruling powers are doing, until what they do impinges on oneself or reaches into one's pocket or directly into one's life. It is also possible to go through life without the slightest understanding of how and economy works. I did so for more than 50 years.

If, in the United States, the federal and state governments were engaging only in their limited constitutional responsibilities, how much of the passionate devotion to the political arena would there be? The politicians would certainly not be the celebrities they are today. If Congress passed general and clear legislation; if the executive branch simply enforced the few laws that should be on the books; and if the courts made rulings on the basis of law, then we would have governments performing their bodyguard functions. There would also be little problem with permitting them to perform such functions that they could do better than individuals or collections of individuals, such as building the interstate highway system or managing port facilities and airports. The chief responsibility of government is to preserve domestic tranquility (keep crime to a minimum), provide for the common defense, and preserve liberty. In other words, the main responsibility of government is to run itself. Read the Constitution.

The passionate and emotional attachments to the political process exist because our governments have strayed far beyond their legitimate duties. Some of us can remember the rip-roaring political conventions of the past, during which nominees were actually selected. They were even more raucous prior to the 1930s, when the federal government was not as over-reaching as it now is. Our federal and state governments now consider themselves capable of running society, including its economic activities. Elected officials make promises to every constituency, offering goodies of every description and promising to heal any injustices. The federal and state governments, at their executive and legislative levels, have become giant Favor Factories or a Big Rock Candy Mountain, and the primary activities of government are now racketeering and extortion. This is the natural tendency of most governments throughout recent history – to exert as much control over society as possible, by being as appealing and seemingly well meaning as possible. In so doing, governments frequently and deliberately damage their societies. The governments of Europe seem bent on destroying their own societies.

Much is made today of "special interests" having undue influence on elected officials. If these officials were not in the business of providing favors or making threats, the money that the interests provided as campaign contributions (read, bribes) would have no place in either the White House or Congress. Hoping that the federal and state governments would cease playing Santa Claus is vain. The system has ever been as it is now, but it was rarely the threat it has become. Most of the dirty dealing was done within the confines of smoke-filled rooms and did not have a serious impact on society at large. As long ago as 1906 it was possible for David Graham Phillips, during the era of muckrakers, to write *The Treason of the Senate,* laying out for all to see just what kind of deal-making was going on between the politicians and the moneyed powers. Who cared? In the same year, Lincoln Steffens did the same kind of exposé for local government in *The Shame of the Cities*. Again, who cared? Some state governments are so corrupt, it is a wonder they get anything done at all, apart from raking in the loot. (I have not lived most of my life in Cook County, Illinois for nothing.)

I suspect that good government at any level is nearly impossible, but total corruption is more than any society should have to put up with. Corruption is more than simple venality, the grubbing for money. That is almost benign when compared to the corruption that eats away at the form of government itself and turns the country into the opposite of what it was designed to be, the last best hope of earth. The corruption I speak of is vote-buying legislation, such as Social Security, Medicare, Medicaid, the Affordable Care Act, minimum wage laws, rent control, and allowing government workers to unionize. This latter fact has become a severe financial problem for many states, as they try to find money for union pension obligations. Again, Illinois is at the top of the list of mismanagement. In an editorial for February 22, 2019, the *Wall Street Journal* labeled Illinois the Land of Public Unions, with $131 billion of unfunded public sector pension liabilities in 2019. The list of government's lying promises could go on.

On the cusp of the 20th and 21st centuries, the mindset of most of the world is still Marxist, consisting of a yearning for the perfectly just and prosperous society. The utopian message is easy to present and easy to understand. To assert that the utopian and romantic dream is not realizable and actually portends a nightmare is a complicated matter to explain to the public and seems a real downer. Those who have been enveloped in the utopian ideology are blind to experience. The fact that all the attempts to create the New World have thus far failed is not significant, apparently. Keep trying, there must be a way, just avoid the previous mistakes: this seems to be the overwhelming consensus. Why is it that individuals occasionally can learn from their mistakes, but societies seem unable to?

(Parenthetically, there is a reason why the schools are doing such a bad job of teaching. It is by design. Keep the public as ignorant as possible about the past and their institutions, in the hope that everyone will be a willing serf for the state and its good intentions. Economist Walter Williams of George Mason University has said that the inner city schools would be no worse off if run by the KKK. The late Steve Jobs of Apple Inc. asserted in 1996 that as the power of teachers' unions increases, the quality of schooling declines. Public "education" has, in fact, become a racket to enrich the union members and school bureaucrats.)

Congress does actually pass general legislation, most of it unconstitutional. Some bills are hundreds of pages long, and it is highly unlikely that those who vote for them have ever read them, since legislators no longer write legislation. The finished product is handed over to the executive branch to work out the details. Thus, departments of the executive branch create tens of thousands of pages of federal regulations dealing with every aspect of a citizen's life. The courts are also notorious for legislating, often based on the personal whims of the judges. The result is a government with three lawmaking branches that can create regulations on anything at any time, even mandating the proper amount of water in a toilet tank or fluorescent light bulbs containing mercury. This condition used to be called a police state. (A book published in 2018 deals with the legislative failures of Congress: *Judicial Fortitude,* by Peter J. Wallison.)

One can take a contrary view. Why should people have to spend their whole lives looking over their shoulder for potential threats from Washington, DC, or their state capitals (and, increasingly, their local governments as well)? People have lives to live. Who has time to sift through all the nefarious deeds of elected officials and bureaucrats as they are revealed in the less-than-ideal, agenda-driven media? Why can't we just go to the polls to vote and expect to get fairly sensible and honest elected officials who have not promised us a rose garden?

There was, in fact, a time when people could afford to be full time citizens: in ancient Athens and the Roman Republic. This was possible because the citizens – all male – did not have to work. Slaves did the work of society, so the citizens could spend as much time as they wanted in civic affairs. Today, people in the private sector work for a living and devote their time to home and family, to associations of all kinds, and generally try to make for themselves the best life possible.

Our current situation has come about incrementally, with a lot of deceit and demagoguery along the way, because the citizens really have neither the time nor the inclination to follow all the minutiae of federal and state activity. Nor are people able to perceive the great historical trends as they unfold. (Who can? Certainly not their leaders.) Looking back over the 20th century, it does not take much insight to note the nearly simultaneous appearance of the all-pervasive state: the Russian Revolution in 1917, the emergence of fascism in Italy in 1922, the Nazi victory in Germany in 1933, the militarization of Japan in the 1930s, the New Deal in the United States in 1933. None of these was predicted, but each was a long time developing.

The collapse of the Soviet Union and the "end" of Communism in 1989-91 has not altered the situation at all. The utopian mindset struggles on. The 135-year tradition of the welfare state, a gift from Otto von Bismarck, has ballooned far beyond its original modest beginnings. Added to it are the demands for social and economic justice, whatever they are, and it is quite understandable that large segments of every citizenry should have a heated devotion to what a government can do. When Bismarck started his welfare state with a Social Security plan in the 1880s, he intended it as a means of social control. He also wanted to diminish the voting power of the Social Democrats (followers of the Socialist, Ferdinand Lassalle). Strangely, the Marxists and other Socialists originally had no interest in social welfare schemes. It was only when they discovered to what good use such programs could be put – Bismarck's social control – that these programs became part of the overall Socialist plan. Today we live under what can be called Bismarxism.

It really all comes down to two questions. The first is: Can government keep the promises it makes with its ever expanding entitlement programs. The answer, judging from events in Europe and increasingly here at home, is no. The effort to do so is based on the premise that all segments of an economy are meant solely to support government programs. If all economies were robust with high employment and good wages, it would work for a time. But, as Margaret Thatcher observed, eventually you run out of other people's money.

Economies since 2008 have not been robust, yet government keeps expanding. (That changed, probably temporarily, in 2017-19.) Economies may well fall off a cliff again, and our government will have no solutions since it is government that pushes the economy off the cliff in the first place. This assertion is not something I made up. It is based on the work of economists Ludwig von Mises and Murray Rothbard among others of the Austrian School. At last reading, the unfunded debt of the federal government was 86 trillion dollars. State governments, with their vote-buying promises of large pensions for government employees are in serious financial difficulty. A realistic remark from *The Economist* of Feb. 2nd-8th of 2013 is worth repeating. It's from a special report on the Nordic countries: "The welfare state we have is excellent in most ways," says Gunnar Viby Mogensen, a Danish historian. "We only have this little problem. We can't afford it."

The second question is: Can any government run a society? If everything is political, the answer is yes, as some of the already-mentioned 20th century experiments have proved. But what about running a society well for the benefit of all citizens? The answer is a definite No. Ivor Thomas, in the book already quoted, said: "But the idea that the state is somehow wiser and better than the best of its citizens is a metaphysical delusion." Or, to quote from a 2007 novel, *Sovereign,* by C. J. Sansom: "You think you have a holy truth and that if the state is run by its principles all men will become happy and good. It is a delusion." (p. 560)

The best that a government can do is run itself. Why is this true? Because, as noted, every society is fundamentally an economy. Large societies, such as the United States, consist of many economies regionally based. Jane Jacobs has demonstrated this with great clarity in *Cities and the Wealth of Nations*. Economies are complex systems of interpersonal interactions, dealing in producing, distributing, exchanging, financing, contracts, and much more. Fundamental to all aspects of an economy is information, the amount of which varies among individuals. The notion that government can have all sufficient information to operate an economy is ludicrous.

Economies are self-organizing institutions that produce order where one would expect chaos. They are not planned, although a great deal of planning exists within their many facets. That's the amazing paradox of a market economy: unplanned economic activities create order and prosperity, while planned economies create chaos and poverty. As previously noted, Ludwig von Mises has proved this quite adequately in the previously mentioned *Planned Chaos*. Another book by an Austrian economist, *The Fatal Conceit* by Friedrich Hayek, explains that the whole complex of activities that we include under the term Economic were never designed by anyone or by any group. The whole process of economic development was one of trial and error by very flawed people, as it still is. In those numerous places where economic activity was planned, directed, and controlled, the benefits accrued to the few only. Speaking of Hayek, his little 1944 book, *The*

Road to Serfdom, sets out clearly all the arguments against government involvement in and economy.

No government – anytime or anywhere – has ever been able to operate an economy to the benefit of a whole population. Government efforts have always been bent toward securing the greatest amount of wealth for the few. The Soviet, and any other Socialist system, is a prime example, although it was true in ancient Egypt, China, and other civilizations as well.

This is a subject on which Plato and Jane Jacobs are in agreement. In the fourth book of the *Republic,* the philosopher stated that the just society is one in which each citizen does his own work as his intelligence guides him. No one should meddle in the affairs of others. The shoemaker should not tell the weaver how to do his business, nor should the silversmith dictate to the potter. Those who govern should by no means try to manage everything, considering how ineptly they generally do their own work. More recently, in *Systems of Survival* (1992), Jane Jacobs has shown that governmental activities and economic activities are pursued according to mutually exclusive sets of rules; and trying to mix them brings undesirable consequences. If I could print those rules without violating copyright law, I would. Check your local library; it is a brilliant piece of writing.

Why, then, are so many "special interests" spending vast amounts of money trying to influence the decisions and policies of our elected officials? 1. Because elected officials tend naturally to expand the scope of their activities. I suspect that one could count on two hands the genuinely constitutional legislation passed since 1932 (or perhaps, 1890). Governments always grow to fill all available space. 2. Because our elected officials know where the wealth is. They play these interests like a violin, in one shakedown after another. All the while, our noble politicians declaim against the woeful and dangerous influence of these same interests. If we still had constitutional government, the economies of our nation would be left alone. But no, our ever-expanding government has brought all of commerce, industry, and labor within its purview. And everyone contributes. If it's any consolation, Europe is much worse off than we are, but for how long? And the less said about the former Soviet Union's rapid slide into fascism and kleptocracy, the better. Government racketeering is a worldwide phenomenon. It is one of the major outgrowths of modern democracy.

So, what kind of government do we find worldwide today? This is a problem I looked at long and hard, until I arrived at a very unappealing conclusion. It's really a matter of not taking labels for granted, labels such as democracy, republic, or constitutional monarchy. One could put a sign on a cow indicating that it was a horse, but no one would enter the animal in the Kentucky Derby. What is the thing in itself? What is actually going on behind the rhetoric? Can consistent patterns be discerned? Those questions were part of a long and slow process of discovery.

My conclusion will win no admirers and very little agreement. After making my decision, it was with relief that I read William H. McNeill's *The Pursuit of Power* (1982). Speaking of the after-effects bred by the economic dislocations of World War I, he states: "Despite carryovers from the past, what ought to be called national socialism, if Hitler had not preempted the term, emerged from the barracks and purchasing offices of the European armed services, and with the help of a coalition of administrative elites drawn from big business, big labor, academia, and big government, made European society over in an amazingly short time." (pp. 336-337). With that sentence before you, think about our own government.

To confirm this opinion, I was relieved to find in Jim Powell's *FDR's Folly* a supportive statement. He quotes from *The Philosophy of Fascism* by Mario Palmieri (1936), published, of all places, in Chicago. "The proper function of the State in the Fascist system is that of supervising, regulating, and arbitrating the relationships of capital and labor, employers and employees, individuals and associations, private interests and national interests.... Private wealth belongs not only to the individual, but, in a symbolic sense, to the State well."

Can it be? National Socialism, with all the vile historical baggage that term carries. The natural inclination is to focus on the genocide and the concentration camps. But National Socialism was first a political-economic system devised for making war. One may want to consult a little volume, *The Meaning of Hitler,* by Sebastian Haffner (1979) or the more recent volumes by Richard Evans. Germany's chancellor was quite aware of what was going on in the Soviet Union under Stalin. He admired and borrowed its concentration camp system – a system that was invented by the British during the Boer War. But he also knew that, economically, what the Soviets were doing was unworkable. He was not about to place his Brown Shirts and other Nazi thugs in positions of responsibility in manufacturing businesses and banking enterprises, when those who were already operating them did such a good job. Hitler's desire was control without ownership – preserving the illusion of private property instead of having the state take it all over. Hitler may have admired Marx, but he was no fool. Let all businesses function as they do best, but let the government regulate them down to the least detail. Does that sound familiar? In his own words: "After the war, equally, we must not let control of the economy of the country slip from our hands. If we do, then once more all the various private interests will concentrate on their own particular objectives." (*Hitler's Table Talk 1941-1944*, translated by Norman Cameron and R. H. Stevens, introduced by H. R. Trevor-Roper, 2000, p. 559)

Such is the political-economic system that is in place the world over, with few exceptions. Hitler didn't invent it; he had learned the lessons taught by Bismarck and by the economies of World War I. (As did Mussolini and FDR). In Russia, Vladimir Putin has been doing a remarkable job of reconstituting it, as the government seizes control of major segments of the economy. But the Putin system is unworkable in the long run, even without Russia's demographic collapse.

The productive success of the war economies were not forgotten. Thus, when the Great Depression occurred, what could seem more reasonable to national leaders than trying to deal with it in a war-economy fashion? McNeill goes on to note that: "The New Deal, proclaimed by President Franklin D. Roosevelt in 1933, like the Nazi regime in Germany, fell back on World War I precedents in trying to do something about the depression which had put some thirteen million persons out of work since 1929."

The Hitler comparison may seem outrageous to most Americans. McNeill could have also used Mussolini as an example. Mussolini was much admired by many in the West for his ostensible successes in Italy. The admiration faded after Italy's attack on Ethiopia in 1935. The effort was made by our government to put things back together in the only way it knew how, by demonizing the free market, by taking control, by seeming to be doing something. What better way than to create a corporatist state, to cartelize all major industries and leave the rest to fend for themselves under government-managed competition. FDR did try to do this with the National Industrial Recovery Act, but the Supreme Court struck down the attempt. One thing governments can usually do quite well is mobilize for war. That has been true since the days of Sargon of Akkad, Alexander the Great, and Julius Caesar. Napoleon was an expert at it. All effort and resources are then directed toward one goal; and public support is marshaled behind it.

A few lines from Shakespeare's Henry IV, Part II. The king, on his deathbed, speaks to his son Prince Hal:

> Therefore, my Harry,
> Be it thy course to busy giddy minds
> With foreign quarrels, that action, hence borne out,
> May waste the memory of former days.

Let me interrupt the narrative here to remark on the quotation above. Government leaders deal with what are now termed domestic and foreign policy. Throughout most of history, domestic policy was pretty much ignored, and populations were left to their own devices, apart from paying taxes and supplying armies. Foreign policy dominated, mostly in the form of war. It is tempting to say that foreign policy is easy and domestic policy difficult. There can be great complexities in dealings between nations, as presidents of the United States have learned when confronting the Middle East, Islamic terrorism, North Korea, the European Union, Russia's war mongering, and a host of other issues. The easy part is in the fact that negotiations are directly between national leaders. With domestic policy, nothing is simple, because there is such a large variety of diverse interests to satisfy. And citizens vote based almost entirely on domestic matters, not on foreign policy questions – unless there is an immediate threat such as there was during FDR's terms. Now, back on course.

The New Deal did not, of course, end the Depression; it only prolonged it, as anyone who really studies it knows. But it did change the whole playing field of American government. Since that sorry episode, the federal government has been able to do pretty much what it wants, just so it is seen as doing something. Whether the alteration is permanent or not, no one can say. But the country has edged away from constitutional government and rule by law. When laws exist by the millions, there can be no rule of law. What now exists is a modified version of National Socialism, repugnant as the term may be. Democratic procedures remain in place, and they will remain in place as long as enough of the people can be fooled enough of the time. Our school systems are seeing to it that this will be so.

Any economic system needs a textbook. The Socialists have theirs in the works of Karl Marx, most notably in

Capital, a book that very few can stand to read all the way through and that Marx himself did not live long enough to finish. His close associate Friedrich Engels published the last two volumes, and in doing so unwittingly demolished the labor theory of value by admitting that there are costs of production. This mistake was brilliantly exposed by Austrian economist Eugen von Böhm-Bawerk in *Karl Marx and the End of His System.*

The *Communist Manifesto* of 1848 is much more readable. It is also more to the point, since it contains the 10-point program of the Left in America. The free-market also has its theorists, including Adam Smith, J. B. Say, David Ricardo, Karl Menger, Ludwig von Mises, Friedrich Hayek, Murray Rothbard, Milton Friedman, Hans-Hermann Hoppe, and many more. Shouldn't National Socialism also have its text? It does.

When John Maynard Keynes wrote the *General Theory of Employment, Interest and Money* (1935-36), he did not intend it to be such a textbook. In fact, the work was much admired by Hitler, whereas Stalin despised it. Keynes himself, although a very arrogant and brilliant elitist, did not favor totalitarian government and would have been appalled to think that his work was misused to support one. Nevertheless, in the German edition to his *General Theory* he did admit that his work "is much more easily adapted to the conditions of a totalitarian state, than is the theory of the production and distribution of any given output produced under conditions of free competition and a large measure of laissez-faire." (Quoted in Mark Skousen's *The Making of Modern Economics,* p. 347.)

Keynes never did change his conviction that it was the task and responsibility of the experts and technicians, the truly well schooled – the best and the brightest - to oversee and direct economic outcomes. He was certain this was possible. His dry and turgid tome became the handbook for American economists and politicians for most of the decades after it was published in 1936. It still is the basis of most college texts on economics. I can vouch for this, having read many of them. Incidentally, his book is by no means a "general theory." It was designed as a specific theory to deal with the Depression, and in this it failed completely. There are several good refutations of Keynes. The most recent I'm aware of is *Where Keynes Went Wrong* by Hunter Lewis, 2009. (Anyone wanting a good text on economics can find it in Mark Skousen's *Economic Logic*.)

Chapter 7: As Mao Said, "There Cannot be Enough Killing"

As noted above, the first thing to come to mind with a mention of National Socialism is genocide, and specifically the Holocaust. Less frequently mentioned is the far more massive amounts of killing that went on in Russia under Lenin and Stalin, or under Mao Zedong in China. There is a reason for the emphasis on Hitler and a passing over of the crimes of Communism. Leftist politicians have long admired the Soviet "experiment," and some even have said that there is really nothing much wrong with genocide if it is done in a worthy cause. They agree with Mao's verdict: "Those who consider these things to be crimes do not comprehend the overall plan" (*Economist*, March 18, 2000). They refuse to accept the fact that Hitler was also of the Left, and it is the Left that is the point of origin of genocide in the modern world. Had he not been so driven an anti-Semite, he might have salvaged more of a reputation and may even have won the war, but this is unlikely since Germany was the enemy in World War II. (The material on Mao is taken from *Mao* by Jung Chang and Jon Halliday, 2005.)

Genocide has a definite meaning; it signifies the killing of specific kinds of people of a certain ethnic or racial origin. I am arbitrarily liberalizing the meaning to embrace all the mass murders that have blighted the 20th century. The practice of genocide originated in the Terror of the French Revolution. According to Louis A. L de Saint-Just, "A nation regenerated it self only on a mountain of corpses." He was a friend of the more famous Robespierre, who himself fell victim to the guillotine.

Genocide went into temporary retirement during the 19th century but was revived at the dawn of the 20th. It piggybacked its way in on eugenics, which became a popular cause among the "intellectuals" in the West in the late 19th and early 20th centuries. Francis Galton, an English scientist and cousin of Darwin, in his book *Hereditary Genius* (1869), popularized the movement.

The goal of eugenics was to eliminate "defective" human beings by better breeding. The intellectuals of the day were quite perturbed by the quality of life they witnessed among "the masses" and the newer immigrants to the United States from Eastern and Southern Europe and were sure the lower classes would degrade society beyond repair. They were even more appalled to see the lower classes going to school and participating in cultural activities, becoming freer by virtue of prosperity. How readily the liberal clergy of the mainline Protestant American denominations gravitated to eugenics can be learned from Christine Rosen's book, *Preaching Eugenics* (2004).

Paralleling the eugenics movement, and closely related to it, was the emergence of virulent racism. This, too, was a product of the intellectuals and academics of the 19th and early 20th century. The first of these notables was Joseph-Arthur, Comte de Gobineau, who published a four-volume work entitled *Essay on the Inequality of the Human Races* (1854-55). Houston Stewart Chamberlain, author of *The Foundations of the 19th Century* (1899), took up the cause in England, but it became really popular in Germany. In the United States the banner was carried by Madison Grant and Lothrop Stoddard, who feared the "mongrelizing of the good old American stock." Grant published his *The Passing of the Great Race* in 1916, and Stoddard came out with *The Rising Tide of Color* in 1920. The two Americans were promoting immigration restriction, an effort that bore fruit in the so-called National Origins immigration law of 1924, a law that remained on the books for more than 40 years.

Combine eugenics with racism, and the result logically will be genocide. There had to be good soil for these pernicious weeds to grow. Europe had been fervently anti-Semitic for centuries (thanks to Christendom), and this trait carried over into the United States, where it was benignly prevalent among the "better classes" of people. Furthermore, ethnic and religious strife within Europe was not uncommon; it persists today. On this subject, you may want to consult a little book by Stuart Miller, *Painted in Blood: Understanding Europeans* (1987).

In the United States ethnic animosities dated back to the pre-Revolutionary era, but they became especially pronounced in the 19th century. The Nativist movement was directed first against the Irish and their Catholic Church, but in later decades animosity was directed against all immigrants from Eastern and Southern Europe as well as from Asia. Coupled with nativism directed at immigrants was the greater hostility directed at blacks, and after the Mexican War, at Hispanics. (Strange isn't it, how old problems return with a new wardrobe. A century ago the Immigration Restriction League was urging an end to admitting Eastern and Southern Europeans. Today the concern is about millions of illegal immigrants from south of the border.)

In the 20th century the first instance of genocide was occasioned by the American war against Philippine independence immediately after the Spanish-American War. No one knows for sure, but it is estimated that 200,000 Filipino freedom fighters were done away with by the American armed forces in this insurrection. Mark Twain assailed this foreign venture in an essay, "To a People Sitting in Darkness," but the war went on. Then during World War I were the Turkish massacres of Armenians. Hardly had the war ended when Lenin and his associates began killing on a grand scale in Russia. Stalin took up the task with relish. Then came the Third Reich in 1933 and Communist China in 1949.

Since those infamous years, genocide seems to have become embedded in the cultures of the West. It usually passes under the more innocuous terms, abortion and euthanasia. The latter is widely practiced in The Netherlands, while abortions are available nearly everywhere. May it fairly be said that *Roe v Wade* is America's Final Solution? Since genocide now has legal sanctions, who can guess where the road, or the slippery slope, will lead? As long as the rights of the state reign supreme, anything is possible.

Has anyone ever studied the economic impact of genocide? If not, it would be worth examining. In spite of all the nonsense written by the Malthusian population-scare crowd, human beings are still the greatest economic asset in the world. How much did Germany, Russia, and China suffer economically because of all the needless deaths mandated by maniacs? We'll never know. Coming closer to home, consider the Social Security System. (I believe it's the biggest vote-buying scheme ever put over on the American people – Medicare runs second – but that's beside the point here.) My math here is quite inexact, but it is plausible for illustrating the point. We know that Social Security operates on a pay-as-you-go basis. There is no trust fund; Lyndon Johnson and his fellow Democrats took care of that. Today's retirees are paid from money collected from today's workers. Now say that in 1960 there were ten workers supporting one retiree. Picture a broad-based pyramid, with the workers paying Social Security taxes forming the base and the smaller number of retirees toward the top. At the present time, the pyramid is being gradually inverted. The number of retirees has grown. It has grown in absolute numbers because of population increase and because people live longer. As the base of workers per retiree shrinks, the Social Security system is faced with a problem: more people are collecting than are paying in. Can you imagine a society in which one worker has to support one retiree? It's called a Ponzi scheme.

Now consider that, since 1973, there have been about 35 to 60 million abortions. That's 35 to 60 million individuals who were never allowed to be born, grow up, and become productive workers. Had they lived, they could have been paying into that Ponzi scheme called Social Security, and the problem the government faces would not have been as severe. There would probably not have been such a tight labor market in the 1990s or in the 2010s either, had there been that many more workers available. Unfortunately, not all of them would have been available or productive; our school systems would have guaranteed that.

Other countries are facing the same problem. Birth rates are dropping worldwide, and more people are living longer. As I write this paragraph, the *Wall Street Journal* published a lengthy article entitled "Global Baby Bust," about the worldwide decline in birth rates (January 24, 2003). The information in it contravenes the conventional wisdom propagated by the "population bomb" crowd, with its passion for abortion and euthanasia. Earlier, an article appeared in the *Chicago Tribune's* business section entitled 'China population hurtles toward old age.' It states that, in the year 2000, 126 million people, one tenth of China's population are over 60. In 30 years that is expected to be 300 million people. China has practiced mandatory birth control for its population for decades. It's one-child per family policy is notorious. Only in 2001 did those dedicated Communists begin to recognize the folly of this practice, and in 2015 it was abandoned. Coming back to this subject in 2019, I note that the *Wall Street Journal* of February 11 has an editorial entitled "China's Looming Labor Shortage." It states that the Chinese Academy of Social Sciences predicts that the nation's population will start an unstoppable decline in the 2030s.

The March 6-12, 2001 issue of *The Economist* devoted its cover to "Gendercide: What happened to 100 million baby girls?" The article deals with the abortion or intentional killing of infant girls that some Far Eastern nations do not deem worth having, as well as the socioeconomic effects of such a policy.

In the modern culture of death, one can hardly be surprised at the results. The law of unintended consequences always lurks nearby, when government handiwork is involved. But in the long run, it is not the government that pays the piper, but the citizens, while members of Congress stand by as innocent observers and never miss a meal. Citizens end up with outrageously higher taxes and personal privation. The more control a government asserts over its citizens under the guise of compassion, the more their lives are diminished. I wonder if, in the long run, the population will be satisfied with less and less. Government, as we know, will never accept less and less for itself. Even as the Soviet Union and its satellites were collapsing, their masters lived very well. Our masters also do quite well for themselves, especially when it comes to voting themselves and their fellow government workers large, even exorbitant, pensions. And the taxpayers are always on the hook to pay for an extravagance they cannot share in. As I write these sentences in 2013, the state government of Illinois has and unfunded liability of $98 billion for its pension plans, as well as a huge budget deficit. It's said that governments spend like drunken sailors, but at least the sailors are spending their own money. If our federal and state governments had all the money in society, both personal and corporate, they would spend it all and come back for more. They are where greed is firmly rooted, not in the private sector.

One of the shrewdest and most perceptive spectators on the human comedy was a 19th-century Frenchman, little known today, named Frédéric Bastiat. In an essay entitled "What Is Seen and What Is Not Seen," he makes these statements: "Society loses the value of objects [and humans] unnecessarily destroyed." "To break, to destroy, to dissipate is not to encourage national employment." And, "Destruction is not profitable." In the context of genocide, consider what he is saying. Along with all of those who will never lead productive working lives, imagine the great artists, musicians, writers, physicists, biologists, entrepreneurs, software engineers, architects, playwrights, agronomists, economists, historians, journalists, inventors, landscape architects, teachers, and even clergypersons that we will never know.

The problem remains. Government will always become as powerful, wealthy, and deadly as it can, even in a democracy. It will become an object of adulation, if not worship, for huge segments of society. It is now time to look at what Marx might have called "the inherent contradictions of democracy."

Chapter 8: Tocqueville's Dilemma

> Equality may perhaps be accepted as a right, but no power on earth will convert it into a fact. (Honoré de Balzac, *History of the Thirteen*)

> There are many people for whom "thinking" necessarily means identifying with existing trends. (Marshall McLuhan)

> "There never was a democracy yet that did not commit suicide." (John Adams)

> The democratic theory is that if you accumulate enough ignorance at the polls, you produce intelligence. (S. S. Van Dine/ Willard Huntington Wright, in the *Benson Murder Case,* chapter 22)

Alexis de Tocqueville and Gustave de Beaumont came to the United States in 1831 to study the penal system. They produced a book on it in 1833, and Beaumont wrote a book on slavery. But the great and lasting work to come from their journey was Tocqueville's timeless masterpiece, *Democracy in America,* published in two volumes (1835-1840). This work endures and is still read because it is one of the most penetrating analyses of the United States ever written. Those who have not read it, and many who have, regard it as an unqualified paean of praise to democracy and the "equality of conditions" the author discovered on his travels. Those who follow the book to its conclusion will be less sanguine about the prospects for the continuance of democracy and free government in this country. I introduce Tocqueville now, because it will be a bit before I return to him.

Woodrow Wilson wanted to make the world safe for democracy. The joking rejoinder was: first, make democracy safe for the world. Amusing, but apt. This democracy thing was all the rage at the end of the 20th century and even more so in the early 21st century.

If what I have said above about National Socialism being the worldwide political system, what place has democracy in all of it? If people are continually vote willingly or unwillingly against their own self-interest, what value has democracy, except to keep a decrepit and corrupt system working? Can people even perceive their own self-interest, or are they perpetually deluded and gulled? And what is democracy, anyway? And why, when freedom was in the world's grasp with the collapse of Communism, are some of the major nations of the world governed by a collection of ignorant and reactionary Marxist relics? (Even Tony Blair, for all of his admirable qualities, had his "third way?" As Mises pointed out decades ago, the only third way is National Socialism, although he didn't phrase it precisely that way.) Third way and mixed economy are euphemisms to conceal government control.

There are two kinds of democracy: direct and indirect. Direct democracy is simple majority rule, a system applicable to small societies in which every citizen votes directly on issues. Ancient Athens and the well-known New England town meeting are examples. Indirect democracy is what the United States now has: we vote for representatives, and they vote on legislation and other matters. Notice two things. First, no mention is made of the extent of citizenship. In ancient Athens, the so-called first democracy, the citizens all could vote, but not all members of society were citizens. In the United States, until 1920, the female half of the citizen population could not vote; and the black population was essentially voteless until the mid-1960s. Democracy as procedure is not nearly the problem as democracy as form of government.

Democracy, as a word, has been so abused in the 20th century that one wonders it has any reputation left. The People's Democratic Republic of Germany? The Republic of North Korea? The other Communist states also threw the word democracy around with great abandon. Such is the type of deceit one expects from the Left. A viable democracy, if there be such a thing, demands a population in general agreement about fundamentals. If a great segment of a society is bent on injuring another segment, there is no consensus. If segments of society are pitted against each other, men against women, race against race, rich against poor, in what is termed identity politics in modern democracies, then elections become contests to decide who can raid the treasury to their own benefit. This is called mob rule. This is what all democracies are inevitably prey to, unless they make a quick shift into despotism. The latter is the natural end of a democracy. Always.

Democracies are more liable to drastic change than other forms of government, although the change can be incremental instead of sudden. This may seem an odd thing to say, since we have witnessed the apparently sudden disintegration of Communism around the world, save for a few small enclaves. The process of Communist dissolution was certainly incremental. The difference lies in Communism's inherent unworkability as an economic system. Ludwig von Mises demonstrated this quite clearly in his 1922 book *Socialism,* which exposed all the economic fallacies of the Soviet Union. That it took so long to collapse was due to the power of the dictatorship, especially during the Stalin years. Had The Soviet Union been an open democratic system that had willfully adopted Communism, it would have fallen apart much sooner, just as the voluntary Socialist communes of 19th-century America did. As it was, the end came with a crash. Jean-François Revel described the collapse in *Democracy Against Itself* (English edition 1993): "Communism was forced to annihilate itself. But before this it had annihilated all that makes a society, a state, an economy, a system of justice, a civilization. There was no foundation on which to build anything over the wreckage." (p. 113). Actually there was – some old Communists became wealthy oligarchs.

That he was correct about getting out from under the consequences of Communism there is no doubt. One has only to look at the mess Russia has been in since 1991, where the same old thugs and criminals bid for power and wealth by any means they choose. Granted, Vladimir Putin seemed to be making progress in changing the system, although by 2004 even that was doubtful and by 2019 was out of the question. What are Revel's conclusions, as a lesson to the current crop of Socialists and Liberals in Europe in the United States? Why do so many of these intellectual frauds insist that Socialism did not really fail; it was just that the Soviet Union did not do it right. They will apparently never let go of the dream – everyone else's nightmare. Revel explains:

"What was evident was that by whatever name they were called, socialist and communist regimes inspired by Marxist progressivism or 'Third-Worldism' failed to satisfy any human needs, material or spiritual: neither well-being nor liberty, neither social rights nor political rights, neither human dignity nor economic security, neither culture nor nourishment." (p. 9)

Having said all this, I still conclude that the Communist disaster proves nothing in relation to the inherent weaknesses in a democratic system. But this remains to be proved. So I'll have to backtrack and cover some historical evidence.

After its failure in ancient Athens, democracy virtually disappeared as an historical artifact for many centuries, only to emerge as a political force in the 1780s. The Roman Republic had some democratic procedures, but it was basically a very well run military plutocracy. The self-government of the late medieval Italian and German cities cannot be accepted as democracies; they, too, were mainly oligarchies. It is questionable whether the various Peasants' Revolts of the Middle Ages were cries for democracy; they were based in economic misery. Had the rich and powerful of the time not been such imbeciles, the problems of the peasants could have been solved instead of worsened.

The American and French revolutions brought democracy to the fore, but there were decisive differences between the two in outcomes. The American Revolution was not against monarchy per se, but against the specific government of George III and his ministers. There were men, Alexander Hamilton and Benjamin Rush to name two, who would not have been fearful of having a monarchy in the United States. But the French Revolution was directed against monarchy itself. (Before I forget it, may I repeat: the American Revolution was an Enlightenment revolution; the French Revolution was a romantic revolution. Incidentally, for a good lesson in what revolutions really are, chapter two of *1688*: *The First Modern Revolution* by Steve Pincus (2009) provides come challenging conclusions.)

In France, a democracy was quickly established in 1789. Within four years it had degenerated into mob rule and bloody terror. (Anyone wanting to dwell on the gory details can read Simon Schama's *Citizens*.) The leading actors in this spectacle were the Jacobins, the forefathers of all modern Socialists, Liberals, and Leftists. Their broken-down failure of democracy collapsed into mass slaughter and then quickly evolved into an autocracy under Napoleon. In Russia, a democracy was established in February 1917 under the Provisional Government. By the end of the year the Bolsheviks had taken control with what results we know. The unstable and very unpopular Weimar Republic was erected in Germany after World War I. It ended in January 1933, when a new chancellor took office. When democracy becomes nothing but the exercise of the passions of the mob, it will eventually be controlled and eliminated.

In the young United States of 1787, the men who gathered at Philadelphia to make a new constitution were mostly quite fearful of democracy. (Thomas Jefferson was the main exception, but fortunately he was not there.) They created a republic in which democratic procedures were hedged about with protections for the country at large. In his famous *Federalist* No. 10, James Madison explained the difference. He discusses "the mischiefs of faction" to which any populous nation can be subject. He knew from history how easily the passions of the mob could be stirred up to take an action that may be regretted later. How can this be prevented? Madison goes on to say:

> "By what means is this object attainable? Evidently by one of two only. Either the existence of the same passions or interest in a majority at the same time must be prevented, or the majority, having such coexistent passion or interest, must be rendered, by their number and local situation, unable to concert and carry into effect schemes of oppression."
>
> "From this view of the subject it may be concluded that a pure democracy, by which I mean a society consisting of a small number of citizens, who assemble and administer the government in person, can admit of no cure for the mischiefs of faction. A common passion or interest will, in almost every case, be felt by a majority

of the whole; a communication and concert result from the form of government itself; and there is nothing to check the inducements to sacrifice the weaker party or an obnoxious individual. Hence it is that such democracies have ever been spectacles of turbulence and contention; have ever been found incompatible with personal security or the rights of property; and have in general been as short in their lives as they have been violent in their deaths. [He wrote this before the excesses had started in France.] Theoretical politicians, who have patronized this species of government, have erroneously supposed that by reducing mankind to a perfect equality in their political rights, they would, at the same time, be perfectly equalized and assimilated in their possessions, their opinions, and their passions."

"A republic, by which I mean a government in which a scheme of representation takes place, opens a different prospect, and promises the cure for which we are seeking."

"The two great points of difference between a democracy and a republic are: first, the delegation of the government, in the latter, to a small number of citizens elected by the rest; secondly, the greater number of

> citizens, and the greater sphere of country, over which the latter may be extended."
>
> "Men of factious tempers, of local prejudices, or of sinister designs, may, by intrigue, by corruption, or by other means, first obtain the suffrages, and then betray the interests, of the people. The question resulting is, whether small or extensive republics are more favorable to the election of proper guardians of the public weal; and it is clearly decided in favor of the latter..." [I include this paragraph, because it should resonate in the America of the 1990s and beyond.]

How were the excesses of democracy avoided by the Constitutional Convention? 1. By the Constitution itself. It was to be the fundamental law of the land, and it specifically stated the powers granted to each branch of government. 2. By the indirect election of the president and vice president through the Electoral College. 3. By having senators appointed by the state legislatures instead of by direct election. 4. Lack of an income tax. Numbers 3 and 4 were done away with by amending the Constitution during the Wilson administration and thus handing the federal government the means to destroy a free and prosperous society.

Relating to point one: it can hardly be said that the Constitution is still the fundamental law of the land, when Congress, the bureaucracy, and the courts can pass any legislation on any subject that they wish. This is unlimited government. Bismarck and his subsequent enablers were the real authors of our current system.

Relating to point two: the Electoral College persists, but it is fortunately not a rubber stamp for the results of popular elections. There have been many calls for doing away with it, but it endures largely because it is regarded as harmless. Or was, until the election of 2000 and any election in which the winner gets fewer votes than the loser: this happened again in 2016. It is now doubtful that the less populous states will ever agree to an amendment eliminating it. To do so would throw the ability to elect presidents to the great population centers of the East and West Coasts and bring an even swifter end to American liberty.

Relating to point three: the 17th Amendment did away with appointment of senators by legislatures and placed them in the arena of popular politics and direct elections. As such, they represent their states but regard themselves as national figures who can collect campaign contributions from any and all interests in all parts of the country. As I wrote this, the 2000 New York senatorial comedy was under way. (As I got back to writing, it has been resolved in the most unfortunate manner. But Mrs. Clinton went on to become Secretary of State in the first Obama administration and obtained the presidential nomination of the Democratic Party in 2016. Fortunately, she lost, after having been nominated. Donald Trump, the winning candidate, is certainly one of the most unusual men to hold the office.)

Relating to point four: the direct taxation of income was instituted by the 16th Amendment. This ostensibly innocent amendment has, more than any other legislation, allowed the enormous expansion of government with unlimited powers. Chief Justice John Marshall said, in *McCulloch v. Maryland* (1819) that "the power to tax involves the power to destroy." Whether he will be proved right remains to be seen, but that the power of excessive taxation stifles individual initiative and collective well being is undeniable. From Aristotle until today it has been acknowledged that democracy, as a system, is inherently redistributionist because of the envy and greed of the greater part of the population. Ludwig von Mises addressed this issue in *Socialism*:

"Whoever stirs up the resentment of the poor against the rich can count on securing a big audience. Democracy creates the most favorable preliminary conditions for the development of this spirit, which is always and everywhere present, though concealed. So far all democratic states have foundered on this point. The democracy of our own time is hastening toward this end." (p. 66) [To this statement, he adds a quotation from Pierre Proudhon, the 19th-century French author: "Democracy is envy."]

Pardon me for belaboring this subject, but it is precisely on the matter of redistribution of other people's money that democracy is most dangerous. Bertrand de Jouvenal devoted a small book to the subject in 1952, *The Ethics of Redistribution*. Toward the end he makes this attention-getting comment:

"During the whole range of life of commercial society, from the end of the Middle Ages to our day, the wealth of the rich merchant has been resented far more than the pomp of rulers. The ungrateful brutality of kings toward the financiers who helped them has always won popular applause. This may perhaps be related to a deep feeling that the individuals have no business being rich by themselves and for themselves, while the wealth of rulers is a form of self-gratification for the people who think of them as 'my' ruler." (p. 78)

At the end of his little volume, Jouvenal adds an appendix in which he does the mathematics of redistribution. Two basic conclusions: if all present wealth were evenly distributed, each individual would receive a relatively paltry sum; and all economic activity would grind to a halt. To this point Ayn Rand devoted a whole novel, *Atlas Shrugged*. A simpler fact needs to be stated: prior to the 16th Amendment, taxes were collected to keep the government operative. Today, most taxation is for nonrevenue purposes design to buy votes for the next election – and the country be damned.

In contrast to the bloody devolution of democracy in France, the term took on a somewhat different meaning in the United States. When 19th-century Americans spoke of democracy or the "democratic faith," as they often did, they really had in mind liberty, individual freedom. That was the distinctive quality of American life that set it apart from the Old World. Americans had the rights listed in the Declaration of Independence and the Bill of Rights, rights that were natural and not presented to them by their government. They saw their government as limited by the Constitution, not themselves as limited by their government. They took politics and its democratic procedures seriously, as much as any sport can be taken seriously, because the federal government was, for most people, no big thing. It could not arbitrarily take away their money and property, as it does today. And, with the size of the continent, Americans could move farther and farther away from the seat of government. The ever-receding frontier really did have a lot to do with shaping the American character. Frederick Jackson Turner's *The Significance of Frontier in American History* is still worth reading, more than a century after it was written.

As to rights, a small parenthesis. The debate on natural rights has gone on for centuries. In fact, natural rights cannot be proved. Mises, in *Socialism,* says that Nature grants no rights at all (p. 50). Jane Jacobs explored the question a little more fully in *Systems of Survival.* "The contractual law we inherited from those medieval merchants contained radical conceptions. Not only did it apply alike to all individuals, no matter who they were or what their social status might be, but it was available to individuals for no other reason than that they were individuals, making contracts."

Whether human rights are natural, as some philosophers believed, or God-given as some theologians insist, or whether they were a rather modern product of historical development, the notion that individuals do have rights by virtue of being human is generally accepted in some parts of the world. Even nations that deprive most of their citizens of nearly all rights use the correct terminology in their worthless rhetoric. Citizens of the early Republic knew that they had rights, except for the slaves and the Indians, of course. And they did not cease to play up the fact in Fourth of July speeches, as well as in more literary works. The United States was the land of opportunity for those who lived here, and it was so regarded by the thousands of immigrants who arrived on its shores annually.

All rights are not the same. We may accept the theory

of natural, or even God-given rights. There are also civil rights, those specifically resulting from legislation. Of these, the right to vote when one reaches the age of 18 is probably the best known. The right to drive a car after getting a driver's license is another. But when a government starts proclaiming or legislating a whole array of rights that have no basis in history or reason, it is necessary to become suspicious. Are these rights anything more than a cover for more redistribution of wealth and a means of control? (The compassion of Liberalism/Leftism can easily be defined: the eagerness to put your money where their mouths are. But it's not really compassion; it's a determination to keep people in their place. It is Bismarck's old system of social control.)

Numerous aspects of any normal society are suddenly found to engender rights: the rights to housing, health care, education, and grants of welfare. I recall seeing on the news some years ago a demonstration in downtown Chicago by a group demanding welfare rights; these are the rights to have you work to pay for the living expenses of someone who is ignorant, lazy, and incompetent (or, perhaps, someone who is actually in need). When governments start granting rights wholesale, they are really doing nothing more than extending their own reach and diminishing the rights of the majority of citizens, those who foot the bill. American citizens should really learn to understand that the Constitution was designed as a limit on the powers of government, not as a limit on their rights. The Bill of Rights did not grant us any new rights; it only declared the ones we already had and told the federal government to keep it dirty mitts of these areas of our lives.

The Bill of Rights does not, unfortunately, seem as potent as it once was. Supreme Court rulings in the past few decades have put limits on freedom of religion and of speech, the latter most recently under the guise of campaign reform, although a later ruling reversed this trend. Administrative and legislative bodies at all levels of government have seriously compromised property rights. The Supreme Court, in it *Kelo* ruling, recently joined the erosion-of-private-property crowd in its decision to allow local governments to seize private property for the sake of economic development, and, of course, higher taxes.

Every society has recognized the need for a well-schooled citizenry, the need for decent health care, and the need for housing. These needs have always been met by the efforts of the citizens themselves. There is no need for the involvement of government to provide any of these needs. The case has been well and often made that the involvement of government always makes the situation worse, that I'll not bother presenting that massive array of evidence yet. Those who would deny the evidence are those who have a vested interest in preserving obviously failing systems, whether it be public housing, the public schools, or national health care. Now, back on track.

There was a good reason for the optimism that suffused the American spirit in the decades after the Constitution was ratified. The residents of North America had discovered something that was indeed new under the sun: the liberty to pursue one's interests and to improve one's life as well as possible without having to look over one's shoulder at the government or some "lord of the manor" waiting to grab his "rightful share." No one has analyzed these developments in 18th-century North

America better than Gordon Wood in his *The Radicalism of the American Revolution* (1991).

"The social hierarchy seemed less natural, less ordained by God, and more man-made, more arbitrary.... Everywhere ordinary people were no longer willing to play their accustomed roles in the hierarchy, no longer willing to follow their callings, no longer willing to restrict their consumption of goods. They were less dependent, less willing to walk while gentlemen rode, less willing to doff their caps, less deferential, less passive, less respectful of those above them." (pp. 145-146)

So the young United States thrived and prospered for several decades. Of course there were flaws. Nearly all the social ills with which we are familiar today were present then. But, by and large, it was a busy, vigorous, growing, and increasingly prosperous society. It was really, contrary to the *Book of Ecclesiastes,* something new under the sun: a free society where, for the first time in history, individuals could pursue their own happiness without being forced to contribute to someone else's. Now, those were good old days.

Following the Constitutional Convention of 1787, someone asked Benjamin Franklin: "Sir, what have you given us? Franklin: "A republic, if you can keep it"

As Americans approached 1850, there was a stench in the air. In 1820, on the occasion of the Missouri Compromise, Thomas Jefferson had remarked, "I tremble for my country, when I reflect that God is just." With the onset of the Mexican War and the probable extension of slavery into new territories, he would have had renewed cause to tremble, had he been alive. Many grimmer views were being expressed, both about the government and about the prospects for democracy. I could fill up many pages with quotations from famous Americans at this point, but I will make do with a few pointed ones.

First, Henry Thoreau in his *Civil Disobedience,* a speech given on the occasion of the Mexican War. "How does it become a man to behave toward this American government today? I answer, that he cannot without disgrace be associated with it. I cannot for an instant recognize that political organization as *my* government which is the slave's government also."

From the same: "I saw that the State was half-witted, that it was timid as a lone woman with her silver spoons, and that it did not know its friends from its foes, and I lost all my remaining respect for it, and pitied it."

This is Thoreau from 'A Plea for Captain John Brown," a speech delivered in Concord, Mass., on Oct. 30, 1859. "We talk about a *representative government*; but what a monster of a government is that where the noblest faculties of the mind, and the whole heart, are not *represented*! A semihuman tiger or ox, stalking over the earth, with its heart taken out and the top of its brain shot away. Heroes have fought well on their stumps when their legs were shot off, but I never heard of any good done by such a government as that.

"The only government that I recognize – and it matters not how few are at the head of it, or how small its army – is that power that establishes justice in the land, never that which establishes injustice. What shall we think of a government to which all the truly brave and just men in the land are enemies, standing between it and those whom it oppresses?"

John C. Calhoun of South Carolina also addressed

the problem of the war with Mexico. He opposed the war because he believed it would increase the power of the presidency. He had a perhaps-irrational fear of military dictatorship. Speaking in the U. S. Senate in March 1848 he said: "We are a warlike people, rapidly increasing in numbers, population, and wealth – well fed and well clothed, and having an abundance of leisure. Like all such people, we seek excitement; and there is no excitement more seductive to the young and ardent portion of our population than war. It is difficult to prevent such a people from rushing into a war on any pretense; and if they should frequently recur, and this precedent be not reversed, nothing can prevent the Executive power from overshadowing the constitution and liberties of the country." He made another comment the same year. "With me the liberty of the country is all in all. If this be preserved, everything will be preserved; but if lost, all will be lost."

Calhoun has fallen out of favor, because he was a staunch defender of the slave-holding South. Nevertheless, he was one of the most prescient of American statesmen and quite in accord with the creators of the Constitution. In the two sets of remarks, he was right on both counts. In the 20th century, war has been the chief instrument of the aggrandizement of government. And if liberty slowly slides away, everything worthwhile will be lost.

In his *Disquisition on Government,* Calhoun almost seemed to be staring into the 20th and 21st centuries. "But government, although intended to protect and preserve society, has a strong tendency to disorder and abuse of its powers, as all experience and almost every page of history testify. The cause is to be found in the same constitution of our nature which makes government indispensable. The powers which it is necessary for government to possess, in order to repress violence and preserve order, cannot execute themselves. They must be administered by men in whom, like others, the individual are stronger than the social feelings. And hence, the powers vested in them to prevent injustice and oppression on the part of others, will, if left unguarded, be by them converted into instruments to oppress the rest of the community. That, by which this is prevented, is what is meant by Constitution, in its most comprehensive sense, when applied to government."

Next, we have Walt Whitman, and in a much nastier mood than he ever showed in his poetry. He composed an essay entitled 'The Eighteenth Presidency' in 1855. Why he used the number 18, I have no idea, since Buchanan was about to become the 15th president, and Franklin Pierce was ending his uneventful four years of pandering to the Slavocracy. It was, again, the slavery issue that got the poet's ire worked up; and he used plenty of vitriol to malign the objects of his scorn. "The sixteenth and seventeenth terms of the American Presidency have shown that the villainy and shallowness of great rulers are just as eligible to These States as to any foreign despotism. History is to record these two presidencies as so far our topmost warning and shame. Never were publicly displayed more deformed, mediocre, sniveling, unreliable, false-hearted men! Never were these States so insulted, and attempted to be betrayed! All the main purposes for which the government was established are openly denied. The perfect equality of slavery with freedom is flauntingly preached in the North, nay, the superiority of slavery.... The President eats dirt and excrement for his daily meals, likes it, and tries to force it on the States. The cushions of the Presidency are nothing but filth and blood. The pavements of our Congress are also bloody."

Whitman then goes on to describe the process of choosing elected officials. "Whence then do these nominating dictators of America year after year start out? From lawyers' offices, secret lodges, back-yards, bed-houses, and bar-rooms; from out of the custom-houses, marshals' offices, post-offices, and gambling hells; from the President's house, the jail, the venereal hospital, the station-house; from unnamed by-places where devilish disunion is hatched at midnight; from political hearses, and from the coffins inside, and from the shrouds inside the coffins; from the tumors and abscesses of the land; from the skeletons and skulls in the vaults of the federal almshouses; from the running sores of the great cities; thence to the national, state, city, and district nominating conventions of These States, come the most numerous and controlling delegates.

"Who are they personally? Office-holders, office-seekers, robbers, pimps, exclusives, malignants, conspirators, murderers, fancy-men, port-masters, custom-house clerks, contractors, kept-editors, Spaniels well-trained to carry and fetch, jobbers, infidels, disunionists, terrorists, mail-riflers, slave-catchers, pushers of Slavery, creatures of the President, creatures of would-be Presidents, spies, blowers, electioneers, body-snatchers, bawlers, bribers, compromisers, runaways, backers, monte-dealers, duelists, carriers of concealed weapons, blind men, deaf men, pimpled men, scarred inside with the vile disorder, gaudy outside with gold chains made from the people's money and harlot's money twisted together; crawling, serpentine men, the lousy combings and born freedom sellers of the earth."

He did have a way with words, but he was not without hope. "Are not political parties about played out? I say they are, all round. America has outgrown parties; henceforth it is too large, and they too small."

"What historic denouements are these we are approaching? On all sides tyrants tremble, crowns are unsteady, the human race restive, on the watch for some better era, some divine war. No man knows what will happen next, but all know that some such things are to happen as mark the greatest moral convulsions of the earth. Who shall play the hand for America in these tremendous games? A pretty time for two dead corpses to go walking up and down the earth, to guide by feebleness and ashes a proud, young, friendly, fresh, heroic nation of thirty millions of live and electric men!"

Many other quotations could be added. But the point is clear: by mid-19th century the whole nation was in ferment over slavery. That subject has been well covered in so many places that there is no need to plow that field again, except for one reminder. At the heart of the controversy over slavery was the statement in the Declaration of Independence, "all men are created equal." The Civil War and its subsequent Constitutional amendments dealt with the problem of slavery, and the consequences of the Civil War for our government will be the subject of a subsequent chapter. The problem of equality endures, often in quite distorted forms. It's necessary to say a few words about it, before finally getting back to Tocqueville, because he had so much to say about the equality of conditions he noticed in the United States.

Equality exists nowhere in nature, apart from quantum mechanics. Similarity does, but not equality. Mathematics is not part of nature, although it may be derived from it. Yet equality has long been linked to democracy. It certainly was during the French Revolution: Liberty, Equality, Fraternity was its slogan. It was a romantic slogan with little if any cognitive content, but its appeal has never, unfortunately, died. In fact, liberty and equality are in most senses incompatible. The chief exception is equality before the law. A more recent and acceptable one is equal pay for equal work. An attempt to force a society into equality necessarily pushes the whole society downward. Equality never means leveling upward; it's always leveling downward, whether it be in quality of schooling or in quality of life. This is, in fact, the goal of the American Left.

The Nobel Prize winning economist Friedrich A. Hayek elucidated the problem of equality in his *Constitution of Liberty* (1960):

"Equality of the general rules of law and conduct, however, is the only kind of equality conducive to liberty and the only equality which we can secure without destroying liberty. Not only has liberty nothing to do with any other sort of equality, but it is even bound to produce inequality in many respects."

It always comes down to money, doesn't it? If we were all equally poor and miserable, a bunch of Somalian peasants on a wind-blown goat farm with no way out, there would be no egalitarian campaigns. And if such a campaign should ever succeed, those who impose it will not be partaking of the equality. They will be living high on the hog, above it all, as all political charlatans manage to do; which is to say, they would resemble the pigs in Orwell's *Animal Farm*. Some are always more equal than others. Congress is a blatant example. But the remaining socialist nations are even more so. Fidel and Raul Castro never missed a meal. Nor did Hugo Chavez and Nicolás Maduro as they presided over the collapse of Venezuela's economy,

It's always for the "masses" that the great social experiments are proposed; and the same masses are often stupid enough to fall for it and dine on the grubby tidbits that fall from the master's table. Perhaps it is because we are basically a nation of immigrant peasants and their descendants that we've arrived at this sad state. Some security is better than none, apparently. Or perhaps a lot of people have no aspirations. I am always amused by the Leftists I know personally or by reputation; they live like wealthy Republican country club members, while declaiming against the evils of capitalism; and they would not for a minute agree to live in the kind of country they admire – Cuba, North Korea, China, or their beloved Soviet Union. But they'd be happy to see the rest of us living in such a land, provided they were among the rulers or at least the lapdogs of the rulers.

Now, at last, a paragraph from Tocqueville's masterpiece.

"I believe that it is easier to establish an absolute and despotic government among a people whose social conditions are equal than among any other. I also believe that such a government once established in such a people would not only oppress men but would, in the end, strip each man there of several of the chief attributes of humanity." (From Democracy in America, translated by George Lawrence and edited by J. P. Mayer, 1969, Page 695)

That this could have been written during the 1830s is remarkable. Tocqueville looked ahead with more perception and insight than many of our historians look back. To acknowledge that what he said is true only takes honesty. Now it is time to travel down that winding road to the present to see how we got where Tocqueville said we would arrive.

Chapter 9: Externalities

College students who have had the misfortune to study what passes for economics in most of our institutions of higher learning will have heard about externalities. The term is normally used in a pejorative sense, as something businesses do that have bad consequences. Air and water pollution emanating from factories are examples. And we know that the oceans have been used s garbage dumps for centuries. Such externalities are regarded as market failures. Writers of economics textbooks spend much time dealing with market failures. Their purpose is, of course, to promote government programs designed to correct or eliminate such failures.

In his *Principles of Microeconomics,* Harvard professor N. Gregory Mankiw defines market failure as "a situation in which the market on its own fails to allocate resources efficiently." As a market failure, "an externality is the impact of one person's actions on the well-being of a bystander." (p. 10) He does make an admission: "To say that the government *can* improve on market outcomes at times does not mean that it always *will.*" And, a few sentences later: "One goal of the study of economics is to help you judge when a government policy is justifiable to promote efficiency or equity and when it is not." (May I suggest that this is not a goal of studying economics? It has been made the goal in order to structure the teaching of economics around that glorious edifice, the federal government, which seems to lurk behind nearly every page of the textbooks.)

I selected Mankiw's book because it was at hand, and he is one of the most eminent economists in the United States and served on President George W. Bush's Council of Economic Advisors. But the same points are made in all the major economics texts used in our schools. I can say that with some authority, because I have read so many of them, including the two that are most commonly used. There is an underlying assumption in all of them: government must always be at hand and ready to move in to correct errors made in the marketplace. A further assumption is that government and the market must always be partners, with government always the senior partner. A later chapter will demonstrate the falsity of this notion. Here, I want to deal with the worst of all externalities, subsumed under the term "government failure." This term is also used in textbooks, but it is usually covered quite briefly. It is actually amusing to read some of the texts, because of the frequent mention of instances in which the government has completely screwed up when it meddles in the economy. Yet the authors stick with their premise, regardless of the massive evidence.

In a small book called *The Economics of Liberty,* Llewellyn H. Rockwell makes the point of this chapter in two short sentences. "The mainstream claim about 'market failure' is nonsense, of course. It is *government* failure that plagues us." (p. 120) I am going to define government failure two ways: 1. Failure to do what ought to be done for the well-being of society; 2. Taking actions no government has any business taking. So, how have governments failed? Let me count the ways (but not all of them or this would be the longest book ever written. Consider the size of the Federal Register.)

I've already mentioned the pervasive genocidal nature of the 20th century. *The Black Book of Communism* covers in bloody detail the crimes of the several Communist dictatorships. A. J. Rummel has expanded on this theme in his *Death by Government,* in which he says that the 20 most murderous governments killed about 160 million people, all with the best of intentions of course. That number is certainly too small, for there have been deliberate mass starvations in many non-Communist countries. The mess in Zimbabwe in 2003-13 comes to mind, and the calamity in Venezuela persisted in 2019. And, since I do not have the latter book in hand, I don't know if the author included the African bloodbaths of the 1990s. But what is the single greatest government failure? War.

May I abstract from *Encyclopaedia Britannica* data on the costs of the two world wars. In World War I, the Allied and Associated Powers mobilized about 42 million men; the Central Powers mobilized about 23 million. A total of 65 million. Of these, 8.4 million were killed. The monetary cost of this exercise in international lunacy is estimated at $145.4 billion for the Allied Powers, while the Central Powers spent a paltry $63 billion. All those lives and all that treasure were squandered at the behest of the demented leaders of Europe and the United States. The cost in lives for World War II was so great that only estimates are given. The lowest death toll is 35 million, while the highest is 60 million. And the amount of money squandered was, naturally, much greater than in the Great War. In addition to these main attractions, there have also been the Korean War, Vietnam, Afghanistan, Yugoslavia, and numerous civil wars. And now, of course, we have World War III, also called the war against terrorism, to deal with. Think again of Bastiat's "the things that are not seen," all the young lives never allowed to fulfill their potential.

> What passing bells for these who die as cattle?
> - Only the monstrous anger of the guns.
> Only the stuttering rifles' rapid rattle
> Can patter out their hasty orisons.
> Wilfred Owen, killed in action 1918

"There shall be wars, and rumors of wars." Quite true. It is one of the most basic human institutions and has been with societies from the beginning. The British general, Montgomery of Alamein, said in his history of war that the spread of civilization entailed an increase in war, perhaps because of improvements in technology. And it must be admitted that there is a romance attached to war, providing you are not actually in combat. It is one thing to read about and admire the heroism of an Alvin York or Audie Murphy, quite another to put oneself in their place. Histories of wars and novels about wars will remain popular, and they are best enjoyed in the comforts of one's home. For a realistic view, read John Keegan's *Men in Battle,* or in fiction, Norman Mailer's *The Naked and the Dead.* Another suggestion: The great antiwar film of 1969 is now on DVD: *Oh! What a Lovely War,* with an astounding array of British talent. I cannot recommend this film too highly, but it must be watched carefully, because Americans are not nearly as familiar with the genuine tragedy of that four-year debacle as are British audiences. It would help to have a libretto available. Even better, use the English subtitles. For World War I there is also *All Quiet on the Western Front.*

Ordinary citizens do not band together to go off and fight wars; their governments compel them. But certain wars have brought about a great rejoicing at their start. In ancient Greece, Athens launched the Peloponnesian War with great confidence and ended in ruins. Europe, from the time of Charlemagne (died 814) was almost continuously at war until the defeat of Napoleon in 1815, a glorious thousand years indeed. (This was the era of Western Christendom). In the United States, the Mexican War was quite popular with most segments of the population. The Spanish-American War was treated almost as a holiday event, a "splendid little war." At the start of World War I there was massive exultation and celebrating by the youth of Europe. The joy quickly turned to sorrow, as the British poets so eloquently described the horrors of the trenches, while the government in London consistently lied about the incredible suffering of the troops.

The main point stands: governments make wars happen, whether prosecuted by a power-mad thug in Baghdad or the "best and brightest" in Washington, DC. Lest you get the wrong idea, pacifism is untenable. When one's nation is attacked, war becomes a necessity; and pacifists become the enemies of civilization, regardless of political affiliation; and a party that undermines such a war is guilty of treason. My father was in the trenches in France in World War I, while his older brother served in the Philippines. Three younger brothers and my oldest cousin served in World War II. They all made it home.

Let's turn now to some less monstrous examples of government failure. In 1961 Jane Jacobs published *The Death and Life of Great American Cities,* a careful analysis of what is laughingly called urban renewal in the United States. She showed what, decades later, was accepted as fact: the massive housing projects built in our major cities were social disasters, neighborhood-destroying, crime-breeding sores on the body politic. Our leaders, showing their customary wisdom, hooted and jeered, knowing that these projects were the best accommodations they could design for their victims to live in. Old and poor neighborhoods were torn down, and their residents, mostly minority, were forced to move into the new housing. Their "betters" knew what was best for them, so into these high-rise slums they went.

The result of this irrational and misguided policy was to create a generation of victims dependent on the "largesse" of the government. The equally absurd welfare programs compounded the problem by breaking up families, increasing dependence, and encouraging irresponsibility. The story of the disastrous "war on poverty" has been told by others more competent to deal with it. But we know the costs have been monumental. The recipients of the welfare generally remained in poverty, while those who were doling it out did quite well for themselves. How like bureaucrats. Perhaps this was the goal.

Now, fast forward from the 1960s to 2000. On Tuesday, December 19, 2000, the *Wall Street Journal* published a front-page feature article on the status of urban renewal and the disastrous housing projects. "All over the country, some of the nation's biggest and most poverty-stricken public housing projects are coming down. Finally, the inner-city high rise has been declared an irredeemable failure....Over the decades, these dense neighborhoods of poverty bred greater poverty – as well as crime that spilled over into wealthier parts of cities. Unemployment and a sense of alienation from mainstream society grew more pronounced until public housing became like life nowhere else." (Written by Jonathan Eig)

These sentences tell a not always obvious truth. Elected officials and bureaucrats perceive a problem, announce a crisis, and set out to solve it. How much outright racism was involved in their solution is impossible to say, for a great many of those forced into the high rises were African Americans. In Chicago that was definitely the case. Leaving that aside, government did not really perceive a problem, it misperceived one, just as it did with the determination to end poverty. For one thing, public officials regarded poverty and the kinds of housing it entailed as a static condition instead of a fluctuating one. The history of American economic development shows clearly that people who are poor today can become better off tomorrow, as they take advantage of opportunities that come their way. This is the story of every immigrant generation.

None of the generations preceding 1965 sat around waiting for federal handouts. They worked and they studied, and they made sure their children studied and worked. Situations that appear frozen in time to public officials are really always in a state of flux. Scholars who know what they are talking about have examined the employment problems of the poor. Richard K. Vedder and Lowell E. Gallaway have published a highly readable treatment. Its suggestive title is *Out of Work: Unemployment and Government in Twentieth-Century America.* Right there in the subtitle the reader learns who the enemy is. The war on poverty, on the other hand, was promoted by Socialists and their admirers, people who are as clueless about the workings of society as they are ready with their worthless solutions.

For the government to tell a whole generation of those less well off than most: "Don't do anything. We will provide," is the grossest kind of well-meaning but ignorant social malpractice imaginable. It was an opportunity-destroying, education-denying, and - in the end - a life-distorting program, both in its offer of income for nothing and in its dreadful housing decisions. Do we hear outrage expressed against the government for its follies. Not that I've noticed. The victims keep voting for their oppressors. Maybe there really is a slave mentality. And we certainly never hear either party apologizing for the disasters government creates. Good intentions are everything.

While we are in the race neighborhood, let's go back to 1896 and the Supreme Court ruling in the case *Plessy v. Ferguson.* This is the case that established in law the "separate but equal" doctrine of racial separation. The ruling was overturned in 1954 by *Brown v. Board of Education.* Racial and ethnic animosities have existed in every society in which there were individuals different from the majority. Hence the word xenophobia, fear of strangers, derived from the Greek words for strangers and fear. The ancient Israelites, Greeks, and, sometimes, the Romans all took ethnic and racial differences into consideration in matters of law and social policy. Law cannot abolish personal attitudes, but in the absence of law those attitudes can be made unprofitable, unworkable, and unpopular.

The point to be made is this: In the United States it is the state and federal governments that took racism out of the realm of private attitude and made it a public policy. No notice was paid to the "equal protection" clause of the Constitution. Then, in response to the Civil Rights Movement of the 1960s, the federal government once again went into action. Attempting to right old wrongs, it created by law whole new sets of wrongs. Anyone who has paid attention in the past 40 years is well aware of affirmative action quotas, set-asides, and accusations of reverse discrimination. Anyone interested in learning more about this issue can consult *Forbidden Grounds: The Case Against Employment Discrimination Laws* by Richard Epstein (1992) and *Race and Culture* by Thomas Sowell (1994).

May I offer one more case of extreme government imbecility in our land? In 1917 Congress passed and sent to the states for ratification the 18th, or Prohibition, Amendment. It was ratified by January 29, 1919, and went into effect one year later. The enabling legislation, named the Volstead Act, was passed on October 28, 1918, to provide law enforcement guidelines. Such legislation was just what the incipient Roaring Twenties, or Jazz Age, needed. There had always been neighborhood saloons and bars in the United States, probably several thousand of them. Prohibition led to the creation of thousands more, called speakeasies. Drinking became a patriotic act of defiance. Determined to put behind them the grim years of World War I, the American people were going to enjoy themselves. What here is the externality? Organized crime was basically given control of the whole liquor industry. Government policy raised crime to a level of profitability and power it had never known and from which it has never receded. Who recalls the names of Prohibition enforcers, other than Elliott Ness? But the names of the criminals have woven themselves into the fabric of American history, as well as into the workings of all levels of government. In his *Dry Manhattan*, Michael A. Lerner presents a brilliant evocation of the whole Prohibition era and its eventual demise.

Another government-created disaster was the savings and loan crisis of the 1980s, during which more than 700 such institutions failed and which cost the government millions to deal with. This complicated financial fiasco took Kathleen Day 395 pages to explain in her *S&L Hell* (1993), so I am not going to try.

Before moving abroad, there are a few other common American government failures worth mentioning. Price controls come in two varieties. Price ceilings result in shortages, while price floors bring about surpluses. Rent control is probably the best known price control. It has been law in New York City since World War II. The only state to mandate it as of 2019 has been Oregon. Farm price supports have been a long-running price floor. Local zoning laws are frequently used to benefit wealthy landlords and builders rather than poorer citizens. Property taxes are often lowered for the wealthy and politically connected, leaving less well to do residents to make up the losses. (This has been notoriously true in Cook County, Illinois, for years.) The lack of border protection has been highlighted during the Trump administration. New York State, as of 2019, had a shortage of natural gas, owing in great part to the state government's refusal to allow fracking for oil and gas as well as prohibiting pipeline development. This, in spite of the fact that the Marcellus Shale is a huge source of natural gas. Meanwhile, neighboring Pennsylvania was reaping enormous benefits from fracking and creating thousands of jobs in doing so.

I want to revert to a price floor that has become popular in the past few decades: the minimum wage. It first became law under the Fair Labor Standards Act of 1938 during the administration of Franklin Roosevelt, when it was set at 25 cents an hour. The law was quiescent for a long time before it re-emerged as a potential vote-buying scheme. In 2019 the state government of Illinois passed a law raising the minimum wage to $15.00 an hour. Other states and cities have passed similar legislation. Long term results are uncertain, but some economists have suggested three outcomes: automation to replace workers, cutting back on the number of employees, or going out of business. Something politicians fail to recognize is the wages of labor in the private sector are based on productivity. Granted, it was not always so, but unionization changed that. I refer to productivity in terms of goods produced, items sold, and services rendered. This is not a problem in the public sector.

Now may I propose a similar scenario? Suppose that the federal government, in a desire to keep the economy booming, legislated that every individual living alone must spend $50.00 per week on groceries; married couples without children $100.00 a week. So for each additional family member another $50.00 is assessed. Government is forcing people to spend money they may not have, in spite of the fact that in a free society individuals as well as businesses should be able to make their own choices on expenditures, as they are able to – not as they are forced to do.

There are also failures to do what should be done. Rebuilding the infrastructure – roads, bridges, and tunnels. But, of course, there must be money for members of public sector unions. Then there is Amtrak. Have you ridden on European railroads and wondered why we don't have something comparable in the United States?

I must not leave unmentioned a government success: the war on tobacco that has been going on for decades. I recall when the price of a carton of cigarettes was $1.00. Today, in my area it approaches $70.00 per carton, and the bulk of that cost represents taxes. Cigarette smoking has decreased a great deal. Pipe and cigar smoking seem to remain popular, since there is a *Cigar Aficionado* magazine. Now, however, government has decided to turn this success into an absurdity with the legalization of marijuana. Tobacco may be additive, but it is not a mind-altering drug. Marijuana is, especially in its newer varieties with an enhanced THC chemical component. Driving "buzzed" is as dangerous as driving drunk, as some states that have made marijuana legal can testify. What's the reason for this new policy? Money, of course. One wonders whether cocaine and heroin will be next. They were, after all, readily available in the late 19th century.

What was the greatest government failure, apart from war, in the 20th century? It was the Great Depression, something that need not have happened but that was occasioned by repeated mistakes made by the Federal Government.

Does our government do anything well? Indeed it does. There are the armed forces: Army, Navy, Marines, Air Force, and the Coast Guard, all of which perform their duties admirably most of the time. They cannot avoid being sucked into unwinnable wars such as Vietnam. The mail is still delivered. Social Security payments arrive on time. Medicare bills are paid. I suspect most government workers are conscientious in their jobs, apart from time-serving bureaucrats. The FBI has a pretty good record in dealing with crime, especially now that J. Edgar Hoover is gone. Local law enforcement officers do the best they can, considering the huge increase in crime over the past few decades. Fire fighters do excellent work in trying circumstances. How well the federal government does in helping out places devastated by tornadoes, forest fires, hurricanes, and floods, I don't have enough information to say.

Now let us go overseas for a moment. The much-vaunted Japanese juggernaut stumbled and fell flat on its face about 1990. And it had not yet recovered after more than three decades of recession. Many Americans, looking at Japan's post-World War II prosperity, would assume it was modeled on the economy of the United States. It wasn't. When Japan began to modernize, late in the 19th century, it patterned itself after Prussia, the powerful unifier of Germany. Prussia was a statist society, as was all of Europe. Top-down rule was considered to be the only way a country could be governed. Japan never adopted the kind of free-market economy that existed in the United States until the Great Depression. Business-government partnership became the norm.

When an economy fails as badly as that of Japan has, government is called upon to step in and fix it. So the Japanese government launched its own New Deal, and it failed just as Roosevelt's New Deal did. The tried and false prescriptions of Keynesianism were dragged out of that dilapidated economic warehouse and inflicted on the country. "Economic stimulus packages," paid for by taxes, were supposed to revive the fallen economy. Make-work projects abounded, including building roads, bridges, tunnels, and whatever else could be thought up to offer tax-based paychecks to workers. What have all the marvels of Keynesian spending accomplished? The economy has averaged a growth of about 1.5 percent during the 1990s. Even better, as reported by *Wall Street Journal* staff reporter Bill Spindle, "Japan's national debt is gargantuan and growing fast....Japan's government debt as a percentage of national economic output is now the world's largest, surpassing that of Italy." (December 11, 2000) And the economy remained in the doldrums. How it will put itself back together after the massive earthquake and tsunami of March 2011 remains to be seen, but bad old habits die hard. The prime minister who took office in early 2013, Shinzo Abe, has decided to go down the same old path.

The notion that it is possible for a government to spend a nation into prosperity is too ludicrous to need comment, or it should be. But that was the New Deal's answer in the 1930s; it was Japan's answer 60 years later; and it was that of our federal government in the recession that started in 2008. They never learn, and if they did they would probably not understand. Elected officials and bureaucrats seem to have no understanding of capital formation and how wealth is created. Spending it is their game, and they are always surprised when the well-intended waste never attains its goal. But it is quite possible that solving the problem is not the goal. Perhaps it is maintaining control at all costs, no matter what happens to the country. This is certainly the attitude of the leftists in the United States who would like to see radical changes in the economy. It must be a terrible shock to government officials to have as president, as of 2017, a man who actually understands capital formation, despite his other quirks.

I bid farewell to Japan with a sentence from a book review in *The Economist* (Dec. 23, 2000-Jan. 5, 2001, p. 123). "Japan's industrial policy in the last 30 years has been an abject failure, with the government harming virtually every industry it touched."

There is no point in wasting much space on the foreign aid boondoggle. Any citizen who has thought about it knows that trillions of American taxpayer dollars have been flushed down that toilet in the past 50 years. Congress loves to spend our money on worthless causes, the only kind it understands. What politicians, whether in Congress or at the International Monetary Fund or World Bank, fail to understand is that giving away piles of money to another government is not capital formation. The money rarely, if ever, was used to benefit the respective populations of the receiving countries. It went into ill-considered projects or directly into the Swiss bank accounts of the various dictators.

During the Cold War the excuse for doling out the cash was to buy friendship among the "nonaligned" nations. That excuse is now passé, but the money keeps flowing. More recently, our government and the IMF have together poured billions into Russia's pocket-stuffers, with what results we know. Ignorant and misguided church "leaders" and a few celebrities plead for the industrial nations to forgive Third World debt. The same leaders naturally were in the forefront of demanding the money be wasted in the first place. (For a fine summary of what has happened on one continent, get hold of *The Fate of Africa: From the Hopes of Freedom to the Heart of Despair* by Martin Meredith, published in 2005.)

In his *Prosperity Versus Planning*, David Osterfeld in 1992 presented his conclusions on foreign aid. "In short, foreign aid generates incentives that, by their nature, militate against economic growth and development. This should hardly be surprising. Aid has been in existence for more than four decades. If it were in fact effective, by now the demand for it should be declining. In fact the demand for aid is only increasing. Foreign aid is not aid at all, it is foreign harm." Why is it so hard to accept that the way out of poverty is wealth creation, something people will do for themselves if given the freedom?

We may as well pay a short visit to the United Kingdom. Its National Health Service was created under the Socialist government of Clement Atlee after World War II. Currently it is not in the best of health. In 2000 a certain Harold Shipman, physician, was convicted of murdering 15 patients and was suspected of killing from 300 to 500 more in a 24-year career. In an editorial about him, the *Wall Street Journal* noted: "Perhaps as many as 25,000 people die in the U.K. each year because they are denied cancer treatment, according to estimates by the

World Health Organization. Britain has fewer doctors per thousand patients than any other Western European nation. Every day, the British papers seem to have another hospital horror story." A recent article noted that it is far easier for a dog to get hip replacement than a human being. This is the great boon that the Clinton administration hoped to foist on the United States and that the Obama administration did, as we apparently moved closer to his vision of collectivism.

Staying in the United Kingdom a bit longer, it's worth mentioning the agricultural crisis that began in the 1990s with "mad cow disease." Added to this disaster was an outbreak of what we in the United States call hoof and mouth disease among farm animals in 2001. The crisis spread to the Continent. Exports of European meat to the United States, Australia, and other nations were banned. Discussion of this crisis is best left to experts. I only want to note some comments made by a British physician, Anthony Daniels, in a *Wall Street Journal* article (March 15, 2001). Along with the farm problems, he discusses the general deterioration of the quality of life in Britain. His conclusion is fascinating.

"What adds to our misery is the certainty that mere public expenditure will not solve the problem. Indeed, it will make it worse. Our functionaries have no pride or belief in what they do; they are mere collectors of salaries, waiting impatiently for five o'clock, the weekend, and retirement. Our educators don't educate, and our regulators interfere but do not prevent disaster. Throwing money in the sea would be more rational than entrusting money to British officialdom."

Many more examples could be cited: the late Taliban

dictatorship in Afghanistan; the tyranny of the Muslim clerics in Iran; the anti-prosperity governments of India, the sheer idiocy of the Mugabe regime in Zimbabwe; the mess in Venezuela and Bolivia; the failure to come to grips with reality in South Africa; the complete bankruptcy of government in Greece, Spain, and Italy; the frantic attempts of France and Germany to keep the populations quiescent as the welfare state disintegrates. And in the years since 2012 there is the refugee crisis, spawned by the war in Syria.

It's fascinating to watch the government responses in 2011 and 2012 at the national as well as at the European Union level to the plight of the Mediterranean countries – Spain, Portugal, Italy, and Greece – to the bankruptcy of their governments. Borrow more money, raise taxes, and impose austerity programs is the preferred solution. Who bears the austerity? Why, the citizens of course, never the officeholders. It reminds one of the failed, but politically motivated, New Deal programs during the Great Depression. Barbara Tuchman's *March of Folly* is still on the move.

It would be possible to sympathize with the heads of the European nations, if one saw any chance of their changing course. There is none. To change policy and move toward economic freedom would cost them all their jobs, and they would lose their celebrity status. Worse, they would lose control. I find it impossible to explain the mindset of European politicians. Why are they so opposed to a free-market economy? Is it simply an antipathy toward the United States, and to a lesser degree, Great Britain? Why do they hate success?

There are more examples here at home, too, but the

point is made, and it is made without even discussing any of the outright criminal activities of the federal government – and there is no shortage of these. Waco does not stand alone.

Returning to the American follies, politicians declaim against the high costs of medical care. What they will not tell you is that these costs have gotten so high because government jumped into the health care market with both feet with Medicare and Medicaid. When government arrives, it is with bags full of money. Large infusions of cash into a segment of the economy will cause inflation, just as a large infusion of cash into the economy at large will tend to make all prices rise. (Inflation is always an increase in the money supply, thereby decreasing the value of money in relation to other goods.) So when politicians pretend to be shocked at the high costs of medical care, it is much like Captain Reynaud in *Casablanca* being shocked that gambling takes place at *Rick's*, as he pockets his winnings. Of course, the grandiose promises attached to these programs when they are passed fade away as the realities of cost settle in. So Medicare patients see their coverage decrease while the costs of the coverage rise annually. Wait until the "free" prescription drug program is passed. You ain't seen nothing yet. (This new entitlement fiasco became law in 2003.) The federal government's goal, of course, is to destroy the American health system and replace it with a state system, like unto Stalin's and Castro's. Movie stars may cheer the notion, but they are wealthy enough to opt out. As one of our saintly politicians said: We're going to shove socialized medicine down the throats of the American people, whether they want it or not.

Parents are shocked and dismayed at the costs of higher education. Why are they so high? For much the same reason that health care costs have skyrocketed. The benevolent *federales* arrived with moneybags in the form of student loans. A *Wall Street Journal* editorial on March 13, 2010 pointed out that the result was a 400 percent increase in the costs of higher education. Why would the colleges and universities want to resist such a cash cow? The only term I can think of to define these irrational infusions of money into specific segments of society is focused inflation.

There are so many areas of American life that have been harmed by ill-considered government policies. These policies exist because elected officials and bureaucrats are sufficiently arrogant to believe they can run society and make it better. This has never happened in the history of the world. All schemes for the amelioration, or even the perfection, of society will necessarily fail. But what is it that makes these schemes ostensibly feasible in the first place? Taxation, of course. Government programs are devised in great part to get officials re-elected. Remember Harry Hopkins, aide to FDR: "Tax and tax, spend and spend, elect and elect." Whether he actually said it is irrelevant.

The purpose of taxation is to enable the government to function. Being a parasitic non-producer, it must rely on revenues from the citizens. Until the passage of the 16th Amendment to the Constitution, this original tax system worked fairly well. Apart from emergencies such as the Civil War, the federal government made do with income collected from land sales, tariffs, excises, and other taxes. With the arrival of the income tax, the system changed dramatically. Taxation became confiscation of funds for whatever purposes politicians could devise, notably redistribution of income from some citizens to other citizens. Apparently the system has by now become such an accepted feature of American life that few consider it obscene to pay as much as 40 percent of one's income to the state. How far we have come from protests against the British Stamp Act of 1765 and the piddling amounts it was designed to raise. But it is the income tax that has allowed the government to expand its activities far beyond its constitutional boundaries. The old Golden Rule joke says that he who has the gold makes the rules. And that is definitely true of our government, which has managed to accumulate the single largest portion of available gold.

In 1895 the United States Supreme Court issued a ruling in the case *Pollock v. Farmers' Loan and Trust Company* (157 U.S. 429) setting aside a proposed federal income tax. Chief Justice Melville W. Fuller made the following remarks in his opinion: "The present assault upon capital is but the beginning. It will be but the first stepping stone to others, larger and more sweeping, till our political contests will become a war of the poor against the rich - a war constantly growing in bitterness. 'If the court sanctions the power of discriminating taxation, and nullifies the uniformity mandate of the constitution," as said by one who has been all his life a student of our institutions, 'it will mark the hour when the sure decadence of our present system will commence.'"

The incremental descent into statism in the United States is the subject of the next few chapters. The coverage is not comprehensive, but anecdotal. I could have started with Andrew Jackson, since he was our first really bad president. The era over which he presided made a fairly decisive break with the past. From Jefferson until the election of 1828 there had basically been one-party rule in the United States, although a few Federalists still held office. The Democratic Republican Party of Jefferson brought Jackson to the presidency, but his terms office were so divisive that the party split into Democrats and Whigs. His party became the Democrats of today, and interestingly enough, the party has not changed all that much. Under the guidance of the president and his close advisor and successor, Martin Van Buren, party loyalty trumped what was good for the country in nearly every case.

During his Jackson's two terms and the four years of Van Buren, the Democrats solidified their position as defenders of slavery at all costs and permitted no dissent on the either in the North or South. I will leave Jackson by quoting a sentence from a remarkably comprehensive survey of the era by Daniel Walker Howe: "Although Andrew Jackson defended his own authority with resolute determination, he did not manifest a general respect for the authority of the law when it got in the way of policies he chose to pursue." (*What Hath God Wrought*, p. 411). Including Van Buren, Jackson was followed in office by a series of one-term presidents until Lincoln. The significant achievement of the post-Jackson period was the war with Mexico, by which the country gained the whole southwest, from Texas to California.

Chapter 10: The Lincoln Legacy

The Civil War is the most written-about event in American history and Lincoln the most written about president. I can bring nothing new or original in discussing it. Coming back to it after many years, a few things are obvious. The event did not occur suddenly. Talk of secession and even of war between the North and South was in the air constantly after the end of the war with Mexico. The South's determination to protect its peculiar institution and expand it became an obsession, a view that most Northerners would not tolerate. The part of the country that had been for decades a section with slavery became an empire for slavery, as Professor James McPherson has so aptly put it in his *The Battle Cry of Freedom.*

There is some historical writing that suggests that the Civil War started over the issue of the tariff and not slavery. It is true that the tariff was a divisive issue between the sections. But that alone, absent slavery, could not have led to the violence of 1861-1865. It is quite true that the South viewed itself as victimized by tariffs so ardently favored by Northern politicians and businessmen. Prior to the Civil War (and for long afterwards) the industrialized North had favored tariffs as a means of protecting businesses and keeping prices high on manufactured products, thus penalizing consumers. The less industrialized South was primarily a supply region. Since this is as good a place to talk about the matter, I'll devote some space to it before getting to the 16th president.

Jane Jacobs devotes a chapter to supply regions in *Cities and The Wealth of Nations*. The chief characteristic of supply regions is that they produce nonmanufactured materials (cotton, tobacco, wheat, meat, minerals, and lumber) for citified industrial regions to turn into final products. Jacobs says that: "The reason such regions are specialized and narrow is that, in the first place, their production for others so overwhelmingly outweighs production for themselves."

Furthermore, their production for others depends on what the others want. Beyond this, manufactured goods cost more than raw materials. The raw materials and labor for any product, from a can of soup to a new automobile, are factored into the costs of production. In short, it is the manufacturers who call the shots on prices of raw materials (granting the usual supply and demand conditions); and when the final products come back into the supply region they cost more than the products the supply region exported. Supply regions are invariably poorer than industrial areas, unless they cooperate to form cartels such as OPEC or are given special status by government, such as are the sugar producers in the United States. Government ownership of resources will, naturally, tend to make the government richer than the populations who produce the resources. This is the situation today in Russia, Cuba, Venezuela, Saudi Arabia, and other nations that maintain industrial monopolies.

From the first years of the American Republic,

northern manufacturers demanded and got tariffs to protect them from foreign competition. Since a tariff is a tax providing revenues for the federal government, the government was happy to comply. But it was not entirely happy. The South, as a supply region, knew that tariffs were economically harmful to it, while they benefited their northern neighbors. Southern opposition to tariffs was fierce, and it came to a head during the tenure of Andrew Jackson in the presidency.

In the 1820s and 1830s the South was in a severe economic depression. Southerners blamed the tariff because it discouraged the importing of foreign goods. This made it difficult for foreign countries to earn money with which to buy cotton. Jackson's first vice-president, John C. Calhoun published (anonymously) a *South Carolina Exposition and Protest*. This document, contrary to his intentions, was partially responsible for the ensuing Nullification Controversy and Calhoun's resignation from office. Nullification was a procedure by which states believed they could overturn a federal law. The whole story is a complex one that took several years to play out. In brief: South Carolina passed an ordinance of nullification in October 1832. Had the other Southern states rallied around, there might have been a chance of success, but they did not. Jackson issued a *Nullification Proclamation,* declaring this states' rights issue absurd. The president was prepared to use military force against South Carolina, but a compromise was reached and tariffs were lowered in early 1833; and the crisis of the Union was postponed. Now, at last, Mr. Lincoln.

It is impossible not to admire Abraham Lincoln, unless one is a hard-core Southerner with resentments about the Civil War. His flaws, if any, were wiped away in one sentence following his assassination: Now he belongs to the ages. One wonders what his reputation would be today, had he lived to carry out his plans for Reconstruction. Would he, instead of Andrew Johnson, have been impeached? It is certainly plausible, since he was as much in opposition to the Radical Republicans as Johnson was. Strangely enough, in the decades after the war, it was generals Grant, Sheridan, and Sherman, not Lincoln, who were proclaimed as heroes for saving the Union. The Lincoln legend is a creation of the 20th century.

But that is getting ahead of the story. Had he never become president, Lincoln would have still been considered one of the best writers in American literature, on a par with Emerson, Thoreau, Whitman, and Twain. Consider the elegance and eloquence of the following paragraphs.

> "This is essentially a People's contest. On the side of the Union, it is a struggle for maintaining in the world, that form and substance of government, whose leading object is, to elevate the condition of men – to lift artificial weights from all shoulders – to clear the paths of laudable pursuit for all – to afford all an unfettered start and a fair chance, in the race of life. Yielding to partial, and temporary departures, from necessity, this is the leading object of the government for whose existence we contend." [Second Message to Congress]

"I am loath to close. We are not enemies, but friends. We must not be enemies. Though passion may have strained, it must not break our bonds of affection. The mystic chords of memory, stretching from every battle-field and patriot grave, to every living heart and hearthstone, all over this broad land, will yet swell the chorus of the Union, when again touched, as surely they will be, by the better angels of our nature." [First Inaugural Address]

"Yet, if God wills that it [the war] continue, until all the wealth piled by the bond-man's two hundred and fifty years of unrequited toil shall be sunk, and until every drop of blood drawn with the lash, shall be paid by another drawn with the sword, as was said three thousand years ago, so still it must be said 'the judgments of the Lord are true and righteous altogether.'" [Second Inaugural]

"With malice toward none; with charity for all; with firmness in the right, as God gives us to see the right, let us strive to finish the work we are in; to bind up the nation's wounds; to care for him who shall have borne the battle, and for his widow, and his orphan – to do all which may achieve and cherish a just and a lasting peace, among ourselves, and with all nations." [Second Inaugural]

Writing doesn't get much better than that. And, of course, there is the Gettysburg Address. How fortunate Lincoln was in not having attended one of our public schools.

The question I wish to deal with is: Was Lincoln wrong in starting the Civil War? Did he, in fact start it by putting Jefferson Davis in an untenable position by sending supplies to Fort Sumter? Furthermore, would slavery have endured long had the Confederacy been left to go its own way? Residents of the South had no doubts on this at all. When the war started in April 1961 the South was fighting to protect slavery and all of its way of life. The North was fighting to preserve the Union. (A small book well worth reading on this subject is James M. McPherson's *What They Fought For 1861-1865*. It was the discovery by Union soldiers that perhaps they were really fighting to free the slaves that led, among other things, to the New York draft riots.)

Yet neither slavery nor the tariff is fundamental here. What matters most is Lincoln's concept of the United States. There is little point is discussing what might have been: Would Lincoln have called out the militia had Fort Sumter not been fired on? It's a fascinating question, but it cannot be answered. Based on his own sentiments, it seems unlikely he would have let the Secession pass without a fight, even if the Fort had been evacuated, as the president's own secretary of state was promising. The Fort was, by the way, a tariff collection site.

The nature of the United States had been a subject of debate for decades. Was it a Union, or was it a federation of independent states cooperating under a compact called the Constitution. Prior to the Civil War, when one used the country's name in a sentence, it often took a plural verb: The United States *are*. Since the Civil War – maybe even since the War of 1812 - the verb has become singular. Looking at the Declaration of Independence, it is curious to find, in the last paragraph, the term "united States of America," in which the first letter of the first word is lower case. Later in the same paragraph appears the phrase "these United Colonies," which "ought to be Free and Independent States." This grammatical sketch is not insignificant. The founding fathers were quite careful with words and were not given to sloppy thinking.

The two views – centralization versus states' rights – became prominent quite early. The nullification doctrine dates back at least to 1798, when James Madison and Thomas Jefferson proposed it. It was even used successfully in a few instances. But as the decades passed, the tendencies toward centralization were pronounced. By the time we get to Lincoln's election to office, the arguments on both sides have been in place for some time. John C. Calhoun's concept of the Union was expressed in his *Exposition and Protest* on the tariff controversy: "The general Government emanated from the people of the several States, forming distinct political communities, and acting in their separate and sovereign capacity, and not from all of the people forming one aggregate political community." Lincoln took a completely opposing view. That he was firmly on the side of centralization will soon appear. He regarded the United States as an indissoluble Union. In doing so, naturally, he was rejecting some of the premises of the Declaration of Independence. In fairness to Lincoln, it is necessary to admit that the constitution of the Confederate States disavowed both nullification and secession.

In his well-known letter to newspaper editor Horace Greeley of August 14, 1862, Lincoln stated his goal quite clearly. "My paramount object in this struggle is to save the Union, and is not either to save or destroy slavery." What, then, was Mr. Lincoln's view of the United States? It is found explicitly stated in his first inaugural address.

> "I hold, that in contemplation of universal law, and of the Constitution, the Union of these States is perpetual. Perpetuity is implied, if not expressed, in the fundamental law of all national governments. It is safe to assert that no government proper, ever had a provision in its organic law for its own termination. Continue to execute all the express provisions of our national Constitution, and the Union will endure forever – it being impossible to destroy it, except by some action not provided for in the instrument itself."

> "Again, if the United States be not a government proper, but an association of States in the nature of contract merely, can it, as a contract, be peaceably unmade, by less than all the parties who made it? One party to a contract may violate it – break it, so to speak; but does it not require all to lawfully rescind it?"

"Descending from these general principles, we find the proposition that, in legal contemplation, the Union is perpetual, confirmed by the history of the Union itself. The Union is much older than the Constitution. It was formed, in fact, by the Articles of Association in 1774. It was matured and continued by the Declaration of Independence in 1776. It was further matured and the faith of all the then thirteen States expressly plighted and engaged that it should be perpetual, by the Articles of Confederation in 1778. And finally, in 1787, one of the declared objects for ordaining and establishing the Constitution was 'to form a more perfect union.'"

"But if the destruction of the Union, by one, or by a part only, of the States, be lawfully possible, the Union is less perfect than before the Constitution, having lost the vital element of perpetuity."

"It follows from these views that no State, upon its own mere motion, can lawfully get out of the Union – that resolves and ordinances to that effect are legally void; and that acts of violence within any state or States, against the authority of the United States, are insurrectionary or revolutionary, according to circumstances."

> "I therefore consider that, in view of the Constitution and the laws, the Union is unbroken; and to the extent of my ability, I shall take care, as the Constitution itself expressly enjoins upon me, that the laws of the Union be faithfully executed in all the States."

A few sentences later he says "in doing this there needs be no bloodshed or violence," but the construction he put on the word Union make his address a fairly clear declaration of war on the states that had already seceded. Southerners, reading his remarks, can hardly have understood them otherwise. Southerners, too, firmly believed they had the Declaration of Independence on their side in deciding to separate and form the Confederacy. Thus, the question becomes: should the North have let the South go? Seeking an answer, however, leads one down the murky road of what might have been. Would slavery have died out on its own? Would the two sections have merged at some future date to reform the Union? Supposing they did not, would the two nations of North America have coexisted peacefully, and what world role would they have played in the 20th century? These provide material for speculation but not much more.

The issue here is simple: was Lincoln right? If one grants his premise, he was; but for my part, I am ambivalent about his conclusions, even if I agree with the outcome. What possible meaning can there be in his term "universal law" as used in the first sentence quoted above? He seems to be constructing some kind of ontological, or is it metaphysical, basis for the Union. The history of the United States is fairly clear. Thirteen states formed a common front against England to gain their independence. During the conflict they agreed to form a loose association based on the Articles of Confederation. After the war this constitution proved unworkable precisely because the states viewed themselves as 13 sovereignties reluctant to grant to a central government any more power than absolutely necessary. The Constitution of 1787 enlarged the powers of the central government, but it also put specific limits on the exercise of federal authority. One of the chief arguments of opponents to the Constitution was the fear that the new government would become quite like the one they had fought England to be rid of. (How right they were to be proved. Their views have been published in *The Antifederalists,* edited by Cecilia M. Kenyon, 1966.)

Hatred of tyranny was a strong motivator in the 1780s. The notion of a consolidated government that left the states almost no wiggle room was abhorrent. For that reason some of our early statesmen could accept the notions of nullification and secession without qualms. Students of American history know that there was more than a little half-hearted attempt at secession by the New England States during the War of 1812. And, later, some Abolitionists advocated secession to rid the North of the South.

> Lincoln's thesis is a prescription for unintended consequences, for a strong central government that tended toward Statism. He would not have seen it that way, but according to some writers he was

> the most dictatorial and unconstitutional president we've had. Charles Adams, in his *For Good and Evil,* assesses Lincoln as follows: "Lincoln was the most powerful president the United States has ever known. He was often brutal. Civilians were tried by military courts so they could be denied a jury trial and other proper judicial procedures. People who disapproved his policies were locked up without a trial." And, as implied in the Greeley letter, there was nothing the president would not do to achieve his goals. When his assassin, John Wilkes Booth, accused Lincoln of tyranny (*Sic semper tryannis*), he was not wide of the mark in his own mind.

Such an assessment of Lincoln is certainly unfair to the man himself. He was not, nor even intended to become, a power-mad tyrant. We cannot now imagine the agonizing struggle within him as he dealt with the mounting death toll of the Civil War, coupled with his anxiety to find generals who could actually win battles. His plainly stated goal was to save the Union, because he did not regard the Constitution as having within it any clause for its dissolution. And we cannot recapture today the vehemence of the Peace Democrats and his other opponents, who worked tirelessly for defeat of the Union forces. (But they seem to be back with a vengeance in the early 21st century.) As the cliché has it: desperate times called for desperate measures.

Lincoln made his own views clear on several

occasions. In a letter to one A. G. Hodges of Frankfort, Kentucky, of April 4, 1864, he stated: "It was in the oath I took that I would, to the best of my ability, preserve, protect, and defend the Constitution of the United States. I could not take the office without taking the oath. Nor was it in my view that I might take an oath to get power, and break the oath in using the power….I have done no official act in mere deference to my abstract judgment and feeling on slavery. I did understand however, that my oath to preserve the constitution to the best of my ability, imposed upon me the duty of preserving, by every indispensable means, the government – that nation – of which the constitution was the organic law….I claim not to have controlled events, but confess plainly that events have controlled me. Now, at the end of three years of struggle the nation's condition is not what either party, or any man devised, or expected."

The war ended a year later. The Union was preserved at horrendous cost in life and property. Few today would argue that the outcome was wrong. Yet the Union was now on a path that the authors of the Constitution would have found repellent. But neither they nor their heirs, for the next several decades, had found any means of resolving the continuing crisis of sectionalism. As James Bryce put it, "The nation asserted itself at last, but not until the resources which the Constitution provided for the attainment of a peaceful solution had irretrievably failed." (*The American Commonwealth,* Chapter 24) And again, "To cling to the letter of the Constitution when the welfare of the country for whose sake the Constitution exists is at stake, would be to seek to preserve life at the cost of all that makes life worth living." (Chapter 33)

Chapter 11 Post-Civil War America

The Civil War left the United States with a very powerful central government. The Republican Party dominated it until the election of Woodrow Wilson in 1912, apart from the nonconsecutive (but virtually Republican) presidencies of Grover Cleveland. At the time, the Republicans were the party of big government, as the Democrats are today. Fortunately for the citizens, there was no income tax at the time. The attention of the public was drawn increasingly toward Washington DC as the source of law and policies. A new mindset took hold of the American people – look to Washington for the solutions to every kind of problem. Washington was quite willing to oblige.

Late in the 19th century new movements arose to press a variety of issues: farm crises, railroad regulation, the monetization of silver, the control of the trusts, woman suffrage, prohibition of alcohol, immigration restriction, conservation of natural resources, and more. Special interests pressed their concerns (and the campaign contributions) on their elected officials and were often rewarded with legislation favorable to their respective causes; the Interstate Commerce Act, the Sherman Silver Purchase Act, the Sherman Antitrust Act, and others, all passed by Republican administrations.

This "Progressive" era wanted to "advocate government intervention in the free market and over personal liberty at every level and in every sphere." (From Jeffrey Rogers Hummel, *Emancipating Slaves, Enslaving Free Men*, p. 357. This is the best book to read for a view of the Civil War contrary to the conventional wisdom.) Hummel believes correctly that the pressure for federal government absolutism started much earlier than 1860. His conclusion on the war is: "In the years ahead, coercive authority would wax and wane with year-to-year circumstances, but the long-term trend would be unmistakable. Henceforth there would be no more major victories of Liberty over Power. In contrast to the whittling away of government that had preceded Fort Sumter, the United States had commenced its halting but inexorable march toward the welfare-warfare State of today."

As political power gravitated toward the federal government, a shrewd observer might have noted that the Ninth and Tenth Amendments to the Constitution were dying a slow death.

> Article IX: The enumeration in the Constitution of certain rights shall not be construed to deny or disparage others retained by the people.
>
> Article X: The powers not delegated to the United States by the Constitution, nor prohibited by it to the States, are reserved to the States respectively, or to the people.

In addition, the courts and legislatures have whittled away the intent of the Bill of Rights. They have denied rights that are explicitly stated, while finding some that are not even mentioned. There is, for example, no right of free expression mentioned or implied in the First Amendment, nor is there a wall of separation between church and state. Modern "liberal" pressures have also severely compromised freedom of speech. The most recent exercise in "campaign finance reform" shows how far Congress is willing to go to destroy free speech, while Congress itself devises new schemes to keep the money coming in.

Since this coverage is anecdotal rather than comprehensive, we now skip a few decades to look at another fascinating individual. The first Roosevelt in the White House established the principles and attitudes that have guided the federal government in both domestic and foreign policy since he left office. His spirit is still with us.

Chapter 12 Theodore Roosevelt's Bully Pulpit.

This is another president that I find it impossible to dislike as a man. He was, in his generation, larger than life: honest, exuberant, robust, energetic, fun loving, incorruptible, thoughtful, intelligent, forceful, and principled. Certainly he compromised on occasion; to get ahead in the utterly corrupt politics of the day, he had to. He was politician, police commissioner, soldier, rancher, governor, explorer, hunter, and a noted author. His whole life is a fascinating story. Even if it were fiction, his life would be a marvelous tale. His autobiography is still worth reading.

First of all, he came from a strong and close family. As an adult, he created a strong and close family of his own and raised children of remarkable qualities. It is hard to understand how his alcoholic brother Elliott, Eleanor Roosevelt's father, could have been so different. TR's first wife, Alice Lee, died in childbirth, leaving a daughter, the remarkable Alice Roosevelt Longworth, grande dame of Washington society until her death at age 96. An excellent biography of her, entitled *Alice,* was published in 2007 and is worth reading just to get the flavor of the politics of her time and the main players in government.

Roosevelt, after a long period of genuine mourning

married a second time, to Edith Kermit Carow. His second family consisted of four sons and one daughter. The sons served with honor in World War I. The youngest, Quentin, died in action in 1918. It was the death of this son of an admittedly war-loving president that certainly hastened his own demise in 1919. (To learn more about this amazing man and his assorted relatives, two books are invaluable. *T.R. The Last Romantic* by H. W. Brands and *The Roosevelts: An American Saga* by Peter Collier and David Horowitz. The latter volume covers the whole clan.)

As is the case with every president, TR's whole background shaped his terms in office. One of the most significant features of his life was this: he was a trust-fund kid. He never had to work for a living, although he was often extravagant and had to turn to writing to earn money. He attended good schools and was able to travel in style with his family. He was also able to spend large amounts to establish a ranch in what was then the Wild West. His notable cousin, Franklin Delano Roosevelt also descended form "old money," and this fact (along with FDR's determination to outdo his cousin) led to parallels in their views of the power of the presidency.

I can understand the condescending attitudes of people who are "old money." They have had time to become aristocrats and assume the right to look down their noses at "new money." But it seems to me that the merit of their status or attitude is hardly deserved. I would think that those who actually worked and earned the original fortune deserve much more praise than those who live off the interest, and sometimes off the capital. If the Roosevelt, Kennedy and Rockefeller families have taught us anything, it is that trust fund kids should be kept as far as possible from government. It is the much derided *nouveaux riches* of every generation who create the wealth and the jobs that make life better for all citizens. Think Steve Jobs, Steve Wozniak, Bill Gates, Paul Allen, Warren Buffett, Mark Zuckerberg, and Jeff Bezos. If their heirs decide not to work, it is better that they become profligate jet-setters, instead of turning into political busybodies.

In Brands' biography of TR there is a short passage describing the relationship between the old-money elites and politicians. "In the age of the spoilsmen, politics was a low profession to those of breeding and inherited money. Occasionally, one encountered the political classes, just as one encountered muddy streets. At such times there was nothing to do but step carefully and try to avoid getting too dirty. Yet one didn't choose to consort with politicians any more than one went strolling through the slop." (p. 77) TR belonged to the upper class, yet he did consort with politicians. They did not drag him down, but was he unable to raise many of them up to his level.

Since having neither old nor new money has ever been one of my problems, these paragraphs may sound tinged with envy. That is not the case. What bothers me about politicians such as TR, FDR, JFK, and others is not their social status but how that status shapes their attitudes toward the populace and toward "public service." Such attitudes also emanate from "intellectuals" and academics. John Maynard Keynes is an obvious and notorious example. There was also the collection of the "best and brightest" that advised Presidents Kennedy and Johnson and gave us Vietnam. By virtue of status owing either to money or schooling, such individuals are quite sure they can manage society for the benefit of all. That this has never happened in the history of the world is not a deterrent. To get a small glimpse of how mentally isolated these people are from the rest of the country, take a look at a small memoir by Louis Auchincloss, *A Voice from Old New York*, published in 2010, the year he died at 93.

To manage anything, even a household, one must have as complete a knowledge of the subject possible; and even households go awry. To manage a whole society, the manager must know everything about it, down to the last detail. This is impossible. Success at the attempt would mean that every policy worked out to everyone's benefit and that everyone was simultaneously satisfied. To manage a whole economy is beyond the ability of anyone, especially anyone associated with government. Not even economists are able to do it. Just looking at the gyrations of the Federal Reserve System since its inauguration is highly instructive. Objections such as these would not have impressed Theodore Roosevelt.

Turning again to Brands' biography, we can place TR in the context of his political time. "The federal government expanded greatly during the Civil War – partly as a result of the insurrectionary emergency and partly as a result of the Republican takeover, which brought to power people convinced of the possibilities of beneficent cooperation between business and government....Theodore Roosevelt was heir to this tradition of big-government Republicanism." [p. 228]

TR was not reticent in expressing his views of the office he held. "I declined to adopt the view that what was imperatively necessary for the nation could not be done by the President unless he could find some specific authorization to do it."

"My belief was that it was not only his right but his duty to do anything that the needs of the nation demanded unless such action was forbidden by the Constitution or by the laws. Under this interpretation of executive power I did and caused to be done many things not previously done by the President and the heads of departments. I did not usurp power, but I did greatly broaden the use of executive power. In other words, I acted for the public welfare, I acted for the common well-being of all our people, whenever and in whatever manner was necessary, unless prevented by direct constitutional or legislative prohibition."

"While I am a Jeffersonian in my genuine faith in democracy and popular government, I am a Hamiltonian in my governmental views, especially with reference to the need of the exercise of broad powers by the National Government."

"The important thing to do is for a President who is willing to accept responsibility to establish precedents which successors may follow even if they are unwilling to take the initiative themselves."

His is an interesting view of the Constitution. When that document was created in 1787, its aim was to impose limits on those who governed, not on the citizens. The Constitution authorized some few and clear powers for the federal government. TR obviously had another opinion: whatever is not specifically forbidden is permitted. At the bottom of that slope is the police state.

TR, who denounced the "malefactors of great wealth," has been called a trust-buster. This is somewhat true, although his successor, William Howard Taft, prosecuted more trust cases. Trusts were a way of organizing companies, essentially corporations or holding companies, some few of which had achieved great economic power in the late 1800s. American Tobacco and Standard Oil come to mind. Dealing with the trusts was in part an economic issue; but mostly, it was and remains a conflict between government and the private sector. Cases were brought under the Sherman Antitrust Act of 1890 and later under the Clayton Act and other legislation.

The aim of antitrust legislation seems to be the preservation of a truly fictional "perfect competition," and to prevent collusion. It has been half-humorously said that if a company is charging high prices, it is engaged in gouging; if it is charging low prices, it is engaged in predatory pricing; and if it charges the same as everyone else, that must mean collusion.

If antitrust prosecutions have ever achieved anything beneficial, I am unaware of it. True, companies have been destroyed or broken up and jobs destroyed. Where is A&P today? But to whose benefit? My research on the subject, while hardly open-minded, has demonstrated to me that the exercise of government power over the economy is far more damaging than anything an economic entity can do by itself. Anyone interested in the subject can read Dominick T. Armentano's *Antitrust: The Case for Repeal*; Robert H. Bork's *The Antitrust Paradox*; and Richard B. McKenzie's *Trust on Trial*. The last-named deals specifically with the Microsoft case of the 1990s, and Armentano's second edition also covers this case. The European Union has, in recent years, been going overboard with antitrust cases. Government greed may be at the bottom of antitrust prosecutions: successful litigation can bring millions of dollars or euros into government coffers.

It was amusing to see AT&T, a government-created monopoly, brought into court by the federal government, which was "shocked" to learn that AT&T was a monopoly. Actually, the federal government should have been a co-defendant. But this is not the place to argue the merits and demerits of antitrust prosecutions. This issue for me is: government taking sides with one segment of society against another. I noted above how the government did this in the matter of race, coming down heavily on the side of whites against blacks; then it reversed itself (allegedly) in the 1960s to come down heavily on the side of blacks against whites (especially white males).

Into the early decades of the 1900s, government sided with business against labor. This is a very old conflict, one that took place in Europe as well as in the United States. The history of the labor movement in this country is filled with instances of violence and massacre, backed by local and federal forces. In the 1930s, with the New Deal, the federal government did a turnaround and came down on the side of labor in the National Labor Relations Act.

But turnabout is fair play. As Professor Nell Irvin Painter has so well documented in her history of the Progressive Era, *Standing at Armageddon,* the lives of workers from the end of the Civil War until the 1930s were miserable; and they had no recourse for relief. The presidency most of the time and the Congress and Supreme Court all the time were bought and paid for by the business interests, who did everything legal or violent to keep workers in their place. Unions, although they existed, were virtually powerless against court rulings and the use of force by state militias and other agencies. That unions now have gone too far in pursuit of their goals is a problem that may lead to their undoing, but their right to become a "countervailing power" against the large corporations was a long time coming. The most dangerous unions today are those of government workers, large and powerful and living off the taxpayers.

The railroads provide another example of the misguided – but well paid for – use of government authority. During the 19th century the federal government granted many railroad builders money, land, and privileges. Then, when these powerful companies took advantage of their federally-granted position, the government got even by passing the Interstate Commerce Act and other regulations. By World War I, the roads were financially strapped and had to be propped up by the government so the weapons and other war matérial could be transported. Passenger service declined to the extent that the federal government had to take it over to keep it alive. Today, the federally supported passenger rail service is in danger of collapsing. It is very difficult to keep a business going, if one cannot cover costs. If you want to travel by rail with great delight, go to Europe.

In relation to Theodore Roosevelt, the point I want to make is his general ignorance on economic matters. He held opinions on the operation of a business that would delight today's even more ignorant Liberals, and his cousin Franklin was utterly ignorant on economics. In a letter to his attorney general, Charles Bonaparte, TR referred to "predatory wealth, of wealth accumulated on a giant scale by iniquity, by wrongdoing in many forms, by plain swindling, by oppressing wageworkers, by manipulating securities, by unfair and wholesome competition, and by stockjobbing..." (And yes, his attorney general was descended from that Bonaparte family.) There can be no denying that such practices existed during the 19th century, especially after the Civil War. But his denunciation cannot honestly be said to encompass all economic activity. FDR's New Deal dealt with these problems in a forceful way, and he was even more forceful in denouncing the business community.

TR never ran a business, apart from his failed ranching experiment. Starting and operating a successful business takes a great deal of imagination and effort: what business are we starting; where will the financing come from; what is the competition; which government regulations must be followed, and other questions. The proper environment for starting and running a business is liberty, not government regulation. When TR says that businesses must be regulated for the public welfare, what can he possibly mean? Economic activity is what people do by necessity; it is the basis for the living of their lives. Are they too incompetent to assess what is in their best interest? Sometimes they are, because businesses fail. But who, in Washington DC has the ability to make a better assessment than the man on the spot? I suspect that what he really meant by public welfare was government welfare. If that is too harsh, perhaps he just wanted to create the playing field for economic activity. He could not appreciate, apparently, that the playing field existed in what Adam Smith called a "system of natural liberty."

All of this talk about economic matters is taking me far afield. TR left office in 1909, succeeded by his hand-picked candidate, William Howard Taft. As is well known, the latter did not live up to the expectations of the former. When Taft ran for a second term in 1912, TR entered into the fray to get the Republican nomination for himself. When he lost it, he started his own Progressive, or Bull Moose, Party. The platform of his party is basically the charter of FDR's New Deal. Taft and TR both lost, giving the White House to Woodrow Wilson.

It is during this era that I, perhaps mistakenly, perceive the two major parties converging. TR's slogan was "new nationalism," while Wilson preached "new freedom." The political differences between the two men were not great, although their personalities differed markedly. By the end of the second decade of the century, the parties were accused of being "gold dust twins," both favoring business over the general welfare.

On the heels of TR's and Taft's failed 1912 campaign, the nation was introduced to the direct election of senators, the income tax, and the Federal Reserve System. The Seventeenth Amendment, providing for the direct election of senators, turned these individuals into national status-seeking figures who could play to a nationwide audience to gain popularity and funds. The Sixteenth Amendment, creating the income tax, was, as we have seen, the primary means by which the federal government has been able to expand its power. The Federal Reserve System gave monetary policy into the hands of appointed officials. This very flawed system is based on the unwarranted assumption that a small group of individuals can manage the workings of the whole economy. Power does corrupt; it does so by creating a very unrealistic estimation of one's own abilities. The money-grubbing type of corruption is much less harmful.

Chapter 13 Mister Wilson's War and After

Thomas Woodrow Wilson, unlike Lincoln and TR, is not an individual I can admire. Had he been satisfied to be a scholar, writer, president of Princeton, and governor of New Jersey, he might have had some small place in American history. There was a lot of talk among the Liberals during the 2000 political campaign suggesting that George W. Bush was not intelligent enough to be president. A random look back at our presidents does not give one a favorable impression of those who were scholars. Even Jefferson, for all his brilliance, was a man of narrow and unbending views and had a difficult presidency, while men of middling academic achievements such as James Monroe fared far better in the office. They probably did not have that overweening pride that seems to infect academia. Coolidge and Truman come to mind as examples of men who made no scholarly claims, although they were very bright. Ronald Reagan is another president often derided for his lack of brilliance. This nonsense comes from partisans who have never read the man's own writings – and they were his own.

I have no intention of recapitulating the two terms of Woodrow Wilson. What is of significance here is the domestic economy during World War I. Socially and politically the nation came as close to being a police state as it had ever done even under Lincoln. Everyone who has studied the period knows of the fierce anti-German sentiments that pervaded the United States. Dissent from war aims was not allowed; in that matter freedom of speech was abolished, and individuals were imprisoned for stating their views. Socialist candidate Eugene Debs is perhaps the best known of those who were tried and convicted. He received a ten-year sentence. Union official William D. Haywood got twenty years. The whole apparatus of the federal government, including the post office, was ranged against dissent in speech or writing. (The best book I've see on this subject in Ronald Schaffer's *America in the Great War.* A more recent work, Ann Hagedorn's *Savage Peace: Hope and Fear in America 1919,* presents a far more startling picture of how close his country came to being a Hitlerite state – although Germany's beloved chancellor was not yet on the international scene.)

With war mobilization, the United States was introduced to the managed economy. Business-government cooperation became essential, in part, because industry was quite unprepared to manufacture the vehicles and weapons war at the start. Mobilization became an all-out concerted effort, much of which was run from Washington. Schaffer makes the following point:

> "While large profits induced American businessmen to support the war, some of their leaders saw in the wartime-managed economy a way toward a kind of gain

> that would continue long after the guns stopped firing. To these men, advocates of what might be called a New Capitalism, participation in the war effort provided the chance to create a better form of business enterprise." (p. 57).

This can be called fascism or National Socialism from below, but it agrees pretty well with the assessment made by William McNeill in his *The Pursuit of Power.* That businessmen thought they could throw themselves into the arms of the federal government without getting a breath-constricting bear hug is rather amusing. When fascism arrived full-blown in Italy three years after the Treaty of Versailles, businesses were very willing to participate in the Corporate State. In Germany, after 1933, they were given little choice. When Herbert Hoover was trying to deal with failing businesses and rising unemployment in the Depression, he was offered a plan much like that of the New Capitalists and not unlike Mussolini's solution; but he rejected it. His successor did not.

Chapter 14 President for Life

About Franklin Delano Roosevelt I am still ambivalent, because he was so imposing a figure during my childhood, and I admit to being devastated when he died. The appalling results of his administrations are still with us in the warfare-welfare state and the greatly expanded federal government. His terms in office, albeit building on the work of Lincoln, TR, and Wilson, changed the playing field of American political life probably permanently. But no one who was there will ever forget the beaming smile, the panache, the flair, and the best speaking voice a president ever had. His hold on the affections of the American people was incredible. In many ways, he was a genuinely good man; but he was a good man who wanted very much to occupy the presidency and thought he did it better than anyone else.

He came into office on March 4, 1933, promising a "new deal" for the American people. His first inaugural address was inspirational, although I didn't hear it – being only two at the time. The problem he faced was the Great Depression that Hoover had been unable to cope with. FDR came to the presidency almost wholly ignorant of economics. He was, said John T. Flynn, "a man literally without any fundamental philosophy." (In *The*

Roosevelt Myth, p. 71) But, having promised a New Deal, his administration had to do something about economic conditions – banks failing, prices and wages falling, businesses collapsing, and unemployment rising to about 25 percent. Facing such a national disaster – and it was the worst peacetime disaster in American history – it seemed obvious that the only way to approach the problem was through a concerted governmental effort, such as the one that had worked so well during World War I.

Let us now pause to consider economic hard times, whether depression or recession. The causes for a general economic downturn, such as the Great Depression was, cannot be located within the economy itself. (For a full explanation get Murray Rothbard's *America's Great Depression*.) Individual businesses may fail for a variety of reasons; it happens all the time. Whole industries can be displaced by the march of technology; this is what happened to the horse and buggy trade around 1900, to the typewriter makers with the advent of the personal computer, and to many small farms with the growth of agribusiness. Accepting for a moment the notion of a national economy, it has so much diversity in it that it would be impossible for the whole thing to unravel of its own accord. Businessmen do not set out to fail. What are the forces external to the economy itself that can trigger a wholesale collapse?

Focus for a bit on the problem of inflation, something the 20th century saw a lot of. The economic texts I am familiar with define it as a general rise in all prices. It is true that all prices will increase during inflation, but inflation is something else. To settle on price increases is like defining measles as red spots. The reason the economists define inflation as price increases is easy to understand. If they pointed to the real problem, their fond embrace of government solutions would seem ludicrous.

Inflation, as Milton Friedman has defined it, is always and only an overall increase in the money supply. Inflation decreases the value of money in relation to the goods people buy. (The hyperinflation of Germany in 1923 is the most notorious example but hardly the only one. The one in Zimbabwe early in the 21st century was worse.) It is nonsense to think that all businesses will arbitrarily raise their prices at the same time without a very good reason. Competition alone would prevent them.

And speaking of inflation and prices, it is fascinating to listen to the "financial experts" on television business reports speaking of a "rise in oil prices" as inflationary. Prices can rise for a variety of reasons, the most common being the old "supply and demand" situation. A severe frost in the orange groves of Florida or California can send the price of oranges higher. Why is the price of Van Gogh's "Sunflowers" so high? There is only one such painting; if there were thousands, the price would fall precipitously. Nor does an increase in wages portend inflation (the so-called wage-push inflation), although if there is genuine inflation wages will go up. The experts rarely point to the Fed as the author of inflation, especially since that agency is so bold in announcing its war against that very enemy.

Only the federal government can increase the money supply, since only the government controls it. The increase need not be general to have a deleterious effect. I've already noted what has happened to the costs of medical care and higher education, when the government steps in to "help." One means that the Federal Reserve System has of increasing the money supply is through easing bank credit, making it easier for businesses to borrow. Now it gets tricky. Businesses borrow from banks, because that's where the savings are. People have a time preference: either spend and consume now, or save for future consumption. Supposedly it is the stock of savings that is made available for borrowing. The savings that end up as investment by businesses are pointed toward future consumption.

But what if the Fed eases bank credit? Businesses find it easier to borrow, but they have no way of knowing if their funds are coming from people's savings or from an increase in the money supply made available by the government. If businesses expand based on easy credit, they will very likely find themselves holding the bag with overbuilt factories and shops and unsold merchandise. This, as Ludwig von Mises has explained it, is malinvestment. It was he who clarified the nature of the business cycle as far back as 1912 in his *The Theory of Money and Credit*. Anyone can make a bad investment, but the idea that all businessmen in a large nation will do so at once is absurd.

In the late 1990s there was a great deal of malinvestment in so-called Dot-com enterprises, and many of them have since failed or consolidated after the high-tech bubble burst in 2000. The ordinary easing of bank credit did not cause this; the financing came mostly from venture capitalists. Financial adviser James Grant explains: "Prosperity financed with speculative capital must sooner or later hit the wall of arithmetic. Presented with ultracheap funds, entrepreneurs build and then overbuild. Before very long there is a surplus of fixed investment." The business cycle has not been eliminated. Malinvestment will continue so long as there is easy money available, tempting entrepreneurs to keep up the capital investments.

Professor Rothbard put the matter this way: "Ironically, despite the gyrations and interventions of the Fed and other government authorities, recession is inevitable once an inflationary boom has been set into motion, and will occur after the inflationary boom stops or slows down." This is precisely what happened in the 1990s. Credit was eased, then it was tightened. Recession loomed at the beginning of 2000. The same thing happened with the crash of 2007-8, when the housing boom collapsed into the Great Recession. Fine-tuning the economy by the Fed is a joke, but it will never willingly give up its role. Power is meant to be exercised. (Professor Rothbard wrote an excellent small booklet called *What Has Government Done to Our Money?)*

A recession may be defined as an inventory liquidation process: sell off the goods cheap and start again, if possible. For a recession to occur, forces outside the economy must come into play: an increased money supply, a tight money policy, a restrictive fiscal policy (too high taxes), and wrongheaded regulation. The decade of the 1920s witnessed most of these, although there were significant tax cuts. There was an easy money policy by the Fed for most of the 1920s, but in August 1929 there was a severe monetary contraction. This was followed by the stock market crash two months later. Then the Hoover administration went into action.

The most wrongheaded piece of legislation was the Smoot-Hawley Tariff of 1930, which essentially ended foreign trade, and which President Hoover was happy to sign. Desperate times call for desperate measures, and this foolhardy law did great damage and no good. Once the relatively mild recession of 1929 started rolling, it gathered speed with the government's help and became an economic catastrophe. It is ironic to compare the actions of government in 1930 and after with the nearly complete lack of action in the more severe recession of 1920-21. In the latter case, the economy sorted itself out. James Grant has done an excellent analysis of the recession of 1920-21 in *The Forgotten Depression: 1921, The Crash that Cured Itself. (2014)*

Roosevelt and his advisers came into office raging against the capitalists and the financiers who, in their rhetoric, had brought so much misery to the American people. It was, they insisted, these financiers and others who had sinned. But, as Flynn noted, "it is perfectly obvious that he [FDR] did not know what the sins were which had done the damage....There is no evidence that Roosevelt ever put his finger on the real causes that make the free enterprise system fail to work." Or to make it work in the first place.

One of the best works on the Depression that I have read is Jim Powell's *FDR's Folly* (2003). It is very clear on the causes of the economic debacle and the policies that failed to bring recovery. His first chapter contains short biographical sketches of the major players in the New Deal. Two themes run throughout: hostility toward the business sector and a passion for reform. It's easy to look back from the 21st century and say how wrong they were. But for their time, they were not wrong in the minds of large segments of the population. Hostility toward businesses, especially big business, had been building for decades. The huge income gap between the rich and poor had been written and talked about since at least Henry George's *Progress and Poverty* of 1879. The Populist movement of the 1890s was a threat to both Democrats and Republicans, because both parties were regarded as defenders of business and against working people.

The hostility was coupled with demands for reform. The Progressive movement was at the forefront. But there was also a growing attachment to Marxism, notably after the Bolshevik takeover of Russia in 1917. There was as well a movement for incremental socialism that emerged in England late in the 19th century, a movement led by the Fabian Socialists, founded by Sidney and Beatrice Webb. This incremental socialism eventually succeeded in the 1940s, and it came close to destroying Britain's economy. So the impetus for reform of what was seen as a very unfair economic system was many-sided. As Powell makes clear, what the New Dealers intended was not economic recovery, but total reform. If anything good emerged from the New Deal, it was making big business responsive to the public, not only responsive to its own goals.

Speculating on what might have been is not a very useful undertaking – had there been no Civil War, no World Wars, no Great Depression, what would our country be like today? So I wonder, if after World War II a genuine free-market economy had been allowed to flourish with minimal but necessary regulation, might there have been a repeat of the late 19th century dynamism. It's nice to dream.

The New Deal responded with an eclectic barrage of policies, the origin of the famous 100 Days. One must remember that the president's advisers were all big-government enthusiasts who were sure that one remedy or another, or some combination, would bring relief. Many of them were socialists, some were Communists who were sure they were witnessing the final collapse of capitalism and worked toward that goal. Others were gung-ho try-anything types. A blizzard of agencies was created, taxes were raised (precisely the wrong move), public works projects paid for by taxpayers, were instituted, and micro management of the economy became the order of the day. Keep wages and prices high – a recipe for disaster.

The major attempt to create a Mussolini-type corporate state failed (and it was really inspired by Mussolini). This was the much-touted National Recovery Administration, The legislation was struck down by the Supreme Court in the famous Schechter Poultry case of 1935. Had it gone into effect it would have cartelized all American industries, bringing them under government oversight, Under its authority the federal government would have regulated production, including quality and quantity; prices; distribution; every aspect of business. To achieve these goals the antitrust laws were set aside. The Court's ruling enraged Roosevelt and the other New Dealers; it was this case that impelled FDR to try to pack the Court after the 1936 election. Congress rejected this scheme. And FDR was unable to get any significant domestic legislation passed again.

FDR won re-election in 1936. What had essentially been a war against business had failed completely. By 1938 the Depression was back. Throwing money at the problem, pump priming as it was called, had not worked. The president himself realized the whole enterprise of the

New Deal was a failure, and he had no idea what to do about the high unemployment and the huge (for that time) federal debt. Moreover, there were storm clouds gathering over Europe. It was these very clouds that would provide the refreshing spring rains for the American economy, as FDR became increasingly caught up in foreign policy problems.

To shorten this tale, let me just say that it was World War II that saved FDR's skin and allowed him to gain unprecedented third and fourth terms. He suddenly found that he needed the business community if the nation was to prepare for war. Most of the government meddling had failed, although in some places it did some genuine good, as Robert A. Caro has shown in the first volume of his biography of Lyndon B. Johnson, *The Path to Power* (1982). But the myth of the New Deal survived and would haunt electoral politics far into the future. Government now would never stop meddling, and its powers became unlimited by any Constitution. The workability of policies did not become an issue; even long-term failures such as the War on Poverty, public education, and urban renewal had their defenders long after the policies themselves had done their damage. With the public always shrieking, "Do something," the feds were never reluctant to respond. (John T. Flynn's book on Roosevelt was published in 1948. A much more recent volume on the New Deal is Jim Powell's *FDR's Folly: How Roosevelt and His New Deal Prolonged the Great Depression,* published in 2003. An almost novel-like retelling of the Depression, *The Forgotten Man,* was published by Amity Shlaes in 2007.)

A piece of information showed up recently that I was

not aware of. It was Governor Al Smith of New York, in his losing presidential campaign of 1928, who actually put together what came to be called the New Deal coalition: the ethnic groups, including blacks and Jews, the unions, the urban working class. It's in Michael A. Lerner's *Dry Manhattan*, a history of Prohibition, with the focus on New York City. He states: "Smith broadened the Democratic Party and remade the party around a coalition of voters that would endure for the remainder of the twentieth century." (p. 244) The first break in that coalition came with the first campaign of Ronald Reagan in 1980. Today, the Democratic Party is entirely a party of narrow special interests, with perhaps enough voting power to take over the government and remake the nation according to its bizarre agenda. That, at least, was Barack Obama's promise in the 2008 campaign, the total transformation of American society. And in the campaign for the presidency in 2016, it was an alarming sign that Bernie Sanders could win a large number of voters with his openly socialist agenda. The love of failure never recedes.

Now for a shift of focus. I've dealt with FDR only in relation to the Great Depression and his administration's failed attempts to end it. There were, however, other things going on in the world at the time that forced his attention to foreign policy. The main one was Hitler's becoming chancellor of Germany in January 1933. In England, Churchill recognized the danger early; but he was out of office and consistently rebuffed for his warnings. FDR also recognized the dangers of Germany's rearmament, but he was well aware that neither Congress nor the American people wanted anything to do with Europe's problems so soon after World War I. After Great Britain's entry into the war in September 1939 and Germany's astounding victories all across Europe, the antiwar sentiment in the United States only increased – aided by a great deal of German and Soviet propaganda. (Germany and the USSR were on the same side at the time, thanks to the Ribbentrop-Molotov Pact of August 1939.) Great Britain's apparent weakness only served to harden the attitudes of the American people.

In England, a vast network of secret service organizations was set up to monitor everything the Nazis were doing up to and during the Second World War and before America's entry after Pearl Harbor. Because of the powerful antiwar and anti-Europe sentiment prevailing in the United States – led by Congress and the America First organization – it really was necessary that FDR be elected to a third term. This whole story was finally revealed decades after the war in an amazing and incredibly informative book, *A Man Called Intrepid* by William Stevenson (1976). In retrospect, it seems natural that the United States and its Allies would win World War II. How close a call it really was will surprise anyone who reads this work.

Part 4 Miscellaneous Observations on Aspects of Human Nature

Thus far and no further with the discussion of constitutional decline and the degradation of liberty and the exaltation of big government. It is time to take up a few other topics of interest to me. You will notice that I have avoided discussing the financial crisis that started in 2008 and persisted for eight years, in spite of the wonderful stimulus programs passed by the all-wise Congress in 2009 and the "quantitative easing" by the Federal Reserve. That crisis was created by the Executive and Congressional branches. Thus, how preposterous it is that these two members of Congress take it upon themselves to solve the problem with ghastly pieces of legislation such as the Dodd-Frank bill – aptly named for two men who had more to do with creating the mess in the first place than any other members of Congress. Several fine books have been written on the subject, plus a few worthless ones that blame it all on the greed of Wall Street. I recommend John B. Taylor's *Getting Off Track: How Government Actions and Interventions Caused, Prolonged, and Worsened the Financial Crisis*, and Charles

Gasparino's *The Sellout: How Three Decades of Wall Street Greed and Government Mismanagement Destroyed the Global Financial System.*

Chapter 15 Lapdogs of the Rich and Powerful

> "She hasn't' any intellect to speak of, but you don't need any intellect to be an intellectual." (from *The Scandal of Father Brown,* by G. K. Chesterton)

> "The direct, conscious attack on intellectual decency comes from the intellectuals themselves." (George Orwell, "The Prevention of Literature," March 1947)

> "The more we think we are sophisticated sometimes the sillier we get – and certainly the more idle people there are with nothing to fill their minds except making moral rules for everyone else, the more hypocrisy there is as to who keeps them and who doesn't." (Anne Perry in *Highgate Rise,* p. 80)

Again, from George Orwell, in "The Prevention of Literature" (1946): "[The] conscious enemies of liberty are those to whom liberty ought to mean most. The big public do not care about the matter one way or another. They are not in favor of persecuting the heretic, and they will not exert themselves to defend him. They are at once too sane and too stupid to acquire the totalitarian outlook. The direct, conscious attack on intellectual decency comes from the intellectuals themselves."

Which shall it be: the masses with their pop culture, their overall ignorance of the great issues of the day, and their presumption that they are as good as "those of us" who know better; or the "wretched of the earth," who deserve to be lifted up and made whole? In a way, the question makes no sense. In the 21st century it certainly doesn't. The wretched of the earth, of whom Frantz Fanon, wrote live in Africa, Central Asia, Latin America, and large parts of East Asia. The masses are the middle and lower classes of Europe, North America, Australia, and New Zealand, along with some fringe areas of East Asia. These masses have a better standard of living than any earlier generation, going as far back as our cave-dwelling ancestors. Can we possibly blame this on a free-market economy?

Until the 19th century, however, the two groups were much the same the world over. I have earlier pointed out that for most of human history the greater part of a population worked to support the few at the top of society. This mass of humanity had no significant rights vis a vis the state, although it sometimes had some rights in law. This mass was simply there to provide the ruling classes with the necessities and luxuries of life and men for armies. I am well aware that there were some exceptions to this general picture; there were rich farmers, merchants, and traders in ancient civilizations and in the Middle Ages.

By and large, though, the picture is accurate. Ordinary men and women were born into the rut in which they remained all their lives. Law and custom, as in the case of medieval feudalism, often enforced this status. In Latin America it frequently still does.

But there was another group of individuals in every society that was wedged between the rulers and the masses: the painters, sculptors, writers, philosophers, musicians, architects, and others who could contribute their talents to the well being of the ruler and his state. Today we would describe them as academics, intellectuals, artistes, lawyers, clergy, and, sometimes, scientists. They received no direct support from the masses, unlike our celebrities today. The sculptors, painters, architects, and poets of ancient Greece and Rome were well known until the Middle Ages. Their names faded until the Renaissance when ancient Greek and Latin documents made their way into Italy. When we get to the Renaissance the names of great talents become known, although probably not to the general public. Had there been mass communication, Michelangelo, Raphael, Titian, and Leonardo, and others would have become celebrities.

By the Renaissance these talented individuals were not working just for the state; they were working for popes and rich merchants and bankers. The Medici family comes to mind, and it is one of many such families in Italian city-states who hired the best talent around to create art and to write or teach. It was a pope who hired Michelangelo to paint the Sistine Chapel and to design St. Peter's Basilica. It was Francis I of France who lured Leonardo away from Italy, and it was Holbein who painted the best known portrait of Henry VIII. Much as the general public may have appreciated what they were allowed to see of the works by these individuals – it would be hard to miss a cathedral – yet the work done by these often-ingenious men was none of the public's business. The rich and powerful did the hiring and paid the bills (often grudgingly).

The social, political, and economic status of such talented individuals has changed drastically over the centuries. The primary cause of this change was the development, beginning in the 18th century, of a new kind of economy, an economy that gradually put more money into the hands of the masses of humanity in the West. Added to the economic alterations was the reappearance of democracy in North America and eventually in Europe, but especially liberty in the United States. The writers, painters, sculptors, philosophers, musicians, architects, and others were mostly thrown upon their own resources to make a living, although patronage has not disappeared completely. No longer was being an artist or intellectual a sinecure. Suddenly; they found themselves with a literate population beneath them as well as above them.

Several factors contributed to the freeing of the masses from age-old degradation and oppression. The first, obviously, was the somewhat better conditions they lived under during the Industrial Revolution. We are well aware, from Marx and Engels, of the wretchedness of the working classes. Engels devoted a whole book to the subject, as did Charles Dickens. Nevertheless, for the first time in history a huge segment of a population was able to work for wages and gradually improve its condition. By the end of the 19th century a real middle class was present in England and North America, and it was emerging on the Continent as well. It's too bad that Marx and Dickens saw only their NOW and had no premonitions about the directions the new economy was taking.

Secondly, education was for the first time made available to the public at large. The United States was first in the field, led by the public school initiatives of Horace Mann. England followed with the National Education Act of 1871. A variety of forums were available for the workingmen to gain some schooling. Schooling for the masses meant literacy for the masses. Where there is a literate audience there is a market, and newspapers and book publishers were more than willing to oblige by catering to it. A popular press emerged that appealed to the newly literate but not highly schooled masses. As the decades rolled on, the general population found satisfaction in movies, radio, vaudeville, the music hall, and, eventually, television. Last, and perhaps most pervasive, was the Internet. A fascinating and instructive book on this subject is *The Intellectual Life of the British Working Classes* by Jonathan Rose, published in 2001. Similar material can be found in the previously mentioned *How the Scots Invented the Modern World.*

The intellectuals, whose wares had always been designed for the upper class and the governing class, had a problem. For most of them the security blanket was gone. If there were any starving artists during the Renaissance, I am not aware of it, but there were plenty of them during the 19th and 20th centuries. Artists, writers, musicians, and others had to produce for a thin veneer of elites or hope to win popular approval. Those who had entrusted their lives and fortunes to the great among us found themselves cut loose. They did not take it kindly.

The masses had always been despised, but at least they knew their place. The intellectuals (my term for the unusually talented and those who make a pretence at it) had always held them in contempt, but they had never merited any attention before; they were just there, like the dirt under one's feet. Now here they were, demanding all kinds of privileges, like voting and reading and peering at the arts. That they still did the world's work mattered not a whit.

To say that the intellectuals were enraged would be too mild. They decided that art and literature should be made incomprehensible to the masses. (They certainly succeeded.) They spoke out against public education. They also theorized that some means should be found to rid themselves of this plague of humanity. The masses must be dehumanized, reduced to the level of vermin and eliminated. One answer was the eugenics crusade that was so popular in the late 19th and early 20th century. Genocide, a natural outcome of eugenics, was also suggested. All of this is well-documented history, not a figment of my overworked imagination. Two of the best books on the subject are John Carey's *The Intellectuals and the Masses*; and Heather Mac Donald's *The Burden of Bad Ideas: How Intellectuals Misshape Our Society.* One may also want to read the 1930 classic, *The Revolt of the Masses* by José Ortega y Gasset.

The point of all this rambling is the perpetual and ongoing allegiance of the intellectuals to the rich and powerful. They regard themselves as a cut above, by virtue of their learning and talent. They are not ordinary mortals like the rest of us. They create their own moral universe. In the past century the intellectuals have almost uniformly allied themselves with the assorted demonic Statisms that so plagued humanity - Nazism, fascism, and Communism. It was the latter to which most of them pledged their allegiance and which still attracts their admiration. "I have seen the future, and it works," the famous comment by Lincoln Steffens about Stalin's Soviet Union, could have served as the motto for a great number of American Liberals and academics. The hatred of the masses persists, but it is often disguised as altruism and "progressivism". The intellectuals, including members of the media, still view themselves as belonging to the ruling elite. They do so, on the basis of a highly inflated view of their own abilities.

Of these Leftist intellectuals historian Robert Conquest has remarked: "On the intellectual level it is revealing to see some of the most respected minds in philosophy, literary criticism, the sciences, falling into the fundamentally simplistic political scholasticism, and in too many cases into the mental idiocy of pure Sovietophilia. This alone is enough to discredit any idea that the notions harbored at any given time by a section of the intelligentsia are to be taken seriously, except as symptoms requiring treatment." (*Reflections on a Ravaged Century*)

The intellectuals would vehemently disagree. They hold their political views as a religious faith, and any disagreement is regarded as heresy to be stamped out – or at least forced to shut up. They, within their narrow specialties consider themselves wise, certainly much wiser than the man in the street. They are indeed more knowledgeable than the average individual, but they do not have the wherewithal to presume to set the rules by which everyone else lives. Recent autobiographies by

David Horowitz and Norman Podhoretz delineate quite forcefully the ideological passions of the intellectual classes. Horowitz himself was once an ardent adherent of the radical Left, so he knows of what he speaks. One such very bright man who is not of the Left has pondered their strange allegiance. Tom Wolfe, the journalist and novelist who died in 2018, was amused at "the propensity of artists and intellectuals and their hangers-on to embrace the left and all its causes without knowing anything about them." (*American Spectator,* February 2001) Intellectual rigor and genuine knowledge are obviously not needed. Passion will suffice. Hence we get the party liner and the ideologue.

Perhaps intellectuals are utopians; perhaps they just seek to regain their position in the halls of power and luxury. Since most of them already live very well, it is more likely just a desire for power, even shared power. Envy certainly enters in. Why should someone who has studied for years to earn advanced degrees not be rewarded as well as some college dropout who only started a company that made many people rich, enriched the lives of the general public, and became a billionaire in the process? It is not uncommon for those who live from inherited wealth to look down on the efforts it took to create that wealth in the first place. The social attitudes of the indolent rich are quite amazing, and really quite repulsive to behold.

Since the 1960s, the intellectuals have in great part become one of the most anti-American groups in society. What the country really is and can be, with all its flaws, they hate. What they would like to make of it, a Stalinist prison house of economic servitude, they adore. They live like rich, country club conservatives; and they think like a Leninist sycophants. Their presence in institutions of higher learning is most distressing, since what they offer instead of schooling is propaganda for a squalid and unfree way of life, propaganda shrouded in the most heartwarming slogans and clichés. Good intentions are always at the forefront, and we know where that highway leads. These are the descendants of the Jacobins of the French Revolution.

Is it not strange that intellectuals – Robespierre, Mirabeau, Marat, Marx, Engels, Lenin, Mussolini, Mao, and Castro – are always in the "vanguard" of revolutions? Those for whose supposed benefit the revolution is launched are never consulted. And if the masses could see what is in store for them down the road, the intellectuals would quickly be packed off to an asylum. What the masses really desire is to be left alone to pursue their individual lives in peace and harmony, without being put upon or ripped off by their "betters." That will not happen soon. The best source of what the elites have had, and still have, in store for the rest of us is Thomas Sowell's excellent *The Vision of the Anointed: Self-Congratulation as the Basis for Social Policy.* He followed up a few years later with *The Quest for Cosmic Justice.* A book by John Leo examines what is commonly described as the cultural divide in the United States. Its title is *Incorrect Thoughts: Notes on Our Wayward Culture.*

What, then, is the relationship between the masses and the elites today? First of all I must assert that there are no masses. Historically there have always been the Others – the bulk of the population – above whom "We who are the excellent and deserving minority" stood.

The modern economy and the emergence of democracy have changed all that. There are now just people, lots of them to be sure, but just people in all their diversity, their wealth and poverty, their ignorance and brilliance, the myriad wants and needs, their seeking and finding or not finding, sometimes confused and at other times clear-headed, sometimes failing sometimes succeeding, sometimes working and at other times just lying about waiting for something to happen, sometimes honest other times criminal, sometimes responsible sometimes irresponsible, sometimes pleasant sometimes irritable, sometimes money-grubbing sometimes generous. All, elites and non-elite, have one thing in common: they all have at most partial knowledge; and none has the Truth of anything. (Try telling that to anyone on the Left.) Most people find satisfaction in just being able to arrange their own lives with some modicum of decency and order, without taking on the burden of trying to arrange everybody else's. The human brain is really a very fragile organ.

Now, as to the relationship between the few self-anointed (or elected) and the many, there are different but not mutually exclusive views. The old adage has it that a fish rots from the head down. When the government of a nation is corrupt, perverse, lawless, and degenerate, there is certainly a trickle down to the population. This scenario was played out in grand fashion in Hitler's Germany: a whole population can be whipped up into a frenzy of irrationality that can endure for years. How quickly the American population was turned into a ruthless mob during World War I. I asked a very reliable friend recently if it is possible for a whole nation, or at least a majority of it, to go nuts. He said yes.

The fraying of moral codes is ever close at hand among human beings, because there is a natural propensity to evil among those who cannot discern the truly good. The current moral decline probably started in the 1960s – a period that gets blamed for so much, deservedly. Disillusionment with the presidency set in during the Johnson and Nixon eras. But the presidency during the 1990s shredded whatever morality the weak among us still clung to. If the highest elected official in the nation can be flagrantly immoral in a self-justifying manner, why not the rest of us? His term of office may be over, but the stench lingers on. Patterns of behavior that were adopted, especially by the unwitting young, will not easily be changed; and they may in time make their lives miserable. There are other wages of sin than death.

When politicians break the law with impunity, why should anyone else hesitate to lie and cheat? When politicians openly take bribes (pardon me, I meant campaign contributions), what is wrong with trying to get as much for myself as easily as I can? What is most puzzling to a rational individual is the public attitude to all this. The people look on with amazement and disgust as elected officials get caught red-handed and go to jail, or even as in the case of the president commit crimes, but few seem to want to do anything about it. We keep electing the same old same old time and again. (In Cook County, Illinois, this is certainly true.) Such behavior in the private sector is treated harshly. As pointed out above, Jane Jacobs noted that a population will feel a solidarity with and pride in its governing officials, while it harbors only envy for those who by their own efforts have succeeded financially and socially. It is easy to understand why the managers of Enron, WorldCom, and other corporations were so roundly denounced and investigated as criminals, while a government that engages in worse practices is allowed to get away with it. (Read Fannie Mae, Freddie Mac, the United Nations.) Thus it has ever been.

Let us turn away from the political realm to society itself. Do moral attitudes and social values filter downward from the top of society to the bottom, or do they percolate upwards from the bottom? Some years ago a book by Myron Magnet took the former position in his *The Dream and the Nightmare: The Sixties's Legacy to the Underclass*. He made a very persuasive argument: the freewheeling and often immoral behavior of the elites were perceived by the underclass and avidly embraced. This, the author insists, was more than the underclass could cope with. (For those of you who have never investigated it, the upper classes, in government especially, have always been more than morally loose, as we puritanical members of the middle class define morals. The behavior of the lowest class has often not been much better, but they had less wealth to facilitate their revelries. Consider Falstaff in his relations with Price Hal.)

There is no doubt that, as relationships between the classes became more intimate during the 19th century, the lower and middle classes sought to ape the behavior, manners, and achievements of those at the top. When I say "intimate," I do not imply that the classes actually mingled socially, although this did occur. They desired to imitate the best as well as the worst; they wanted to adopt the manners, wear similar clothing, and get decent schooling. The lower and middle classes got their information from the newspapers, their version of our supermarket tabloids. Gossip circulated. The Prince of Wales, son of Queen Victoria and the future Edward VII, was notorious among the English public for his adulterous antics. How easy was it for those not so royal citizens to feel that he had put a seal of approval on such behavior? If a president commits adultery, how wrong can it be for the rest of us – although the rest of us rarely need much encouragement? All of this is in line with Daniel Patrick Moynihan's phrase, "defining deviancy down."

I have no doubt that Magnet is right. But his is not the only viewpoint. Do loose behavior patterns and values percolate upward to the higher reaches? Charles Murray insists that they do. (He is the author of *Losing Ground: American Social policy 1950-1980,* an examination of the failure of government welfare programs.) On February 6, 2001, he published an article entitled "Prole Models" in the *Wall Street Journal.* Murray implies that it is also possible to "define deviancy upwards," although he does not use the term. His subject is "the proletarianization of the dominant minority." The dominant minority is, of course, the collection of wealthy and cultured elites and their allies in government.

(At this point I must redefine elites, so as not to create a false impression, because the word elite suggests that they were elected to something. There are a lot of hard-working men and women who attained great wealth. They are the "movers and shakers" of society, those who keep the engines of prosperity humming. I have met a few of them, and they are fine citizens. The elites I speak of are academics, artistes, those who live on inherited wealth, or who have attained the heights of wealth in show business or professional sports – and not even all of these have fallen in with the Left.)

Murray bases his argument on a chapter from Arnold Toynbee's multi-volume *Study of History*. "The growth phase of a civilization is led by a creative minority with a strong, self-confident sense of style, virtue and purpose…. In a disintegrating civilization, the creative minority has degenerated into elites that are no longer confident, no longer setting the example." He goes on to say that a rejection of the responsibilities of citizenship and vulgarizations of manners, the arts, and language "are apt to appear first in the ranks of the proletariat and to spread from there to the ranks of the dominant minority, which usually succumbs to the sickness of proletariatization." (Some of these quotations are from Toynbee.)

I believe that Magnet and Murray are both correct in their analyses. I believe so because in our very open society, where everyone seems to know about everything and everybody else, there is a reciprocal movement of values and attitudes. It is really difficult to discern causes and effects. What is a cause; what is a consequence? It's easy to confuse the two. We are all familiar with the Tonight Show. Steve Allen was the first host, but I rarely saw it then, because I didn't have television in those years. My recollections go back to the Jack Paar years. The guests were always well dressed. On today's late evening shows and other talk shows, anything goes, from blue jeans and sweatshirts on down. The slob look arrived with the Sixties. Did it percolate up from below or down from above? We see wealthy Hollywood stars showing up for an interview wearing jeans; and we also see ordinary middle class citizens popping into church dressed the same way. The same can be said of men's hairstyles. The long hair and ponytails made their appearance first, as I recall, among the denizens of Hippie-dom. These were mostly doped up middle class youth rebelling against authority; some were "intellectuals." Did their hirsute preferences ascend to the higher classes? They did descend to the blue-collar class.

Years ago a critic named Dwight MacDonald defined three levels of culture: high, mid, and low. As a definition, it was clarifying, but I am not too sure that it is relevant any more. With nearly everyone, by virtue of income, being able to participate in the culture at large, the whole may be easily defined as pop culture. The audience for rock and heavy metal concerts is not necessarily the same as that for Mozart at Lincoln Center; but neither audience is passing judgment on the other, much as they diverge in tastes. Museums that once housed only the works of great artists and sculptors from centuries past now include examples of every type of contemporary art. One wonders what, in fact, art is. The English journalist-historian Paul Johnson has called the transient phases of modern aesthetics "fashion art," in his *Art: A New History* (2003, chapter 29).

Do the masses have a future? Silly question? In the John Carey book mentioned above, I found it fascinating and instructive that so many of the "great issues" that the intellectuals dealt with a century ago are the same ones they are talking about today. There are too many people, said H G. Wells; something must be done. Now we have Paul Ehrlich with his *Population Bomb,* predicting doom unless something is done to halt population growth.

Eugenics is back. Environmentalism was also very big around 1900, although it was then called conservation. Women's rights were much in the news, both in England and the United States. Prohibition of alcoholic beverages was on the horizon; today we have frenzy over tobacco (it helps to take our minds off the drug problem, while politicians urge legalization of marijuana). Gay rights was not an issue, but Oscar Wilde brought the problem to the attention of society in a somewhat unfortunate way. Socialism was very big as an idea in 1900, and it still is. Does history repeat itself, or what?

"Che sera, sera", as Doris Day sang, "the future's not ours to see." From the vantage point of 2018 and later, it seems unthinkable that the bulk of the population in the West could be driven to become a mass once more, impoverished and under the thumbs of government. With the unlimited government we now have, however, and with all its millions of detailed regulations of everything, once can foresee a similar situation arising. It would be full-blown National Socialism, at least at first.

Somewhat related to the discussion of intellectuals is the notion of world improvers. In the week following the death of Steve Jobs in September 2011, the *Economist* had a cover with his picture on it, along with two words, "The Magician." It was a brief and decidedly appropriate assessment of a man with great abilities who left us far too soon. And it set me to thinking about the many individuals who do improve the world inadvertently as opposed to those who make it their life's purpose.

Decades from now someone may look back at our time under the old Genesis rubric, "In those days there were giants in the Earth." It would be a considerable list.

Certainly Steve Jobs and his partner in founding Apple, Steve Wozniak, would be on it, along with Robert Noyce and Gordon Moore of Intel Corporation, Bill Gates and Paul Allen of Microsoft, Larry Ellison of Oracle, Larry Page and Sergey Brin of Google, Jeff Bezos of Amazon, and Mark Zuckerberg of Facebook. Going back more than a century we can add Thomas Edison with his light bulb, movie camera, phonograph, and ticker tape machine; Alexander Graham Bell and the telephone; the Wright Brothers and flight; Marconi and radio; Philo Farnsworth and television; John D. Rockefeller, who created the oil industry; Henry Ford, William C. Durant, and Alfred P. Sloan, Jr. for automobiles; Thomas Watson of IBM; and John Bardeen, Walter Brattain, and William Shockley, the inventors at Bell Labs who devised the transistor, which eventually led to the microprocessor that made our computers possible. And who can forget that one-man Federal Reserve System, J. P Morgan, who saved the national government from embarrassment more than once.

The list is tiny, considering all the names that could be added for improvements in agriculture, medicine, architecture, space exploration, and many other fields. And we cannot forget the novelists, short story writer, playwrights, sculptors, composers, and performers whose works have given pleasure to millions. From these and many more the lives of Americans are much better off, and increasingly also for millions in other countries. Yet I seriously doubt than any of those named and countless others omitted ever said to himself, "I'm going to make the world a better place to live in." Their goals were narrower and more proximate, but their achievements were far-reaching. They worked incrementally toward often uncertain results. They took time to get where they were heading, benefiting from failure as well as from success.

A lot of names are missing, because they don't belong here. They have been mentioned previously in this narrative, so there is no reason to tarnish the reputations of those listed here with rascals and monsters of years gone by or present-day ones.

This brings me to my next point. It's time to tear society apart and see what makes it tick.

Chapter 16 The Way the World Works: In Praise of Blue Collars

The time has come to separate the parasites from their hosts. The pre-colon in the chapter title is also the title of a book by Jude Waninski, the late supply-side economist. And, before I forget it, there is a very enlightening book on this subject: *How the West Grew Rich* by Nathan Rosenberg and L. E. Birdzell, Jr. (1986)

Rather late in life, due to suggestions from a friend, I got started studying economics for real. It was with Adam Smith's *Wealth of Nations.* This is the first truly modern book, and it made me feel like a lifetime ignoramus. I had never been able, nor did I even try, to comprehend what was right in front of me all the time. Economic transactions go on all around us daily, how had I missed their import? (Fortunately, I was not alone in this gross ignorance.) The economic realities were there, it was only a matter of paying attention and sorting them out.

Fear not, I am not going to give a course in economics, but it would be nice if someone would. That sarcastic remark is mostly valid. There are a few, very few institutions in this country where one can study the real thing. George Mason University and the University of Nevada at Las Vegas are two of them. In Las Vegas there a brilliant scholar named Hans-Hermann Hoppe who presides over an excellent program formerly run by the late Murray Rothbard. Economics is one of the most basic of Humanistic studies, because it pertains to what people must necessarily do in all times and in all places. The text to read is *Human Action* by Ludwig von Mises. A more recent introduction to the subject, without all the frills, is Mark Skousen's *Economic Logic*. It requires no knowledge of mathematics to learn economics well. I can testify to that, based on my lack of mathematical skills.

The point of all this is simple. As long as humanity has been around, it has by necessity engaged in economic activity. It has not by nature engaged in political activity.

We are all consumers, but we are not all producers. Wealth is what is produced. It's too bad there is not a better word, but wealth it must be. Wealth is not money, it is stuff, from the computer I type on, to the car I drive, to the pen I write with, to the chicken I am baking, to the building I live in, to the chair I sit on, to the window I gaze through, to the clothing I wear, to the tinsel on the Christmas tree, and to the can of pipe tobacco on my table. I am grateful that I passed my career in the productive sector of the economy.

Is there a nonproductive sector? Yes, it is occupied by all those who perform services while creating no new wealth. You go to the dentist to get your teeth cleaned; nothing is produced. Visits to the doctor's office yield the same result. You sit in class at school; nothing is produced. You attend worship services, go to the movies or rock concert or theater; nothing is produced. You go to baseball, football, hockey, and basketball games and receive no product, unless you buy from the vendors wandering the aisles. The policeman on the beat and fireman hosing down a burning building create no products. Certainly, products are used in all of these ventures, but they are not created by those who use them.

If services were unavailable, we would all feel deprived. We need dentists and doctors and teachers, and we definitely need policemen and firemen. For our national defense we depend on the armed services. We do not need, but we desire the array of entertainments we subject ourselves to. But it is the producers of wealth who make possible the rendering of these services. Without productive activities, there would be no money, because money is derived from the productive sector of the economy. It is the economic equivalent of wealth. Money originated to facilitate the exchange of products, because it could be a substitute for products in value. Money that is left over after we cover our basic needs is available to pay for services. Some people obviously have a great deal more money left over than others. That this becomes a problem for some is too bad, since being devoured by envy is not good for one's mental health.

A clarification on the previous paragraph is necessary. Since 1971, when President Nixon ended the relation of gold to money, the whole world has become what Milton Friedman called a "fiat world." This means that money has no inherent value; it is based on nothing except the government's decision to decide what money is. *Fiat* is Latin for "let it be." In the book of Genesis God said "Let there be light." So, today, government says "Let there be money." Friedman's book, *Money Mischief,* explains how we got to this challenging situation, one that has caused so many economic problems since 1971.

From the discussion above about the masses, we know how the producers of wealth have stood in society for many millennia: they were at the bottom. In this, at least, Marx was right, for all the failures of the rest of his analyses. The wealth-producers were themselves not allowed to become wealthy until the Industrial Revolution, and then only very gradually. (It took about 200 years to get beyond subsistence wages.) For decades it was the owners, not the workers, who gained the lion's share. And government always took its "share". This institution has always lived on involuntary handouts from the private sector, taxes, in other words. Government creates nothing and provides very few services that could not be better discharged by the private sector. To put it bluntly, the government is a parasite on the body politic. In the so-called private sector, some lawyers are the parasites; they produce nothing yet demand everything. Their pernicious alliance with the government is a real threat to the continuance of freedom and prosperity in the United States. And let's not forget that other great parasite, Christendom's medieval church, which has been rightly compared by historian Paul Johnson to the Soviet Union.

In the Soviet system, as we have seen, the parasite devoured the host to such an extent that the latter collapsed. In the American system the government takes an unprecedented share of the Gross Domestic Product, while piling up unsustainable debts. Were such enormous sums required to operate the government, perhaps no one would complain. But the sums are really there for the elected officials and their bureaucrats to remake society according to their whims. All governments at all times live well, even in the poorest nations and in the most tyrannical ones. The lifestyles of the rich and demonic in the Soviet Union, China, Cuba, North Korea, Haiti, and the African backwaters would incite envy in Louis XIV, were he around to witness them.

It was noted above that the private and public sectors each function according to their own sets of principles. These are mutually exclusive. Jane Jacobs has clarified this matter quite well in *Systems of Survival.* For further information on the differences between a government and an economy, consult *Bureaucracy* by Ludwig von Mises. For what happens when the two sets of rules are blended, see the latter's *Planned Chaos.* The Soviet "experiment" is the supreme example of such chaos, of what happens when the two sets of guidelines are mingled.

We are constantly confronted with news stories about terrible problems of poverty in all parts of the globe. Yet, who asks the source of these problems? As Jane Jacobs demonstrated in *The Economy of Cities,* poverty is the original state of mankind; it has no causes, but the perpetuation of it does. Only wealth has causes; it has to be created and built. There are no inherent obstacles to wealth-creation, apart from those imposed by nature itself. People have always voted with their feet in seeking out better environments in which to prosper. Why else would so many illegal aliens come here from those miserable economic backwaters south of the Rio Grande? Were everyone everywhere left free to do so, the prosperity of each would be assured. If the "intellectuals" would stop agonizing over poverty and look to the possibilities inherent in wealth-creation, they and we would be better served. One does not end poverty by handing out money, either as welfare or as foreign aid. Poverty is ended by wealth creation only.

But, as stated much earlier, there are two historic obstacles to the continuing prosperity of the masses: religion and government – the two chief world parasites. A country-by country survey is hardly necessary. Today, apart from the Muslim lands, the obstacle is government, not institutional religion, although in India religion is still acts as a drag on the economy. When those who have the power and the prestige can take as much as they want from the producers, the ongoing poverty of the masses is assured. When philosophers in ancient times, notably Plato and Aristotle, decreed the essential human worthlessness of the producers in contrast to the ruling authorities, a secular dogma was devised that lasted in theory until the late 18th century and in practice until now. It was, in fact, a worldwide dogma, because less-than-great minds think alike. Only in the United States was the old superstition first overcome. Only here, as the quotations from Gordon Wood showed, did people first discover that it was not only possible to work for oneself alone, but even noble.

Christendom, as opposed to Christianity, has hardly been faultless when it comes to the working man and woman. It lived as a parasite for centuries, using fear to keep the public in line, while taking its presumed share for itself. The insatiable greed of the Latin Church was one of the causes of the Reformation. That greed began when the churches became allies of the state. Ironically, it was the growth of the state that in the later Middle Ages that led to conflicts over control of wealth. Henry VIII's sacking of the monasteries is well known. The outrages of the French Revolution against the church came much later. Medieval history is a treasure trove of the mistakes made by the Christian religion, mistakes that led to its being so thoroughly discredited in the modern era. Yet it was the church that held up the admonition *Ore et labore,* pray and work. Was this complete hypocrisy? Recently, Pope Benedict XVI whined about the decline of Christianity in Europe. Whose fault might that be? As a recent cartoon suggested to the pope: look in the mirror.

In my mind, the greatest crime against humanity in all its history has been the relegation of the producers of wealth to the lowest rung of society, while the parasites feasted at the top. Power, backed by guns, kept them at the top; and it still does. The blue-collar workers are still at the lower end of the socioeconomic totem pole, in spite of labor unions and the good wages many of them make. The sad fact about these workers is that their unions try to create enmity between them and the companies they work for. Earlier in our history, this was understandable, because owners made themselves enemies of the working class. I cannot see such an era returning. What I can see is furtive government attempts to control more and more of the economy, including the workers. We can never be reminded enough that it was in the "workers' paradise" that their rights were most circumscribed. Lenin and his fellow butchers lost no time in getting unions outlawed.

Why do the producers put up with it? In spite of revolutions, the old scenario replays itself. I don't know if there is a clear-cut answer. Part of the solution goes back to the matter of religion: people must have something to pay homage to. There is the old argument: well, we must have government; we need the police, the fire departments, and the armed services. Fine, if this were all that government did. I can get no further than an innate flaw in humanity. People seem genuinely unable to discern their own best interests at all levels of their lives. It seems to me that to live free and prosperous in a land with limited government would be a boon devoutly to be cherished. Perhaps the insecurity of it all makes people afraid. Government does at least pretend to promise security, even if at a low level. The Soviet citizens were generally secure in their poverty and squalor. To think that, after centuries of improved human well-being, a system such as that could appear in the 20th century. It was nothing more than the same old vicious Statism that has plagued the earth for millennia.

There is a problem facing unionized blue collar workers that they seem unaware of. Were this country ever to get the kind of government their leaders desire, the unions would be the first thing to go; and the rest of civil society would go with them.

I found the following statement in Jonathan Roses' *The Intellectual Life of the British Working Classes.* "I had actually arrived at the conclusion that if there was any good life, and freedom from insecurity, and beauty, and knowledge, or leisure, then the men who did the world's dirty, sweaty, toilsome, risky work, and the women who shared the life with them ought to be the first entitled to these things." These are the words of a man named Jack Lawson, who worked in the coal mines.

I leave this subject with two statements. The first is by Richard P. Feynman, the outstanding Nobel-Prize winning physicist. In a letter to his wife in 1962 he wrote. "The real question of government versus private enterprise is argued on too philosophical and abstract a basis. Theoretically planning may be good etc. – but nobody has ever figured out the cause of government stupidity – and until they do and find the cure all ideal plans will fall into quicksand." (*Perfectly Reasonable Deviations from the Beaten Track: The Letters of Richard P. Feynman,* edited by his daughter, Michelle Feynman, p. 137. I can't recommend this collection too highly – he was an amazing individual who departed too soon.)

The second is from Aldous Huxley, of *Brave New World* fame. It is from a letter to George Orwell in 1949 and it is quoted in the recent biography, *Orwell: Wintry Conscience of a Generation* by Jeffrey Meyers. "Within the next generation I believe that the world's rulers will discover that infant conditioning and narco-hypnosis are more efficient instruments of government, than clubs and prisons, and the lust for power can be just as completely satisfied by suggesting people into loving their servitude as by flogging and kicking them into obedience." (Pp.288-289)

Sorry, but I am not quite ready to leave this subject without adding some thoughts that came to me after writing the above two paragraphs. A reading of history will show that the "upper classes," whatever their composition – from ancient empires to the British class system –have always looked down on the millions who actually did the work of the world, whether as producers of wealth or as slaves or servants. Why this condescending attitude? It occurred to me that those in the higher reaches of a society always had everything provided for them by someone else. They didn't get their hands dirty making things or waiting on themselves. Nearly everything was done for them, although they ate their own food. What attitude was more natural toward providers and servants than condescension, if not outright contempt? Having everything provided and being waited on for every desire became viewed as a right. That right was maintained by wealth and power, as it still in is many places. Any study of the British upper classes will prove this paragraph true. Or you can just watch Downton Abbey.

Chapter 17 An Empire of Liberty

The term is Jefferson's, but he was far from alone in perceiving the potential of all the land to the west of Virginia. George Washington was more familiar with the early frontier, having traveled through much of it in his surveying duties and in his French and Indian War adventures. As president, he was determined to incorporate the area up to the Mississippi River into the United States. And during his presidency the need to have an outlet from the Mississippi River at New Orleans began to be an imperative for trade. This problem was eventually solved by Jefferson's purchase of the Louisiana Territory.

Jefferson, as president, went even further – he sent the Lewis and Clark expedition out to explore the vast territory he had purchased from Napoleon. From the very beginning, in colonial days, the focus was westward, and backs were turned on the Old World. That attitude persisted as long as there was a frontier, even if no one really knew how far it extended. To go west, as Thoreau suggested, was to go into the future. The United States was always, and still is, about the future. Why else do so many immigrants come here from the world's many economic and political disasters? Even our native crop of

America-haters cannot dissuade them, legal and illegal alike.

But first, a new government had to be made to work. That it succeeded in the tumultuous years from 1789 to 1815 borders, for me, on the miraculous. All the odds were against success. The first task was winning the Revolutionary War; that took eight years and was a close call. Basically, the war was won by not losing it. Following it, thanks to the shallowness and self-interest of state politicians, came the very unsettled years under the Articles of Confederation. Then, getting a new Constitution written and adopted came close to failing. Hardly was the first president in office than the French Revolution broke out. The founding fathers found it was much easier to theorize about government than to make it work.

The events in France were a calamity for American politics, because the citizens were sharply divided over them and became more so as with the descent into the Terror and execution of Louis XVI. It is no exaggeration to assert that what happened in France was instrumental in the formation of our first political parties, the Federalists and the Republicans (now Democrats). This division was personified in two members of Washington's cabinet: Hamilton and Jefferson. The latter had been minister to France when the revolution started, and he looked fondly upon it. In this he did not waver, even during the Reign of Terror. Hamilton viewed the events in France with disgust, seeing clearly where they tended. Writing more than a century later, James Bryce puts the origin of parties at the door of the Constitutional Convention itself, or certainly in the months following, when the Federalists emerged as strong defenders of the Constitution and the Jeffersonians and Anitfederalists as opposed to a too-strong federal government. (*The American Commonwealth*, chapter 2, and again in chapter 52.)

With England and France once again at war, the new nation was caught in the middle of a conflict over which it had no control. This international mess lasted until the end of the War of 1812 and the downfall of Napoleon in 1815. The bitter partisanship of those years, as recorded in the press, has rarely been equaled, although the current adherents of the Far Left have provided some consistently venomous competition. This is understandable: they have no need to engage in discussion, since they already have all truth. Therefore, name calling and character assassination become their best tools.

Foreign policy was not, however, the only problem facing the Washington administration. The new government had to be made both to work and to endure on the basis of domestic policy. To accomplish this was a singular achievement under very trying circumstances.

The attitudes of Americans toward the federal government were far different from what they are today. All loyalties were local. People regarded themselves as citizens of the respective states, not of the United States – that entity was viewed as a composite and was always referred to with a plural verb. Fortunately Washington was a nationalist, in contrast to most of his Virginia compatriots, most notably Jefferson and Madison.

It is now taken for granted that no one other than Washington could have held the federal government together during very trying times. For one thing, Americans generally had a hard time understanding why there should be one chief executive heading the government. Wasn't this what they had escaped from by winning the Revolution? No one of lesser stature, as perceived by the public at large, could have succeeded in the task; and Washington's stature was immense. But he also had the wisdom and integrity to make the right decisions in a job that he never wanted and tried to duck out of after one term. A good one-volume biography of him by Joseph J. Ellis is entitled *His Excellency* (2004).

He was not alone in the formation of the federal government. He had as secretary of the Treasury Alexander Hamilton. If the word "genius" can be applied to any of the founding fathers, it belongs to him. The famous and somewhat notorious French diplomat and survivor, Talleyrand, said of Hamilton: "I consider Napoleon, [Charles James] Fox, and Hamilton the three greatest men of our epoch and, if I were forced to decide between the three, I would give without hesitation the first place to Hamilton. He divined Europe." (Quoted in Ron Chernow's 2004 biography *Alexander Hamilton,* p. 466) Sometimes this quotation replaces Fox with William Pitt the Younger. The point is the same.

For the time Hamilton lived in, when economics was a very new science – the *Wealth of Nations* had only been published in 1776 – his grasp of economics, banking, and finance was extraordinary. In this country his brilliance was not equaled until the 20th century. (I'm thinking of J. Pierpont Morgan, who acted as a one-man central bank, in the absence of any official institution. He saved the federal government's bacon twice, once in the 1890s and again in the Panic of 1907. Morgan died the same year the Federal Reserve System went into operation.) At the end of a recent "American Experience" documentary on the life of Hamilton on PBS, one historian noted that there is in Washington, DC, no memorial to him; no problem, he commented – the whole country is his memorial. (There is a statue of him on Wall Street, however.)

Within a period of barely more than a year, Hamilton sent three reports to Congress for approval: The Report on the Public Credit, the Report on a National Bank, and A Report on the Subject of Manufactures. Over vehement opposition by some members of Congress, they were all accepted. It was the fate of the second report that had the most lasting effect.

Banks were not popular with the first Americans, largely because they didn't understand them. For Hamilton, a national bank was a necessary means to stabilize monetary policy and make banking honest, among other things. I make a point of this, because eventually his work was undone by Jefferson's Republican Party – today's Democrats. When the bank charter expired during Jefferson's term, it was not renewed. A Second Bank of the United States was chartered in 1816 and lasted until 1836, when Andrew Jackson made sure it expired for good. With no federal control over banks and the money supply, easy money proliferated, and the United States had the most volatile economy in the West during the 19th century. It was a sequence of boom and bust every couple of decades. And many of the downturns were very severe, deserving the name depression had not the catastrophe of 1929-1940 taken that title for good. This was but another example of damage done by government based on ideology, short-sightedness, ignorance, and partisanship. This point is made clear in John Steele Gordon's *Empire of Wealth,* chapter 7, referred to in the next chapter.

Another reason for making so much of the bank issue is to lead into a comparison of the founding fathers. As a group, it was perhaps the most brilliant collection of men to get together at one time, considering their accomplishments. Washington himself was not well schooled, and he knew it. But he had a soundness of character and hard-won wisdom that made him capable of forming the executive department from scratch – the details were not spelled out in the Constitution. Each of the others was brilliant in his own way: John Adams, John Jay, Thomas Jefferson, and James Madison, to name but a very few. But it is one thing to think and another to act.

Washington was an outstanding president; his like would not appear again until Lincoln. Jefferson and Madison were, at best, mediocre presidents. There is no denying Jefferson's brilliance in some matters, but his grasp of economics ranged from slim to none. Furthermore, he was a romantic ideologue, a man who had a view of society and was sure that somehow society could be made to conform to his notions. He saw the United States as a nation of "yeoman farmers." (Yeoman is a Middle English word meaning, among other things, freeholders – farmers who owned their own acreage.) Jefferson hated cities, viewing them as congested and filthy agglomerations of humanity; and he was a freeholder at his beloved Monticello. But he was a much in debt freeholder. He stated his view of a farmers' paradise in his *Notes on Virginia*: "Those who labor in the earth are the chosen people of God, if He ever had a chosen people, whose breasts he has made his peculiar deposit of genuine virtue."

Madison was not so naïve, but he was too tied to the

landed gentry of Virginia and its states' rights views to govern wisely. It was not the fault of either man that they had to deal with the Napoleonic conflicts during their terms, but they showed little expertise in foreign policy; as a result they made a hash of domestic policy as well.

But there was another individual who is not counted among that august group known as Founding Fathers - John Marshall. He did serve during the Revolution, but he became a national figure when named Chief Justice by John Adams. He was brilliant in both thought and deed. It was he, through a series of Supreme Court rulings, who cemented the political and economic nationalism of Washington and Hamilton into place. His biography, by Jean Edward Smith, is entitled *John Marshall: Definer of a Nation*. Rarely has a subtitle been more appropriate. In his *The American Commonwealth,* James Bryce remarks of Marshall, "It is therefore hardly an exaggeration to say that the American Constitution as it now stands, with the mass of ringing decisions which explain it, is a far more complete and finished instrument that it was when it came fire-new from the hands of the Convention [of 1787]. It is not merely their work but the work of the judges, and most of all of one man, the great Chief-Justice Marshall." (chapter 23) At his death in 1835, the Liberty Bell tolled for the last time.

And now, a few words about Patrick Henry. When the Founding Fathers are listed, his name does not normally appear. He was not at the Continental Congress in 1776, when the Declaration of Independence was issued, nor did he attend the Constitutional Convention of 1787. He was actually a strong opponent of the Constitution at the Virginia ratifying convention of 1788. But he was neither last nor least. To my way of thinking, he was first. In his eloquent resistance to the Stamp Act in May 1765, he lit the little bonfire that a decade later became the conflagration of the American Revolution. When his anti-Stamp Act resolutions were published in the other colonies, his was immediately hailed as an American hero. Rightly did fellow Virginian George Mason call him "the first man upon this continent." (Quoted in Henry Mayer's *A Son of Thunder*, p. 189). He was always far ahead of the learning curve on the issues that faced the colonies in those troubled years.

Although Thomas Jefferson is rightly given credit for the Virginia Statute of Religious Freedom, Henry pushed a similar law through the House of Burgesses several years before Virginia was a state. He favored religious tolerance and took the side of the Baptists and Quakers, who were frequently persecuted, tortured, or jailed for setting up houses of worship in Virginia. In 1776, when he helped composed a bill of rights for the new state government, he improved and expanded religious toleration.

He had a knack for knowing which way the wind was blowing, accepting well ahead of his fellow delegates to the Continental Congress that independence was inevitable, as was the need for military preparation for fighting the British. But unlike Benjamin Franklin and George Washington, he was not a master of calculated image management. He appears to have been a very honorable and straightforward individual, who spoke his mind with more eloquence than his peers.

Whether he was the best orator and public speaker in our history, there is no way of knowing. Only snippets of his speeches have endured, partly because those who could have taken them down in writing were so enthralled by listening to him that they forgot to write. When it was noised about town that he would speak in court or in the legislature, the whole town would shut down, and everyone would rush over to listen. He did not need to be a self-promoter. His opposition to the Constitution was highly principled and tended to get him placed on the back burner of American history. Considering that, in the long run, he was correct on the evils of a powerful central government, he should be now moved to the forefront of our national history. He was, for me, the first American. Now, back on subject.

With the end of the War of 1812, the United States could finally begin to be itself. Regardless of claims made by Henry Luce for the 20th century, the 19th can also be called an American Century. The horrendous problem of slavery was solved at enormous cost, but the Union was preserved. Following it the Second Industrial Revolution arrived and a period of invention that, by the time the first Roosevelt was president, had pushed the United States to the forefront of prosperity, as well as liberty. (For an in-depth and very understandable history of the Second Industrial Revolution, one can hardly do better than reading *Scale and Scope: The Dynamics of Industrial Capitalism* by Alfred D. Chandler, Jr.)

As noted in the Lincoln chapter, there was also an Empire for Slavery. Anyone interested in a tour through Southern dementia should read at least the opening chapters of McPherson's *The Battle Cry of Freedom.* He has done it so well that no recap on my part would do it justice.

Chapter 18 An Empire of Wealth: The American Dream

> "Countries are rich or poor, have a great deal to consume or very little, mainly because they work well or badly, not because some outsider is adding to or stealing from a God-given endowment." (Deirdre N. McCloskey in *The Bourgeois Virtues*, p. 453.)
>
> "Everyone wants to live at the expense of the state. They forget that the state lives at the expense of everyone." (Frédéric Bastiat), whose *Selected Essays on Political Economy* are incredibly worth reading. Although written more than 160 years ago, he'll never be out of date.)

The title for this chapter, which follows logically on the previous section, is brazenly taken from the book *Empire of Wealth* by John Steele Gordon, a very satisfactory survey of economic development from the colonial era to the present.

That there is an American Dream cannot be denied, and one must grant that there was a great deal of Romance in apprehending it from afar. The fantasies that percolated in the minds of prospective immigrants spoke, if not of streets paved with gold, at least of endless acres of land waiting to be developed. For the millions of utterly destitute Europeans, and later Asians, anything was better than the circumstances under which they barely survived.

If not for hope alone, why else did many thousands of individuals leave their homelands to come here every year for more than a century? And they still come, looking for a good life that their native environments deny them. Immigrants originally came by the millions for a variety of reasons – to escape religious persecution, to escape military conscription, and perhaps most of all, because of the breakdown of the land tenure system of Europe. This was a theory that the immigration historian Marcus Lee Hansen intended to develop, but he died before being able to complete the work. One of the better known examples was the enclosures of farmland in Great Britain to make way for the raising of sheep. This action drove thousands of families off the land and set them to roving in look for work in an economy that could not provide it. One such family was that of the young Andrew Carnegie. The Irish potato famine of the 1840s provided a very forceful impetus for departure. When Europeans of no economic means heard of the opportunities available in the English colonies – and later in the United States – they fled their homelands.

In spite of all the multicultural nuttiness being peddled in our schools, let's face it: most of the countries on earth apart from Europe Australia, New Zealand, and North America, are miserable places to live, none more so than the lands dominated by Islam. The issue of Islam has been dealt with so well by Bernard Lewis that there is no point in covering that ground again. Inquiring minds will want to get hold of his *What Went Wrong: Western Impact and Middle Eastern Response,* Oxford University Press 2002. Anyone wanting to read a powerful Western response to the attack of 9/11 can enjoy, as I did, Oriana Fallaci's *The Rage and the Pride,* issued in late 2002 or Sam Harris's *The End of Faith* in 2004.

Back to the subject. In the 1960s, large segments of the Boomer population made the astonishing discovery that the United States was not perfect. That generation has consistently made astonishing discoveries of matters that were known to the rest of us all along. America, they said, had not lived up to its ideals. Hence their involvement in the Civil Rights movement and the anti-Vietnam protests. It would have been admirable if the Boomers only wanted to adjust reality to the ideals. Instead they decided to junk the ideals and find a set of replacements.

(I know I'm speaking in generalities about what was certainly a minority, a very loud minority of a very large generation, but the point has to be made. More than 55,000 of those Boomers died in Vietnam, after all. I may be wrong, but it occurred to me that a large number of the college-age population adopted an ideology before they had gained any significant knowledge. When the knowledge came it was either very selective or made to fit into the pigeonholes provided by the generally Marxist, or at least anti-American, way of thinking.) If ever there were generations wrapped in Romanticism, it is those born after 1945.

A sizeable part of the American population decided

that the United States was the real villain on the world's stage, and many of the citizens persist in that belief, urged on by allies in government, especially the president elected in 2008. The question arises: what other nation has had such significant ideals founded on liberty and the individual pursuit of happiness? What is the French dream, the German dream, the Chinese dream? France invests its dream in the Napoleonic *gloire*, now more than 200 years dead. We know what the German dream of the 1930s to 1945 was. If there is one now, apart from finding ways to avoid working, I have not noticed it. As to China, who can say? Let's hope it is not the same as the dream of the now-defunct USSR. That China has far surpassed the former Soviet Union in prosperity is an amazing achievement, considering that its government still calls itself Communist.

That this country could ever live up to its ideals perfectly is quite unlikely. There are probably many regrets that the United States was not born perfect. Nor was the free-market economy ushered onto the scene without blemish, struggle and strife, and occasional bloodshed; and it still undergoes great stress from time to time. Globalization is not without its painful readjustments. It is rather bizarre to see the intellectuals blame the free market for what are really flaws common to human nature in all times and places. They are, of course, ready to set us straight on everything.

When one considers how far both the nation and the free market economy have come in 200 years, it is far better to focus on the progress toward realizing ideals than in deciding to trash them. Perhaps the United States would be perfect, if its citizens shared that quality. It is not, nor ever will it be. The immigrants came here from everywhere else, bringing with them loads of cultural baggage, including all the ethnic animosities that we encapsulate in the word xenophobia – the fear of foreigners. Added to these were their own cultural ideologies, including Socialism and Communism. Recent immigrants still do so. The problem with cultural baggage and Old World mindsets is the unawareness of the roots of American constitutionalism – the British background in the "rights of Englishmen" that the colonists held so dearly. This is especially true of those who come from Latin America, the mindset of which is rooted in late medieval Spain.

How potent xenophobia was can be illustrated with many episodes, past and present. Leaving the treatment of Native Americans and the ghastly slavery episode aside, one of the best known is the anti-immigrant movement led by the Native American party in the mid-19th century. This sentiment grew, even as the party itself expired, and became potent enough to bring about the Natural Origins quota system passed by Congress in 1924. Our literature has captured a good deal of this immigrant squalor. An early description was given by Danish immigrant and social reformer, Jacob Riis in *How the Other Half Lives* in 1890 or Walter Rauschenbusch's *Christianity and the Social Crisis* in 1907. One can see it marvelously displayed on the screen in the 2002 film *Gangs of New York* by Martin Scorsese. I had to read the reviews before I realized that Herbert Asbury's book on which it is based was part of my research 35 years ago. Another fine literary work, now sadly seldom read, is the *Studs Lonigan* trilogy by James T. Farrell.

It is possible to trace all the sordid events in American

history, and there have been many; and I have done so myself in a few historical studies. But they are not all of our history, nor are they its defining characteristics. An Indiana journalist, John L. B. Soule (not Horace Greeley), is credited with the advice, "Go West, young man." Henry Thoreau put it better: "Go west, as into the future." The American dream is always about the future; it is always the work in progress. The immigrants did not come here so that not only their present would be better, but that their future would be. There are plenty of stories and pictures depicting the wretched poverty of the first generations of Europeans and Asians. But this did not prove to be a static condition. Even the gangs of New York are much better housed these days. Those who came in the 17th through the 20th centuries built a nation like no other. Most of them were unknown then and are unknown still. There is an American exceptionalism in spite of the sneers of many politicians.

Many pejorative comments have been written about how the American economy was built. We have heard of the Robber Barons and the Malefactors of Great Wealth. Both charges are much overstated, and it would pay anyone who wants to sort out the facts from the agenda-driven fiction to look into the matter. Two suggestions come to mind: *The Entrepreneurial Adventure* by Larry Schweikart and *The Myth of the Robber Barons* by Burton W. Folsom, Jr. Gordon's *Empire of Wealth* also had good coverage of the period and the myth. Whether these or works like them can counteract the junk history now taught in our schools is doubtful, but it's worth a try.

The industrial might of the United States was brutally constructed. Given the time, the temper of the people, and the social values, one wonders if it could have been otherwise. It was certainly no different in England, home of the Industrial Revolution. Had those who built industries practiced in society what they heard preached in their churches, things might have been different. (I guess they couldn't all be Rockefellers.) Coal mining, railroad building, and making steel were dangerous and difficult jobs. That has not changed significantly. What has changed is the matter of countervailing power - the labor movement.

Owners of trusts and other companies used private property rights as a way of preventing workers from bargaining for wages or hours collectively. To gain strength and bargaining power, the workers formed unions, which were for so long viewed as conspiracies against the public. It was only when the unions were put on an even footing with owners and managers that labor-management strife could be mitigated. It was a decades-long struggle, entailing a good deal of violence on both sides. This eventual outcome has been one of the few benefits of government regulation, albeit a regulation that went too far the other way. The tilt toward labor power was somewhat diluted by the Taft-Hartley Act of 1948 and subsequent state right-to-work laws.

Whether the day of industrial unions is over is hard to judge. (The United Auto Workers has certainly made a mess of the domestic auto industry.) The government should never have put itself wholeheartedly in the corner of management, nor should it now align itself with labor. That it has done both is merely a tribute to the perfidy and greed of elected officials. Public sector unions have no place in this discussion, since they are part of the current problem and should never have existed in the first place. They may well be the prime movers in ending our freedom and prosperity. Can one call racketeering and extortion what has been made legal by government action?

To lament the errors of the past is one thing, to dwell on them to the exclusion of the results is another. To decry it all as crass materialism is sheer folly. As long as we are of material ourselves, we will be very materialistic. It is a worldwide phenomenon, apart from those few who live solely from the bounty of nature as hunters and gatherers or who are the beneficiaries of trust funds.

A judgment must be made, and it is a simple one. Are we better off than our predecessors of a century ago, of fifty years ago? The question answers itself, except for those who will dwell only on the negatives they see and abhor the positive. For me, it is better to live in freedom with the opportunity for prosperity than to dwell in the squalor of nations tied to old and failed ways of life. Perhaps it is prosperity that has made us better. There is a lot to be said for wanting to improve one's condition in life and for working to do so. An improved condition impels one to want to preserve the gains and prevent losses. On a purely secular level, can this be bad? If so, it is a universal human failing. We cannot go back to a simpler time, regardless of its romantic aura, which is always really a fiction. But we can always descend into a much worse time, a revived Middle Ages of permanent status for nearly everyone and power and wealth for the few. Would that the America haters could provide even one instance of a country whose whole history is nothing but rose petals and lollipops. But, of course, we have the

Big Rock Candy Mountain in Washington to console us in our troubles. Thank you, Burl Ives.

Lincoln said that America was the last, best hope of earth. Those who study the New Testament seriously may beg to differ. But in a secular sense, he was certainly correct. The alternative is to let the "best and brightest" push us into a statist purgatory and allow them to design our lives for us. This is an agenda that even the Roman emperors did not attempt. Our politicians, unfortunately, have the means and the will, as well as an apparent contempt for the citizenry.

What has been the outcome of four centuries of economic development? Is it too much to assert that it is whatever prosperity exists in today's world? The great part of the technology that made progress possible originated within the United States. And it still does. Levi Strauss started making blue jeans to clothe the miners of California during the Gold Rush. What is the most popular item of clothing worldwide today? Coca-Cola signs have been found worldwide for a century, as are McDonald's Golden Arches today – to say nothing of Starbucks, KFC, and Wal-Mart. The contributions made by immigrants and their descendants are so numerous that it takes whole books to describe them: electric power systems, the telegraph, the telephone, the movie industry, the airplane, television, computers, to say nothing of Brooklyn Bridge or the sculptures on Mount Rushmore. What has happened since 1900 is no less that the Americanization of the world, something that much of the rest of our planet resents.

Nothing said above is intended to denigrate or deny the contributions made outside of this country to our well-being. The First Industrial Revolution began in England, after all. The first railroads began operation there. The idea for television was first developed by a German, Philip Nipkow, in 1884; but the real development of it was in the United States by Philo T. Farnsworth. The inventor of radio was an Italian, Guglielmo Marconi, but it was here that radio became the vast entertainment medium that it was until television displaced it. Need I mention the computer? (Yes, I am familiar with Alan Turing.) In his *What God Hath Wrought*, Daniel Walker Howe sums up the American achievement nicely. In his discussion of the Erie Canal, he states that, "Changes from the rustic to the commercial that had taken centuries to unfold in Western civilization were telescoped into a generation in New York State." Reflecting on this quotation, it is interesting to consider how many centuries passed after the fall of the Roman Empire for decent road building and plumbing to appear in the West.

Resentment of all of this, as well as America's allegedly poor image in the world, is grounded in the same envy, resentment, greed, and hate that comprise the bases of all Leftism here and abroad. This envy is certainly based in part on: Why can they do it, while we can't? They rarely point to themselves and their wretched governments or demonic religions as at fault. How curious it is that the two most hated nations in the world are the United States and Israel, also two of the most economically successful.

Finally, no one should doubt that those who have of late attacked the United States have as their goal the destruction of Western civilization. We live in a new century and face a new kind of war. Our armchair generals, most of whom have never donned a uniform, will have to bring their thinking up to date and cease dwelling on the wars of the past. Meanwhile Europeans, populations of a continent that lost its status in the world after 1918 and their wretched governments sit idly by, ignoring the threats to everything they have built up in more than 1500 years. Are they really willing to see all of their culture – the paintings, the sculpture, the museums, the music, the cathedrals, the literature vandalized? The outcome of the 2015-18 immigration crisis in Europe will take years to play out, but the result will not be attractive.

A question poses itself: Will the American dream fade, or even die? It is certainly possible. Anyone who is awake to current events must have noticed that the economic structures of the globe are shifting. The American dominance that lasted from 1945 until the end of the Cold War has rapidly diminished. The most populous nations in the world, China and India, have made enormous strides toward economic development and growth, especially China. In a recent book, *Planet India* (2007), by Mira Kamdar, the author notes that: "People are being propelled away from a world they understood toward a new world they have yet to define." (p. 230)

That quotation applies as well to workers in the United States who see their jobs transferred overseas, workers who watch their unions lose membership, and consumers who purchase an ever-increasing amount of foreign goods. But it applies also to populations in developing countries who are seizing new opportunities they long believed would never come their way. What citizen of China could have foreseen during Mao's Cultural Revolution that his country would become the great economic dynamo it now is? (It certainly helped that China could appropriate

American-made technology.) The same may be said of India's citizens. These two, as well as other developing countries, are able to get where we in the United States are now very quickly, without the need to tackle the challenges that earlier Americans faced. What has been invented and produced here can be easily transferred elsewhere. In economic terms, it's called convergence. It can also be called theft of intellectual property.

Consider just one example: the cell phone. In most parts of the world, getting a land-line telephone was a matter of waiting generations, after putting in an order – if it was possible to have one at all. Today that problem is irrelevant, as millions of Chinese, Indians, Vietnamese, and Africans have been able to obtain cell phones and smartphones. Both Apple and Nokia have built plants overseas to reach those huge markets. In the United States, cell phones called smartphones have become in great part a frivolity – taking pictures, playing music, and more. In other places they are used more seriously. An article in *The Economist* (May 12, 2007, p. 83) discussed the economic growth and prosperity the phones brought to fishermen off the coast of the Kerala region of India. The fishermen are able to contact the markets offering the best price for the catch of the day, thus avoiding a great deal of wasted fish and time. This, and other methods of creating prosperity for the poorest populations of the world is the subject of C. K. Prahalad's *The Fortune at the Bottom of the Pyramid* (5th anniversary edition, 2010), one of the best works on economics I've read in a long time. He also demonstrates that traditional methods of dealing with poor – giving them money and making them dependent – are worthless. The same can be said for all of the trillions of dollars wasted on foreign aid over the past 60 years. But as long as the West is devoted to the wretched Keynesian economics, no other means are deemed acceptable or even understood.

All is not sunshine in these economic shifts. Consider, for example, the enormous demands that will be made upon the Earth's resources as more millions emerge from poverty into prosperity. Oil comes first to mind, and a recent (but temporary) large gas price increase in the United States seems to have caught the public's attention. Whether this will have a beneficial outcome remains to be seen – the politicians will certainly rant against the oil companies and their huge profits, all the while pocketing the huge taxes paid by the public. Fortunately, fracking has changed the American oil industry over the past few decades, making this country basically self-sufficient in fossil fuels. The Saudis became angry.

In India the water supply is currently the chief problem; and it will be so for the foreseeable future. Both China and India have enormous pockets of poverty, and I mean real destitution, that need to be dealt with. Communication and transportation infrastructures need to be built. School systems need to be built or reformed. The problems these societies have to solve are mind-boggling, if internal prosperity is to be spread more evenly. With such wretched governments, one wonders if the problems can be solved at all. China and India are both proving that governments cannot run and economy.

And, of course, there is the anti-globalization crowd, whose slogan ought to be, "We've got ours and we're gonna keep it, and if you don't like it, that's tough." Anyone with a shred of decency would applaud the development in places that have been sunk in poverty for literally centuries. But there is a bizarre mentality abroad, fostered by some economists, that development is a zero-sum game: if they get more, we must get less. It is quite understandable that union members in North America are more than a little distressed as they see factories built overseas to house work they once did. Would that union members had a knowledge of basic economics. If labor costs are high here, employers will seek out places where they are lower – even Japanese workers are learning this dreaded truth, and Chinese workers will not be far behind – greetings from Vietnam. It's hardly more than comparison shopping. But the unions in North America have been playing a losing game for decades, in cooperation with their friends in government: they all thought the party would never end. Now they move into the future looking into the rear-view mirror. So many really competent authors have dealt with this subject, it is presumptuous of me even to broach it; but apparently it is a problem that is not going to disappear soon.

Now that the antiglobalization movement has been mentioned, there is a side to it not often considered. I found mention of it by an author I'd not heard of until late in 2007, Larry Eubank. His book is *A Critical Inquiry into the Case Against Capitalism* (2001), but the article I read was published in *Chronicles* in the fall of 2005. He distinguishes between free trade, which nearly all economists embrace, and the alienation of capital. By the latter, he means the transfer of capital goods – the manufacturing base – overseas, to the extent that we become a nation of consumers without being also producers. This is a genuine and serious problem, and it is no wonder that

American workers are disturbed when they see their jobs sent abroad. How it will work out in the future is debatable. It is a problem President Trump has tried to deal with, but his success or failure is yet to be seen. At least his administration was able to get the economy back on track.

Chapter 19 Human, All Too Human

Before getting to the quotations, I must mention another book by Isaiah Berlin: *The Crooked Timber of Humanity: Chapters in the History of Ideas* (1991). The first statement is taken from it.

> "An exceptional being, the hero and genius to whom Carlyle and Fichte paid homage, can lift others to a level beyond any which they could have reached by their own efforts, even if this can be achieved only at the cost of the torment and death of multitudes." (p. 231)
>
> From Plato: "We can easily forgive a child who is afraid of the dark; the real tragedy of life is when adults are afraid of the light."
>
> "Fools and fanatics are always so certain of themselves, and wise people are full of doubts." (Bertrand Russell)
>
> From Chekhov: "When you don't' have a real life, you make do with dreams. It's better than nothing". (Uncle Vanya, Act II)

> From President Grant, on a visit to Galena, Ill., after leaving office: "These people were satisfied to pursue lives empty of accomplishment. There was no burning curiosity there, no restless desire to embrace the world or to challenge it." (Geoffrey Perret, *Ulysses S. Grant; Soldier and President,* 1997, p. 449)
>
> This title of this chapter has been swiped from Friedrich Nietzsche, whose views on human nature left a lot to be desired.
>
> We begin with Alexander Pope's *Essay on Man (*1733*),* an Enlightenment document. From Epistle II:
>
> Know then thyself, presume not God to scan;
>
> The proper study of Mankind is man.

First, a bit of interpretation. Know thyself. This is the famous Socratic exhortation, originating with the oracle at Delphi, and it is a worthy goal, if only it were possible. God, of course cannot be scanned. All human knowledge of God, apart from revelation, is a presumption. Moses Maimonides demonstrated this in his *Guide for the Perplexed* in the 12th century. If one does not accept revelation, all notions of God are pure human inventions. The second sentence is reminiscent of the ancient dictum: Man is the measure of all things, spoken by Protagoras in the 5th century BC.

Stated as an endeavor, the study of man is a worthy one. But in what framework is mankind studied? What is the context? Does acknowledging that humans are but one class of Nature's many animals help at all? We can perceive that fact without much difficulty. We can also perceive that we are a bit more than the other animals by virtue of brain power and the faculty of speech. (I do not mean to denigrate the brainpower of animals; it can be amazing. I do watch the nature programs.) All this doesn't tell us very much. By what means do we account for origin and purpose? Can these even be posited, or do we just assume them?

But Pope is not finished. A few lines later he says:

> Created half to rise, and half to fall;
> Great lord of all things, yet a prey to all;
> Sole judge of Truth, in endless Error hurl'd;
> The glory, jest, and riddle of the world.

There we have it. Nothing has been solved. Pope is stating poetically conclusions that any perceptive individual could reach by observing people over a period of time or by reading the histories of civilizations. And, as Yogi Berra said, "You can observe a lot just by watching." The ancient philosophers could do no better. Theirs is all speculative philosophy, which when focusing on humanity usually dwindles down to practical philosophy – advice on how to behave. Nor do we get any help from the alleged wisdom of the East. Where the East is not purely mythological and fantastic, it denies the merits of the transitory material world in favor of an unseen eternal spiritual existence. (Plato, any one?) The

East does indeed offer a great deal of advice on how to live, but the living, apart from Confucius, is pointed away from our fragile earthly life to an eternal realm. These are considered higher truths. Confucius is at least more down to earth. He did not deny God or the gods, but he preferred to leave the matter alone and prescribe rules of conduct. Ludwig Wittgenstein offered the same advice in his amazing *Tractatus* about 1920: Whereon we cannot speak, thereon let us be silent.

No religious system has yet explained human nature or the meaning of human life. Regarding this last phrase a word must be said. Life either has a meaning, or it doesn't. If it does, it has one meaning only, not many. To say it has many is virtually to discount the search for meaning altogether. The teachings of evolution would have us do away entirely with the questions posed here. To Darwinians we are accidents of biology and purely material. All plant and animal life is self-creating or the result of amazing, very complex, and as yet unexplained processes. The meaning of everything must be devised, made up, if you will. Everything that human societies have built up over the centuries has thus been contrived for our convenience by trial and error. What works out is preserved, what doesn't is discarded, except for bad ideas – they never seem to go away. It's all quite arbitrary, as are all the other wonders of nature. Birth is the beginning and death the end. Period. I am unable to find much that is satisfactory in all this. But perhaps I am hoping against hope, just as those Egyptian kings longed for an immortality they could never verify. Perhaps, too, wishful thinking is better than despair. But I am quite unprepared to accept that everything "just happened."

Just happened? Here we wander into a carnival of absurdity. When we look at the astounding diversity of life forms, plant and animal; when we consider the enormous complexity within life forms, how can we not marvel? It is not only the heavens that declare the glory of God. If it all just happened, why bother with more than one kind of tree? Why not just only one type of cat, dog, snake, or butterfly? Why have fleas and mosquitos at all? The controversy over evolution cannot be solved by theological arguments. There can be no such discipline as Creation Science. Nor does Intelligent Design fare better, since it is a faith assertion, not science. The arguments belong to science alone, so long as it does not become a cult of science.

As long as I'm on the subject, let me say that writings by evolutionists are abundant, and some of them predate Darwin. Those presenting an opposing view are, fortunately, increasing in number. They are not always an easy read, but the effort is worth it. I will list four that I have found helpful: *Darwin's Black Box* by Michael Behe; *Tornado in a Junkyard* by James Perloff; *A Case Against Accident and Self-Organization* by Dean L. Overman; and my favorite, *Darwinian Fairytales* by the late Australian philosopher David Stove. The more I examine it, the more Darwinian evolution seems to have become a science-based religion to be defended against all comers. It has become part of the Conventional Wisdom. If you watch nature programs on PBS, you are aware that evolution gets frequent mention as an accepted and indisputable fact. Global warming gets much the same uncritical treatment, and it will get even more now that our former vice president has been awarded the Nobel Peace Prize and picked up an Academy Award. (Lately, in 2010, the global warming assertion seemed to be falling on hard times, as the deceit underlying it becomes exposed.) None of the above is meant to deny evolution or climate change as such.

Thus far I have asserted that no religious or philosophical system has yet contrived a convincing explanation of human nature. This statement is, of course, debatable; but I will stick with it based on what I believe. The Hebrew Bible is the notable exception.

If there has ever been a coherent assessment of human nature that was completely positive and upbeat, I am unaware of it. There have been many "utopian" writings portraying much-improved societies; but the same type of people history has always shown us inhabit these societies. So if a Utopia is to be better, force, or at least heavy-handed persuasion, must do it. Utopias also have more than a whiff of socialism about them. (Thomas More's is the classic *Utopia,* but there have been others. Sir Francis Bacon wrote *The New Atlantis* and Tommaso Campanella *The City of the Sun*. In a real sense, Plato's *Republic* is a utopian work. An American, Edward Bellamy, created his own futuristic scenario in *Looking Backward,* in 1888. And Aldous Huxley's *Brave New World* was hardly a ringing endorsement of the future.)

Until someone informs me of the research proving the unqualified excellence of humanity, I must look to the dark side. First, a thoroughly secular figure, Frederick the Great, 18th-centry ruler of Prussia; and I believe he was next to the last to whom the term "great" was applied. (Catherine of Russia was probably the last. Remembering Herod and Alexander, Frederick was not in the best of company.) He apparently saw only the dark side. Speaking of his own kind, he said, "Deceit, bad faith and falsehood are sadly the dominant characteristics of most of the men who govern nations and who should be examples to their people. The study of the human heart is a truly humiliating subject." Of the generality of humanity he complained: "Human intelligence is feeble: more than three-quarters of mankind is made for slavery or the most absurd fanaticism. The fear of the devil or hell fascinates them, and they detest the wise man who attempts to enlighten them. The lion's share of our species is stupid and vicious. In vain I search for that image of God of which theologians assure us they carry the impression. In every man is a wild beast." (from *Frederick the Great* by Giles MacDonogh, pp. 190, 299.) This all reminds me of a poem by e. e. cummings, "Pity the Monster, Manunkind."

Ah, yes, that old image-of-God problem. This concept is the property of Western civilization. Is originated specifically in the writings of ancient Israel and was carried forward by Christianity. The famous story of the Fall is told in Genesis 3. This ostensibly religious story is has nothing to do with religion. I regard it as a parable or a bit of wisdom literature, but even if one takes it literally the point is the same. It does without all the fantastic and mythological trappings of other stories of origins, Hesiod's *Theogony* and *Works and Days* for example. The Genesis narrative is an attempt to provide a fundamental explanation for why humanity is the way it is. And I do insist this is not a religious matter. It might be called The Case of the Disappearing God. The God who appears in the early Genesis narratives is the Creator (and the case for Creation is looking better all the time.) This God is not described; he only creates, speaks, commands, and reproves. Most of all, He makes things happen. When Adam and Eve are shoved out of the Garden, they find themselves on their own, with no one to give them instructions about anything. The God with whom they formerly conversed is absent. The ignorance concerning human origins is complete, as is the ignorance of purpose or meaning. This is what St. Augustine called Original Sin, admittedly not a biblical term.

We are left with human beings who have no idea of their origin, no certitude about what they are to do here, no assurances concerning the future, an enfeebled ability to get along with one another, a propensity to evil – however it is defined – and an inability even to understand themselves thoroughly. We fortunately do not have to take the word of Genesis or the rest of the Bible for it. The historians, from Herodotus to now have told us. Today's psychologists and psychiatrists virtually shriek it at us. The economists know it, as do the sociologists. Artists have painted and sculpted it. Composers have celebrated or bemoaned it. The generals and their armies know it. And, best of all, the great literature has declared it. We have Homer's *Iliad*, the dramas of the Greek tragedians, the tragedies of Shakespeare, the *Essays* of Montaigne, *Gargantua* by Rabelais, the *Pensées* of Pascal, Milton's *Paradise Lost*, the novels of Dostoevsky, Tolstoy, Dickens, Thackeray, the less well known George Meredith, William Faulkner, and the darker writings of Mark Twain, to list a highly select few. Here is a statement that I found in novelist Iris Murdoch's *A Fairly Honorable Defeat* (p. 216)

> "What passes for human goodness is in reality a tiny phenomenon, messy, limited, truncated, and as I say, dull. Whereas evil.... reaches far far away into the depths of the human spirit and is connected with the deepest springs of human vitality."

> Anthony Burgess is even more pessimistic in this statement from *Earthly Powers* (p. 427): "Man has not been tainted from without by the prince of the Power of the Air. The evil was all in him and he was beyond hope and redemption."

> Should anyone need any convincing, a quick perusal of the 20th century should do the job.

Here I insert St. Paul's powerful case against human nature. It's from the second half of Romans 1; I do not think this section of verses, 18-32, forms part of the liturgical churches' annual lectionary.

> "[S]ince they did not see fit to acknowledge God, God gave them up to a base mind and to improper conduct. They were filled with all manner of wickedness, evil, covetousness, malice. Full of envy, murder, strife, deceit, insolent, haughty, boastful, inventors of evil, disobedient to parents, foolish, faithless, heartless, ruthless. Though they know God's decrees that those who do such things deserve to die, they not only

> do them but approve those who practice them." (Revised Standard Version)

Is this disagreeable? For a lot a people, it is, because they do not regard themselves as acting in such ways. Most of us don't. Honesty, however, forces us to admit that such actions and attitudes do exist, as all of human history, two world wars, and several holocausts testify. On the other side, it is true that most people do not spend their days indulging in contemptible behavior. They just go about their business, tying to make decent lives for themselves and their families. Within the limits of their knowledge, they are doing right, as the world around them defines right.

Is there a contradiction between St. Paul's indictment and the generally civilized human behavior we encounter every day? I do not believe so. The Apostle and theologians since his day spoke and wrote in terms of the God-Man relationship. The "total depravity" asserted by John Calvin is nothing more than the complete ignorance of God and the consequences that flow from it. Being unable to know the truly good, we must "assume a virtue," define good in any way we can, seek whatever meaning we can, and do the work of the world as best we can. (It would help to know what the work of the world really was.) There are no other options. I am not going to deal with those segments of the population who embrace evil deliberately, calling it good – who are we to be judgmental?

It is now time to admit there is a third obstacle to human wellbeing, an answer to why all the political, social, and economic systems devised over the millennia never achieve perfection: human nature itself in all its muddling ways, in all of its determination to perfect a world without the proper tools or talents.

Is there a solution? The religions have obviously not found one to provide a this-world cure. They insist on pointing us to the next world or to the nothingness of Nirvana. Christianity has, in my very partisan view, given the answer to what it means to be truly human; and it has done this despite carrying the awful burden of Christendom on its back. But Christianity has never given a blueprint for human society – only for the kind of people who should be living in it. "You are the light of the world," not the rebuilders of it.

No matter how much some Christians delight in singing the hymn by Jim Reeves, "This world is not my home, I am just passing through," it is on this earth that we live. This world is all we know about, however imperfect our knowledge is. Humans have always developed their institutions by trial and error. This process created the earliest economies, and by it also came government. That evanescent thing called progress also insinuated itself at some point. I firmly believe that humanity was not put on earth to be religious. At this point, among others, Islam and Christianity are polar opposites.

Progress describes the march of technological improvement. It does not apply to human behavior or to the arts. It certainly does not apply to religion or government. These may improve and change, but they may also revert and change back. Technology moves in one direction, forward. The wheel never needs to be reinvented; technology builds on itself, just as the sciences do. Technology is as fundamental to economic growth as capital formation, freedom of exchange, and the obligation of contracts. The lessons about all of these took humans a very long time to comprehend, and the end is not yet.

A great misconception about progress emerged in the West in the decades following the Napoleonic Wars. The view was abroad that the whole world was progressing and that humanity would see a new day, a heaven on earth. The obvious improvements and inventions of the 19th century encouraged this belief. Democracy made people feel freer, while schooling made them feel more self-sufficient and proud of their own accomplishments. Complainers about the plight of the working class, such as Marx, Ferdinand Lassalle, and Pierre-Joseph Proudhon, sought to assure the masses of a brighter future through proletarian revolution.

Social Darwinism, which did not originate with Darwin, took a different view. Utilizing the theory of evolution, it portrayed society going through a process of natural selection, after which only the fittest would survive. Herbert Spencer popularized this philosophy in England, while William Graham Sumner preached it in the United States. The latter's book, *What the Social Classes Owe Each Other* (1883), is a classic of its kind.

The dream of social progress came crashing to earth on August 4, 1914, and by the Armistice of November 11, 1918, nothing of it remained – except for the temporary triumph of Communism. Here, so many hoped and believed, was the promise of the future. The story of that great human tragedy has been so well told by others that there is no point in wandering over that old cemetery. Readers interested in the verdict of history on that system will find it brilliantly told by Martin Malia in *The Soviet Tragedy* and in *Requiem for Marx,* edited by Yuri N. Maltsev.

Robert Conquest sums up the drearier segments of the last century in *Reflections on a Ravaged Century.* A magnificent review of the whole 20th century has been undertaken by Paul Johnson in *Modern Times,* while a much grimmer version is presented in Niall Ferguson's *War of the World.*

Yet it was not all guns, bombs, and concentration camps. The telephone, the airplane, the radio, the automobile, television, and the computer, the cell phone, and the smartphone all came into their own. So we are back to technology. The medical profession made gigantic strides, as did the pharmaceutical industry. Better nutrition and the affordability of better food led to longer life expectancies and lower infant mortality rates. People affected by all the gloom and doom that pervade the news media and one of our political parties might well want to get a volume entitled *It's Getting Better All the Time: 100 Greatest Trends of the 20th Century* by Stephen Moore and Julian Simon. Why does such good news get so little popular acclaim, while the bad old ideas march on?

With all the good and the bad, my two pet demons - religion and government - linger on unreconstructed and reactionary, and contributing so little to the betterment of society. These two seem to darken or enervate the minds of mankind, preventing human beings from discovering their true self-interest. Now, self-interest is a variable; it belongs to the self and is quite subjective. (Self-interest is not selfishness until it degenerates.) With all the passions, lusts, desires, and appetites that enfold us and steer our actions, with all the voices calling out conflicting advice, with the huge diversity of information available, one wonders whether self-interest can be enlightened. Can the great mass of individuals that comprise a nation be guided by any outside force to perceive what will really make their lives good? If so, will the result be a peaceful and cooperative society?

It depends on incentives. These may be either subjective or objective. On the first page of Steven E. Landsburg's book, *The Armchair Economist,* he writes, "Most of economics can be summarized in four words: 'People respond to incentives.' The rest is commentary."

We all have the incentive to keep living, and we tie this incentive to our self-interest when we seek food and shelter and defend ourselves from harm. Such actions are common to all of humanity. Nor are incentives limited by economic activity, in spite of the quotation. Think, for instance of the word "temptation." It signifies an incentive to pursue flawed, often irrational, behavior: to choose what seems good, rather than what is really good. Tabloid newspapers are filled with stories of celebrities who, freed by wealth from any constraints, behave in the most self-destructive ways: drugs, alcohol, and promiscuous sex, to name the most popular. Then, to cover their tracks, they often embrace a popular "cause" to compensate for their guilt at having done so well in life.

The question arises: how can individual self-interest, always capable of error, sift through the plethora of incentives, evaluate them, and latch onto the precisely correct ones to serve that self-interest for genuine benefit? Must there not be some inner faculty that can assess and judge, weigh the incentives and pronounce them good or bad, helpful or harmful? After all I've already said, it would seem that such an inner faculty must also be flawed, unless it is conscience. Certainly there is an external "faculty." We can call it law, custom, or tradition.

Have these, singly or together, managed to provide a roadmap for positive human self-realization? The question either answers itself or must be left unanswered.

Now, to complicate this somewhat opaque narrative, let's return to the famous three: life, liberty, and the pursuit of happiness. As noted, we naturally seek to hang onto life and to better our individual circumstances. We do this within the confines of our abilities, talents, and imaginations in accord with the incentives presented to us and the circumstances in which we find ourselves. Since we all engage in the identical pursuit, for well or ill, may I suggest that this a general, pandemic, self-interest, since everyone shares it?

Yes, it is general, but the results are obviously not uniform. Within the general self-interest, individuals do not necessarily respond to incentives in the same way or get identical results. Nor do they necessarily perceive the same incentives, or perhaps they perceive them differently. An incentive, after all, is the first step toward a goal. We are differently endowed with abilities, for one thing. This alone rules out equal outcomes. In some persons ambition and the desire to achieve are paramount. Some are driven by the desire to know, others by the desire to produce. Some few see a challenge and respond to it – Lindbergh's flight to Paris comes to mind. Artists, writers, musicians, and actors work at their careers until they reach a desired level of excellence – or fail. The bulk of humanity simply does the work of the world and will not find itself written up in tabloid journals or anywhere else. And quite a few fall by the wayside, neither trying nor achieving.

Granted, all this goes well beyond just hanging onto life. I've inadvertently strayed into the pursuit of happiness. But can they be separated? Having a life and making something of it are very close. Just having the right to life achieves nothing, although it is a singular achievement for civilization to announce the fact after so many centuries.

With the pursuit of happiness, or the good life, we are back to subjective judgment. My happiness goal is not necessarily the same, or even similar to someone else's. I am sure that most people would be driven to distraction by my quality of life, satisfactory as it is to me. Conversely, I've not seen many other shoes I'd care to walk in. Envy is pointless. There must also be a large number of individuals who will never describe their lives as happy or contented in spite of striving, ambition, achievement, and wealth. We have all responded to specific incentives and made our ways accordingly. One of the problems any of us can have is the realization that it takes so long to be sure we made the right choices. For Christians, making choices is a faith-based operation, but that does not make the choosing easier.

No, I have not forgotten liberty. It is the rock upon which this whole discourse may well be shattered. In highly structured societies self-interest is naturally present, but the range of permissible incentives is necessarily narrow. Think of the feudal era of the Middle Ages or Stalin's Soviet Union. In fact, one can assert that for most of human existence the great bulk of any population lived quite circumscribed lives, confined mostly to making a living. The full development of potential was left to the privileged few who had the freedom to oppress.

Since the late-18th century American and French revolutions, this situation has changed markedly. Whole populations now have the option to fulfill themselves in ways of their own choosing. Such is one result of liberty. As the range of options has expanded exponentially, the variety of perceived incentives has swelled to previously unheard of proportions. Prosperity in the West has augmented the possibilities for most individuals.

This prosperity, accompanied by liberty, must be a good thing, since so many people emigrate from the world's many poverty traps to reach it. This suggests that there is a commonly shared desire for the good life. The question I am seeking to answer is: given a general common desire, can a general consensus of self interest ever be arrived at by a whole – or a large portion – of a given population. That is, can a whole population in a given country ever agree on what is really good for it? Are there shared values, as there once were in the United States? I do not know the answer, but my reading of history and human nature says no. And it looks unlikely in the United States for the foreseeable future.

It says no because I look at the many sources of incentives, and I realize there are many questionable sources. Consider a moment the recent history of China. Once a totalitarian society, Chairman Deng announced that to be rich is glorious. This was an incentive from the top. In other words, he changed the circumstances in which the population lived. The Chinese people have taken it to heart and have increased their prosperity beyond anything thought possible – or even permissible – during the Cultural Revolution. It remains to be seen whether this result will entail an expansion of political liberty, but if it does the results may very well be mixed, as society divides into mutually antagonistic factions. That is precisely what the Communist leadership fears.

Liberty does allow for a narrowing of self-interest, as well as an expansion of it. One has only to go back and read Madison's 10th Federalist to appreciate the easy division of society into interest groups, each of which wants what is best for itself. In so doing, a general consensus self-interest is negated. In a society as large and diverse as the United States, it is inconceivable to me that a consensus about the good life and how to achieve it is possible. We all belong to some interest group, if we realize it or not; and we do not relish seeing our private way of life threatened by other factions. Just look at the current tensions between physicians and the tort lawyers. The people are naturally caught in the middle: some few want to sue, while most want decent health care. This problem, like others, is only worsened when a large portion of the government takes sides.

This is just one illustration of the many things that go on above us, in government or the private sector, over which we have no control. Yet these powers manage to direct and distort our incentives, even if we only want to be left alone.

Many pages ago I mentioned Aristotle's conviction about how difficult it was for individuals to make choices that were really good for them, in contrast to choices that were only apparently good. Candy good, spinach bad is the choice any normal child will make. Adults can be just as inept in their choices, and they can persist in making the same kind of wrong choices until their lives end in a heap of rubble. Whole societies can err in the same way, as Europe has proved time and again, as have all the socialist experiments.

I think I'm making this too complicated. Let me summarize by saying that the outlet for individual self-interest is very much conditioned by the sociopolitical environment. For most of its history, the United States was a nation devoted to liberty. This allowed freedom for self-expression and self-fulfillment. The results were often negative, as liberty permitted license. (We did have a Wild West.) No other country has had such a degree of liberty under law (and lawlessness) to allow for personal growth. This nation alone had the institutions that made civilization possible – in the sense that I mean civilization. Simply, the direction an individual's self-interest takes is due mainly to the *circumstances* in which he finds himself. The population of China, under Deng, found itself confronted with a whole new set of circumstances.

Today, unfortunately, liberty is being constricted. Many citizens have latched onto the nefarious notion, propounded by Plato and Aristotle and continued by Fichte and Hegel, that the state (read, government) is humanity's greatest achievement. The entitlement mentality spreads, and it must be government that gives us that to which we feel entitled. Should this view become dominant, the country cannot remain either free or prosperous.

A comment by James Bovard seems appropriate here: "Politicians are dividing Americans into two classes – those who work for a living and those who vote for a living." (*The Austrian*, January-February 2016, p. 8)

Must the same old scenarios play themselves out repeatedly, or is it possible to move in new directions? I have no answer, not being a futurist. As far as religion in our day goes, people seem to live their lives in and around it, if they bother with it at all. (I am speaking here of institutional religion, not the human flaw.) Even the power of Hinduism has not proved an insuperable obstacle to economic progress in India. Those who live under the dead hand of medieval Islam are probably the worst off when it comes to the religious issue. In the West generally, and this includes Europe, North America, Australia, and New Zealand, the Christianity has been losing its hold for some time, thanks to Christendom. There are predictions that it will disappear in Europe altogether. Christianity, fortunately, is growing in some unlikely places, such as South Korea, Africa, and China.

That leaves us with what Albert Jay Nock years ago called *Our Enemy, The State*. It is ironic to recall that Marx had predicted the withering away of the state, with what results we know. More recent writers have been predicting the breakup of the all-powerful nation-state. James Dale Davidson and Lord William Rees-Mogg did so a few years back in *The Sovereign Individual*. The quirky machinations of Quebec in Canada lend some small credence to the opinion. There have been projections for a complete realignment of North America in what would amount to a wholesale secession from the mess in Washington. Would that it were so. Can Russia survive, can China, or even India? Indonesia has not remained in one piece.

At the end of Voltaire's one-joke novel *Candide,* the simpleton hero gets good advice: stay home and tend your own garden. There is merit in smaller political units. The ancient world had only small city-states, until warlords like Sargon began the empire building, which led to endless wars. The Roman Empire was in many ways an historical anomaly; it embraced so much and was at peace for so long, except on the borders. When it disintegrated, the smaller units reappeared, followed by more centuries of empire building. The results of those centuries have endured to the present. Jane Jacobs, in *Cities and the Wealth of Nations,* has praised the benefits of localism; because all economies are fundamentally local. There is really no such thing as a national economy, certainly not in so large a country as the United States, and perhaps not even in so small a state as Singapore. The United Kingdom is a collection of small economies, some rich, some middling, and some in desperate straits.

So we come back to the question: is a change of direction possible? Can the sociopolitical environment be altered? There is no doubt that if governments in every nation – starting in Europe and North America – got out of the way with their excessive taxes and over-regulation, the nations would flourish in some semblance of Adam Smith's system of natural liberty. Such a move would not require the spreading of any kind of enlightenment to the populations involved, only a change of circumstances. They have it within themselves to respond and take advantage of freedom under law, just as the Chinese have. (That seems to be diminishing.) And it must be freedom under law. A certain type of "institutional" garden is requisite if an economy is to flourish. Professor John P. Powelson, University of Colorado, has explained all this in his *Centuries of Economic Endeavor.*

Is the solution put forward in the previous paragraph enough? I do not believe so. Somewhere above I quoted a clergy acquaintance of mine: "You have minds, use them." That is the case: we all have minds. Are we willing to use them or shall we walk around with blinders on focused on only what is immediately before us – work and school and home and family – remaining in desperate ignorance of what we really ought to know and being incessantly bombarded by all the drivel the media pour out? We ought to know something valid for our own protection, at least.

Looking back over the results of schooling in the past 200 years, the results are not encouraging. Teaching is one thing, learning another. People will learn what they want to learn and forget the rest. The inspiration to be more must originate within. To "be all that you can be," as the Army recruitment slogan had it, is a self-generated process. A boy or girl can enter the Army and come out mature, or each can remain a boy or girl who has managed to conform to regulations. This brings me to the most audacious command Jesus gave. "You, therefore, must be perfect, as your heavenly Father is perfect." (Matthew 5:48, Revised Standard Version). This is not a religious command; it is a command to be fully human.

On the face of it, and in its context, this would seem to be a call to moral excellence. It may be that, but I believe it must be more. For one thing, God has no need for moral excellence: He is beyond that, not divided within Himself and forced to make choices after weighing the evidence, in spite of some peculiar passages in the Hebrew Bible. I suggest that this command – and it is a command, not a choice – means "be fulfilled," be accomplished, yes, be all that you can be. Make the most of whatever talents you have. This takes strenuous effort, more apparently than the bulk of the population is willing to exert. It's not enough to say, "Maybe next year," unless you are a baseball fan. Nor is it enough to be deeply specialized in one thing, while remaining ignorant of all else. All of us can marvel at individual excellence in one field, be it Michael Jordan in basketball, Babe Ruth in baseball, Vladimir Horowitz (or Victor Borge) at the piano, Mikhail Baryshnikov or Fred Astaire dancing, Ella Fitzgerald singing, Albert Einstein in physics, or the numerous talents that work in films or on stage. But the one-note life is stunted – and I am by no means implying that these are one-note people. Most of us are multi-note types, but the notes are so often small ineffectual ones.

In his novel *Rogue Herries,* Hugh Walpole has the following lines. (p. 462)

> "He supposed that in human beings there was always through life the search for fulfillment, and through life to death most men never found it. They managed well enough without it, had no time to speculate, snatched whatever substitutes they could find and made the most of them."

Is obeying this command for individual excellence within the realm of the possible for the majority of human beings? I do not know, because the possible belongs to the future. Is there any way to inculcate motivation? Obviously there is, or there would not be motivational speakers or sales conferences. How to reach a whole population, how to help them enlighten themselves about their true self-interest – now there's a challenge. Traditional teaching will not succeed, because the self must learn what it wants to learn. To do so, it must lift its eyes from the ground and look up at the wider world and ask itself: does this make sense and if not why not? One must also ask, does my life make sense, and if not, why not? After all, the best way to improve the world is to go home, look in the mirror, and straighten out the mess one sees there.

Talk to the animals – if only we could. But it could prove a significant embarrassment. Those creatures that have opportunity to examine us closely – our cats, dogs, and farm animals – may well have a few adverse comments. Kittens grow up to be cats, puppies become dogs, and foals become horses. They may well wonder why we can't do the same: grow up to be what we are supposed to be. Apart from stories, such as Orwell's marvelous *Animal Farm,* they do not sit and ponder the meaning of life, their goals, desires, and ambitions. They do not create for themselves stress, anxiety, and neuroses. They simply are what they are by nature and instinct. We hardly know our own nature.

So, having spent all these words, I am left with this. What shall it be: a little lower than the angels or a bit higher than the vermin?

There is no hidden door by which we can sneak back into Eden. But the United States would do well to resurrect its Constitution.

And finally, from George Orwell: "The fact to which we have to cling, as to a life-belt, is that it is possible to be a normal decent person and yet to be fully alive." (from a review of Cyril Connolly's *The Rock Pool,* July 23, 1936)

Chapter 20 There Is a Nonchalance

"Everyone, including the young, lived with the certain prospect of death, and no one believed it." C. P. Snow, in *A Coat of Varnish*

"In Philippe's eyes, the whole universe began at his head and ended at his feet, and the sun shown only for him." Balzac, *The Black Sheep*

"You believe you're making choices and all you're doing is slotting in the pieces of a foreordained conclusion." Ken Bruen, *London Boulevard*.

"Old age, if it's nothing else, should at least be theatrical, don't you know?" Martha Grimes, *The Old Contemptibles*.

"Those who depart from this world without knowing who they are or what they truly desire have no freedom here or hereafter". *Chandogya Upanishad*

"Now the trouble about trying to make yourself stupider that you really are, is that you very often succeed." C. S. Lewis, in *The Chronicles of Narnia*

"Alexander the Great and his mule driver both died, and the same thing happened to both. They were absorbed alike into the life force of the world or dissolved alike into atoms." (Marcus Aurelius, *Meditations*)

"I don't blame them [the younger generation], and I don't want to. They had a chance after the war that no generation ever had. There was a whole civilization to be saved and remade –and all they seem to do is play the fool." Evelyn Waugh, *Vile Bodies,* p. 183.

But at my back I always hear
Time's winged chariot hurrying near;
And yonder all before us lie
Deserts of vast eternity.
Andrew Marvell, "To His Coy Mistress."

"Poor and old is a terrible combination. You become so unimportant. Your past achievements are forgotten. No one believes you. Your life is trodden on by strangers. You've nothing to show anyone who you were." Christopher Fowler, *The Water Room*

"I go to seek a great perhaps." Attributed to Rabelais, as he lay dying.

Yet one more quotation from George Bernard Shaw, still from his Preface to *Androcles and the Lion*.

> "[We] pass our lives among people who, whatever creeds they may repeat, and in whatever temples they may avouch their respectability and wear their Sunday clothes, have robust consciences, and hunger and thirst, not for righteousness, but for rich feeding and comfort and respect and consideration: in short, for love and money." To think that this was written in 1915.

Getting fired from a job can bring on panic, anxiety, and fear – the usual effects of the fracturing of security. (I speak from experience here.) The future, once seemingly assured, is now blank and forbidding. In economic good times, of course, the likelihood of getting another job is great, as it was during the 1990s and the early 2000s; but it suddenly became less so after 2008. (After the election of 2016 the chances for employment improved a great deal, and suddenly there was a labor shortage.) But just being let go from a place where one had spent years of endeavor must still bring with it a flood of emotions. Blue-collar workers, who had counted on working in auto assembly plants until they retired, have been particularly hard hit. Their jobs were so often passed from one generation to the next. Now, they face a bleak future, since they and their union coerced the auto companies into becoming miniature welfare states, with all the failed promises that entails. As I continue this in 2016, the coal miners are worse off because the president wants to end coal mining in this country, regardless of the costs. President Trump has promised to reverse this decision, with what results time will reveal. The environmental movement would like to do away with all fossil fuels. What fuel would the airlines use? Imagine, no cars, no trains, no trucks. Must we really go back to the 14th century, as the Green New Deal of 2019 promises? If the program came to fruition, there would be one immediate problem – there would not be enough horses.

Breaking up is also hard to do; although it sometimes is quite easy for one of the partners. Sudden separation, especially in divorce cases, provides an outlet for all sorts of negative emotions, including anger, resentment, frustration, and some desire for revenge. Even in amicable breakups, there must be a few twinges. Again, security is disrupted, and the future is blank and bleak – at least for one partner.

We've all witnessed on television news shows the rapid loss of security for whole communities, as a result of tornadoes, hurricanes, floods, or earthquakes. The complete loss of all the artifacts of one's life cannot but have devastating effects. Much the same thing happens when a house burns down.

Disease also has a way of ruining one's life. We've seen the results of the AIDS epidemic. Worse, in my mind, is meeting or hearing of some young man or woman who has learned the terrible truth: "I have an inoperable cancer." Those of us well past our prime expect such things. That it should happen to the young and the handsome and the beautiful strikes one as utterly unjust.

The previous four paragraphs present a few of the events that can hit an individual unexpectedly and tear apart the fabric of his life. In some cases, we insure ourselves against these crises: health insurance, home insurance, earthquake insurance, flood insurance, and so forth. But we would all much prefer never to have to collect.

Acts of nature, losing one's job, breaking up, a fearful disease – these are all unexpected and painful interruptions. What, then, about the eventuality we can be absolutely sure of? We each arrive in this world at Point A, and we leave it at Point B. This is indisputable. How can we account for the carefree attitude about the inevitable termination of our time? Why is there a nonchalance toward dying, as though it were hardly of consequence? Here again, I have no answer, at least as it relates to Western society. In cultures that look upon our time on earth as a veil of tears to be escaped, the heedless attitude toward death can be partially understood. But only partially, because I believe even in these cultures there is a desire to hang onto life as long as possible. One need only see on television the tears and anguish after a plane crash, earthquake, or the 2004 tsunami in Japan to realize that even otherworldly religions fail in the most desperate situations.

I am not talking about the fear of imminent death that preoccupies the minds of those with terminal diseases, strokes, or heart attacks, nor about the fear that men in battle have. This is a proximate fear and to be expected. I am talking about the lifelong nonchalance of come-what-may, I'll always be around for the good times. And so I'll hoard as many of those times and the rewards I can gain, without paying any attention to the darkness at the end of the tunnel. This attitude is not prevalent within

Christianity, as the letters of St. Paul so well document. See especially the last verses of Romans 8. How the atheists feel about their own life endings, I have no idea. Materialists assume death is a complete ending. If they are right, we will never know. If they are wrong, we all will.

We watch our elected officials going about their business so seriously, each one certain that he or she is indispensable to the well being of society, as FDR thought he was until April 12, 1945 and as Adolf Hitler did until 12 days later. Each is determined to hold onto power and its rewards as long as possible. Charles de Gaulle said that the cemeteries are filled with indispensable men. Some religious officials are not much different from our elected ones.

One also cannot miss the propensity for fun that really dominates Western society. Fun became the operative word for how to live sometime after World War II. It replaced duty, obligation, honor, integrity, self-respect, and common sense for many of our citizens. Its pursuits are everywhere. That the young, of whom I must now be presumed to be envious, indulge themselves to such amazing extents is hardly surprising. It has ever been so. They know they will live forever. And suddenly they are old and out of it and looked at by the new young as irrelevant old croaks who should please get out of the way.

As I said, I don't have answer, but there may be a couple of plausible ones. If, as the evolutionists insist, we are merely animals made of the stuff of earth, the end is the end and should just be postponed as long as possible. The theory of evolution does not, to me at least, provide much of a basis for creating a culture or seeking a good life. But perhaps I've missed something. Maybe animals do what animals do, and that's the end of it.

There is little point in wasting space on reincarnation, but I'll waste some anyway. It has always seemed an absurd doctrine, but perhaps I am uninformed. As selves, we have a self-consciousness and a specific identity. If that is obliterated by death and some essence of self moves to another life form, what has happened to anything that can really be described as a self? If a self in one life commits offenses or performs good deeds that are to be punished or rewarded in another life, why would there be no consciousness of the past life and of a continued identity? How could the punishments or rewards have any justice involved in them? If self-consciousness has departed, where is the fact of guilt or fidelity to be located? What has happened to personal identity? Reincarnation weighs in for me somewhere between fatalism and hope.

There is another far more popular doctrine in the West, immortality of the soul, which has gained a very wide acceptance. This is not at all a biblical doctrine. (Read Mark 10 or Luke 18.) It was highly significant in ancient Egypt, and it played a role in the philosophy of Plato and his followers. The Old Testament seems to know nothing of it, although phrases about the departed are ambiguous at best. There is a brief indication of an afterlife in the Book of Job. The book of Daniel would seem to suggest some future life by implying resurrection, but this is not the same as immortality. The book of Ecclesiastes denies the whole concept. Nor is the immortality of the soul a New Testament doctrine, despite the many verses that can be made to fit. The New Testament does insist that God alone has immortality.

We know that we are mortal, and that is all we really know. Everything beyond that is a matter of speculation or faith. All the testimonies concerning near-death experiences prove precisely nothing. So much philosophy, so much theology, and so much religion have been summoned to allay fear of death and to propose palatable solutions. Nothing can be demonstrated, no matter how tightly held a belief. Christianity has proposed resurrection. In that I believe, else the whole body of belief collapses into pleasant ethical doctrines. St. Paul said it in I Corinthians: If there is no resurrection of the dead, our faith is in vain. He also said: Whether we live or whether we die, we are the Lord's. When Jesus said: "Go and sin no more," he must have meant something by it. Were death the absolute end, good and evil would be no more than a choice made for practical ends. And neither would have long-term personal consequences.

But resurrection of the dead does not mean or imply immortality of the soul. My own theory about resurrection is fairly simple, some would say simple-minded. The New Testament only gives us pictures heavily rooted in their own time and against the background of Jewish teaching in the intertestamental period. I believe that God is the God of the living, not of the dead. Secondly, I believe, along with the author of Hebrews, that we are surrounded by a great host of witnesses. Those whom we perceive has having died as Christians (and we cannot know for certain) leave the church militant and go to the church triumphant, and they do it now. To be alive in Christ is to be alive always. The notion of a resurrection at the last day, after individuals have been dead for years, centuries, or millennia is incomprehensible to me. It would mean a cessation of individual existence for whatever period of time involved. The counter-argument is that the immortal soul is floating around somewhere, waiting to be united with a new body. To each his own. We simply do not know, and "know" is the operative word.

For Christians, there is no nonchalance. There is only trust. In matters over which we have no control, trust is the only option.

So why the very prevalent nonchalance? Is it fatalism? Is it complete lack of concern for something that seems far removed – until old age creeps up or the guns of war start firing? Is it credulity, a conviction that no matter what, things will go well? Is it the silly notion that we'll leave it up to God to judge the quality and merits of our lives when He gets around to it? Worse, is it being taken in by certain spurious doctrines of the Christian religion, with false assurance of immortality or even more pernicious assurances that the church can somehow save us – when it cannot even save itself? Perhaps it is just "spirituality light," a self-delusion that "I am a good person." Once there is no chance to turn back, are there credits for good intentions? Or is their simply so much living to do that there is no time along the way to consider the end zone? (On good persons, also see Mark10 or Luke 18.)

Perhaps it is really simple. Nihilism was given a name back in the mid 19th century, but it is as old, at least, as ancient Israel. Then, in the period of the Judges, everyone did what was right in his own eyes. From the Latin *nihil,* meaning nothing, it connotes an attitude toward life much like that of Balzac's Phillipe, quoted above: it's all about me; and as an old rock song has it: It's My Life. This is the self centered on self and perceiving no greater good. It is, in the end, a life rooted in its own demise.

Perhaps the problem is nothing more than affluence. Individuals who have more than any previous society could offer by way of wealth would not seem to need what Christianity suggests. Vast, or even middling, wealth tends to focus the mind and keep it attentive. It also offers opportunities to do pretty much what one wants and to go anywhere. Should a wealthy individual feel guilty over his good fortune, there are always causes for the betterment of the rest of us to attend to. Jesus spoke of good news being preached to the poor, but he seemed to insist that wealth posed problems simply because it makes one so earthbound.

But I approach here an issue which has become a conundrum – the relation of the Biblical message to everything we know as culture and civilization. The relation of Christianity to popular culture is one I cannot deal with. I'll leave it for someone who can make sense of it.

So I'll leave the discussion with a few words from W. H. Auden's *For the Time Being.*

> Nothing can save us that is possible:
> We who must die demand a miracle.

Chapter 21 Civilization and Its Discontents, and finally, Adam Smith

This is the title of a book by Sigmund Freud, one that I read too long ago to recapitulate now.

> "At every step the history of civilization teaches us how slight and superficial a structure civilization is, and how precariously it is poised upon the apex of a never-extinct volcano of poor and oppressed barbarism, superstition, and ignorance." (Will Durant, History of Civilization, vol. 1, p.67)

Will Durant opens the first volume of his *History of Civilization* with two definitions of civilization. In the first, he incorporates all facets of a society – its literature, music, painting, sculpture, architecture, economy, religion, politics, legal system, and more. In the second he simply says that civilization is what people do between ice ages.

I prefer the latter definition but cannot completely agree with either one. There has been a lot of discussion over the centuries about culture, and the word civilization is thrown around with reckless abandon to describe every coherent, large, and fairly prosperous society since the last ice age.

Every society has a culture, the features of it that have emerged and grown up over the generations; for cultural creativity is inherent in human nature. All such cultures have similarities. They all have music and dance, along with costumes proper for the specific occasions. They have specific kinds of food. They all have their indigenous arts and crafts. The more advanced ones learned writing and created a literature. They all have religion, political and judicial systems, and economic arrangements. Cultures are strong, cemented by age-old ties and traditions that people will carry with them all their lives. Cultures can withstand wars and other disasters, and they can reconstitute themselves afterward. The wars and disasters become part of the communal memory – reflect for a moment on Homer's *Iliad,* Virgil's *Aeneid,* or the historical books of the Hebrew Bible.

Now, all large societies of the ancient world are called civilizations – that of Egypt, Mesopotamia, Greece, Rome, India, and China. There is a sense, I admit, in which the appellation is valid. They all were, or pretended to be, places where the respective populations could sometimes live together in peace and concord. Civility, is after all, the fundament of civilization.

But I desire to broaden the definition and at the same time make it more exclusive. I want to set aside the elements that pertain to culture in Durant's broader definition. Cultures are natural human developments, or growths, if you please. They are based in human nature itself. There is a propensity to create. Civilizations are built; they are the achievements and the rewards of much effort. Civilizations are the result of long processes of trial and error. Therefore I must be hesitant in awarding the unqualified honor of this distinction to the ancients. The so-called civilizations of the past were bottom heavy with poverty and oppression, as I've noted elsewhere in these pages. My definition is derived from Adam Smith's system of natural liberty, a system of broad freedoms for everyone. This is a very modern invention.

Smith developed this theme in Volume II of the *Wealth of Nations*, Book IV, chapter 9. "All systems either of preference or of restraint, therefore, being completely taken away, the obvious and simple system of natural liberty establishes itself of its own accord. Every man, as long as he does not violate the laws of justice, is left perfectly free to pursue his own interest his own way, and to bring both his industry and capital into competition with those of any other man, or order of men. The sovereign is completely discharged from a duty, in the attempting to perform which he must always be exposed to innumerable delusions, and for the proper performance of which no human wisdom or knowledge could ever be sufficient: the duty of superintending the industry of private people, and of directing it towards the employment most suitable to the interests of society. According to the system of natural liberty, the sovereign has only three duties to attend to; three duties of great importance indeed, but plain and intelligible to common understandings: first, the duty of protecting society from the violence and invasion of other independent societies; secondly, the duty of protecting, as far as possible, every member of society from the injustice or oppression of every other member of it, or the duty of establishing an exact administration of justice; and thirdly, the duty of erecting and maintaining certain public works and certain public institutions, which it can never be in the interest of any individual, or small number of individuals, to erect or maintain; because the profit could never repay the expense to any individual or small number of individuals, though it may frequently do much more than repay it to a great society."

Consider for a moment that Smith's work was published in 1776, and the U.S. Constitution was created eleven years later.

The streams that feed into this system of liberty are, in some cases, quite old. But they never met until the modern era. The system has several distinctive qualities: rule of law, the right to make contracts and have them honored, and freedom of exchange. This is obviously a mostly economic definition. It should be, because economic activity is what people do by nature. This system is very fragile; it can easily be shredded, as it was in many places during the 20th century. It is always facing threats in the United States, the first place where it came to fruition. To maintain a system of natural liberty takes continuous effort. As Jefferson remarked, "Eternal vigilance in the price of liberty." Most significant for our time is the insistence that government cannot run an economy without destroying liberty.

Why go way back to Adam Smith, whose book was published in 1776? Actually, it is a going forward. He is so far ahead of us, we may never catch up. As the powers of government increase, and as rights are diminished, the likelihood of ever attaining a system of natural liberty grows slimmer. P. J. O'Rourke has an appropriate comment: "Politics is unreceptive to the obvious and simple system of natural liberty" (*On the Wealth of Nations*, p. 154)

Liberty rejects any broad definition of equality, and it has no need of fraternity. Liberty also provides no guarantees of security. For this reason, those who live under it are often ready to bargain it away, just to gain more assurance of their place in society or to hold onto the gains they have made. Political systems tear at liberty always, because it undermines their power and prestige. Office holders want to run society, but a system of natural liberty can never be run from the top. Religious systems look askance at it, because they desire the honor of bestowing whatever security humans need. Rules are bent, laws are multiplied until they become impossible to honor. Bureaucrats regulate. Legislatures perceive crises where are none exists and determine to solve them. What crisis has government actually solved, compared to all those it has created? It has been truly said that government solutions only create problems. Recall President Reagan's comment: "The most ominous words in the English language – 'I'm from the government and I'm here to help'"

The discontents of civilization originate within it. Its main flaw is that it is always a work in progress. Unlike the much-ballyhooed utopian systems we've heard about, civilization can never reach perfection, it can never create the new humanity that Communism promised, or even that National Socialism envisioned. It is an ongoing battle with itself just to stay on a relatively steady course. This makes it unsatisfactory for all those who would like a sound finished product they can rely on in perpetuity.

This can never be. It is impossible to get perfect and equal outcomes from a wholly imperfect humanity. There will always be economic upturns and downturns; there will always be wars; there will always be crime and civil strife. There is simply no gated community to provide the permanent protection and security that people desire. The discussion of human nature has already proved it. Human beings themselves are unfinished products. Civilization can not be planned, any more than can the good life.

Will Durant made a few comments worth quoting on the fragility of civilization. "Civilization is the precarious labor and luxury of a minority; the basic masses of mankind hardly change from millennium to millennium." (Vol. I, p. 59) "From barbarism to civilization requires a century; from civilization to barbarism needs but a day." (Reformation volume, p. 190)

For an example bearing out the last quotation, consider Germany in 1933, as Chancellor Hitler took office. Culture survived, civilization (supposing there was any) disappeared; and it only took a matter of months. The Soviet experiment was even worse. In China, the certifiably insane Mao determined to obliterate Chinese culture. He did not live long enough to do so, and recently there has been a revival of its ancient roots. President Xi, in 2019, seems determined to prove that his version of National Socialism cannot work by making untenable and unworkable economic decisions, based naturally on the conviction that government knows all.

Culture, thus, is forever. Liberty is a chancy proposition. It takes guts to keep it going. It also takes good schooling, resolve, and never-ceasing effort, because it is always a potentially losing battle. Culture is exclusive to a specific society. Civilization cannot be so quantified. It is open to anyone who wants to participate. It knows no ethnic, social, economic, or religious limits. It breaks down all such barriers, just as Christianity does. But everyone must play by its few rules. It invites cooperation, not strife. It is the world's only peaceable kingdom. Only the king is absent. I wonder if it too strong an assertion to say that the free-market economy is the basis of civilization, because it too breaks down all humanly-devised barriers.

Based on my restrictive definition, I find very few civilized places in the world today. In Europe, culture dominates, but civilization is weak and always has been. Since World War II the question has often been asked: How could German civilization have fallen for Hitler? The answer is: It didn't; its culture made Germany wide open to his arrival, and that really happened during World War I. Latin America, South-central Asia, and Africa are rife with culture. So is the Far East. Whether the great "civilization" of China will ever attain to the real thing is too early to tell. Signs are ambiguous. Japan tried to make a go of civilization but failed; its government was too domineering. It loved authority, feared freedom, and embraced tribalism too much. Russia is a shambles; few of the necessary ingredients for civilization are present, despite its great historical cultural achievements. In North America civilization hangs on, but it has been under constant attack for most of the last century. The chance for survival is anyone's guess. Meanwhile much of its culture has descended into an abyss.

For a whole population to be devoted to a system of liberty is difficult in the best of times, as Durant implies.

The system offers so many challenges, but people do not necessarily love the kind of challenges it presents. In all societies that I am aware of, the stability and security offered by the accoutrements of culture will prevail over the insecurity and dynamism of civilization, if push comes to shove. In those vast areas of the globe that have never quite reached civilization, one can understand the powerful hold of centuries of cultural conditioning. One can even respect, if not admire, the number of adherents Stalin still has in Russia or the occasional wistful longing for Juan Peron in Argentina. The powerful hold of religion is apparent in the Muslim lands as well as in India. Where institutional religion is weak, as in the West, the equally powerful hold of politics as its counterpart is as great. In his volume on *The Age of Reason,* Durant said, "The conflict of religious creeds has given way to the conflict of political creeds." (p. 554).

Religion and government are both integral to culture. Neither pertains to a system of liberty, although such a system can flourish with them, but without their aid. Religion, politics, and civilization each operate according to a specific set of rules and norms. So we are faced, at the end, with the same issue: the two obstacles to human well being. To which we must add the third, human nature itself, which has such a tough time assessing its own best interests.

Is it plausible that a large population cannot deal successfully with liberty, when it involves taking responsibility? The free-market economy, which is this system of liberty, has consistently been criticized for its uneven results, the fact that great disparities of wealth persist. But there are disparities of talent, ability, intelligence, and ambition as well. Every system of Marxist derivation that has tried to leapfrog over these human disparities has failed. Equality of conditions is an unattainable goal and an undesirable one. The problem is not that Smith's system of liberty is flawed. It is that human nature is flawed but unwilling to admit that no type of perfect sociopolitical arrangement can be devised to mask the fact.

Is there an underlying cause for the decline of civilization? One may want to look at government itself as a plausible cause.

Chapter 22 Isn't It Romantic?

"It is not only what we have inherited from our fathers and mothers that exists again in us, but all sorts of old dead ideas and all kinds of dead beliefs and things of that kind. They are not actually alive in us; but there they are dormant all the same, and we can never be rid of them." (Henrik Ibsen, in *Ghosts*, Act II)

"But anyone who after the twentieth century still thinks that thoroughgoing socialism, nationalism, imperialism, mobilization, central planning, regulation, zoning, price controls, tax policy, labor unions, business cartels, government spending, intrusive policing, adventurism in foreign policy, faith in entangling religion and politics, or most of the thoroughgoing nineteenth-century proposals for government action are still neat, harmless ideas for improving our lives is not paying attention." (Deirdre N. McCloskey, *The Bourgeois Virtues*, pp. 50-51)

"The more I see of the world, the less hope I have that humanity as a whole will ever become wise and happy. Among the millions of worlds which exist, there may, perhaps, be one which can boast of such a state of affairs, but given the constitution of our world, I see as little hope for us as for the Sicilian in his." (Goethe, *Italian Journey,* Letter to Herder, May 17, 1788)

"A fault we must never again commit is to forget, once the war is over, the advantages of the autarkic economy." (*Hitler's Table Talk,* ed. By Hugh Trevor-Roper, p. 73.)

"I don't interfere in matters of belief. Therefore I can't allow churchmen to interfere with temporal affairs. The organized lie must be smashed. The State must remain the absolute master." (*Hitler's Table Talk,* p. 143)

"I always believed that America's government was a unique political system – one designed by geniuses so that it could be run by idiots. I was wrong. No system can be smart enough to survive this level of incompetence and recklessness by the people charged to run it." Thomas Friedman, quoted in *Forbes,* Nov. 10, 2008.

And, finally, from Turgenev's *Fathers and Sons.*

> "He's a nihilist," repeated Arkady.
>
> "A nihilist," said Nikolai Petrovitch. "That's from the Latin, *nihil, nothing*, as far as I can judge; the word must mean a man who… who accepts nothing.?"
>
> "Say, 'who respects nothing,' " put in Pavel Petrovitch (chapter 5).
>
> "There are no general principles – you've not made that out even yet! There are feelings. Everything depends on them." (Chapter 21).

If government is the primary new-age god, should it not have the attributes that belong to divinity – omnipotence, omnipresence, and omniscience? All governments do well on the first two. China, North Korea, Cuba and Russia are the most effective, and the United States is rapidly catching up. The dictatorships are also trying to become omniscient. The point of having all three characteristics is to demonstrate to citizens that government is all that matters. For party-line Democrats and Republicans in the United States, this seems to be a conviction. Unfortunately, genuine omniscience is not possible for any government. It is certainly impossible when it comes to running an economy, as has been shown by the former Soviet Union and today's Cuba and Venezuela.

No, it isn't romantic any more. It is all about power .It is certainly not so for many elected officials and bureaucrats whose great desire is to get a stranglehold on the American economy and run it as a command and control system. All Marxist "reforms" have proved worthless. The delusions persist among the "better informed," of course, but socialism and communism have proved unworkable both in theory and practice. National Socialism, under which most nations now live, has more durability, because it has generally been put over incrementally among apathetic and ignorant populations. The fact that, so soon after the fall of Communism, National Socialism is in a state of crisis is surprising. I thought it would take longer. As of now, all the governments in the West are getting stronger and intruding into each citizen's life increasingly. That is precisely the problem, as – with all their power – they cannot solve the dire economic problems of the respective societies for the benefit of all citizens.

Europe is in a double bind. Its citizens depend on government to take care of them – a fatuous promise if there ever was one; and each nation has its own Islamic threat living within it and growing bolder every day. The Europeans have grown so apathetic in their social democracies that they no longer have the will or the courage to defend themselves against enemies without or within. One would hope that the United States would extract itself militarily and never return to extricate the foolish from their folly. Two world wars were enough.

Speaking of Europe, I recently had the pleasure of reading a remarkable book called *The Middle Sea: A History of the Mediterranean,* by John Julius Norwich. In the closing chapter he has the following sentences: "Some six or seven thousand years ago the Mediterranean gave birth to Western Civilization as we know it. Its relatively small size, its confined shape, the gentleness of its climate, the blessed fertility and the manifold indentations of its European and Asiatic shore, all combined to provide a uniquely protective environment in which its various peoples could develop and flourish."

Somehow they did, but what a struggle it was. From beginning to end, the book is a chronicle of endless wars and massacres, especially so once one reaches the Middle Ages. One it tempted to ask: has the region ever had good government? My answer would be no, with the slight qualification of Napoleon. When he wasn't waging war, he did prove an able administrator. And the less said of the medieval popes the better. Neither Christendom nor Islam proved themselves friends of humanity, and the latter does not do so to this day. Today Europe is governed by a stifling national socialism under an incredibly corrupt bureaucracy, which the various populations are apparently unwilling to abandon. Security trumps freedom. The unwillingness to allow open economies is the greatest weakness. I wonder if they know how.

In the United States, the federal government has, ever since 1887, found a way to interpret the Commerce Clause of the Constitution as entitling it to manage the economy. Clauses that were intended as limits have been turned into avenues of more and more control. And every piece of legislation, every administrative ruling, and every court decision is premised on good intentions, as doing the right moral thing.

Today it is no longer a question of imposing an ideology; it is a matter of attaining power and holding it at any cost. The unworkable ideologies and party lines are trotted out during election campaigns, with the intent of fooling all the people all the time. Somehow it works; while the populace, distracted by making a living and enjoying itself, is led incrementally down the garden path.

If a large enough segment of our population ever accepts the fraudulent notion that "everything is political," it will become so. How ironic it is that in the early 21st century there is more information available about everything than ever before, while at the same time we have generations that are more ignorant than at any time in the recent past. I'd like to see any college senior pass the 8th grade tests that my parents did a century ago.

How sad, to write so many words and pose so many problems, and be unable to speak of solutions. That's not the way it's supposed to work. But I never intended to write a self-help book to clutter up the best-seller list with. And this certainly won't. So, where are we?

Chapter 23 The Road to Dystopia

It's not a road picture with Hope, Crosby, and Lamour. There is no song, nor are there camels, as in *The Road to Morocco*. It's where we are headed, and where large segments of the world have arrived.

In my *Webster's New Collegiate Dictionary*, dystopia is defined as "an imaginary place which is depressingly wretched and whose people lead a fearful existence." Let's forget the word "imaginary," and picture to ourselves Cuba, Venezuela, Zimbabwe, Somalia, North Korea, Syria, or the Sudan. Dystopia is considered the opposite of Utopia, which means one of two things: either it is no place, or it is a place of general human well-being, depending on which Greek-based prefix is meant by the U. In the literature about it, Utopia is nearly always presented as an ideal country, although my reading of them must have missed something. They are basically slave states, or nations in which government calls all the shots. Thomas More's 1516 book *Utopia* is, I believe the first to use the word in the title: it's not a very appealing read, but it may well have been when it was published.

The 19th-century utopian experiments in the United States nearly all failed. The Amana Colony Iowa still exists; but it is a well-run business enterprise and not a closed utopian society. The glorious 20th-century utopias – Mussolini's Italy, Lenin and Stalin's Soviet Union, Hitler's 1000-year Reich, Mao's Great Leap Forward, Castro's Cuba so beloved of the Hollywood crowd, Venezuela's dreadful condition, and many lesser but disastrous experiments (read, dictatorships) all have failed. Cuba and North Korea hang on by dint of sheer idiocy. The Muslim societies do not present themselves as utopias, and they certainly aren't. Why is it that when Muslims flee war zones such as Syria, they do not go to other Muslim nations? They go to Europe or the United States.

Can one not conclude, therefore, that dystopia and utopia are identical in outcome? The nations of the West are marching along in a National Socialist parade, on the way to who knows what. In the United States a new crop of Democratic Socialists is on the march to go the whole Soviet way. The malevolent effort by governments to control everything is far advanced, more so in Europe than here, although one of our political parties is determined that we emulate Europe in all its follies. Why? Because in Europe everything is political. Some of our politicians have alleged the same. If the population of the United States becomes satisfied with this idea, we will have arrived. How ironic it would be to see China, India, and even Vietnam heading the other way. I was delighted to find, in *The Economist* of October 24, 2009, the following statement: "Even if John Galt is under threat in the West, he is back in business in China and India." Galt is the protagonist in Ayn Rand's *Atlas Shrugged,* and the article mentioned was a commemoration of the 50th anniversary of its publication.

Which brings me, finally, to the end of this undertaking.

As I write in early 2019, twenty-one years after starting, the United States has elected and re-elected its first black president. That, in itself, is a stunning achievement, one that must pain the race-baiters such as Jesse Jackson and Al Sharpton no end. At the same time, a severe economic crisis has erupted – although years in the making. So the country elected a man of the far Left just as news reports are daily wondering whether there can be another Great Depression. Then, surprisingly, in 2016, voters elected someone who sought to undo the previous eight years.

The outcome of all this is not predictable, but there are unwelcome signs. The *Economist* of October 18-24, 2016, had on its cover the headline "Capitalism at Bay." As with the Depression I grew up in, the politicians will eagerly blame the private sector, the place where most of us live and work, for the crisis and seek to bring it under even more control. (Parenthetically, I recall a local television news interview with Bobby Rush, a former Black Panther thug who now represents an Illinois district in Congress. He stated: "Remember, the private sector is the enemy." Such rare truth-telling by a Democrat is remarkable. It was restated by vice-president elect Joe Biden during the recent campaign of 2012 to his union and lawyer supporters.)

All recessions and depressions are manufactured in our nation's capital, by presidential administrations, the Federal Reserve, and Congress. This was clearly demonstrated a century ago by Ludwig von Mises in his *Theory of Money and Credit*. When the crisis arrives the guilty parties in government all stand around in wonder, assuring themselves they had nothing to do with it. It was all those evil capitalists. This big lie got great play during the Great Depression: FDR constantly returned to it. It is making great headway today, as Congress conducts a series of show trials, hauling the allegedly greedy executives before it. Anyone wanting to understand how the mess happened would do well to get two books already mentioned. Charles Gasparino's *The Sellout* reads like a novel, a very good one. For analysis by a first-rate economist, there is John B. Taylor's *Getting Off Track: How Government Actions and Interventions Caused, Prolonged, ad Worsened the Financial Crisis*. Taylor followed that up with *First Principles: Five Keys to Restoring America's Prosperity* in 2012. It's unlikely his recommendations will be accepted in Washington.

In fact, the market system worked quite well. The market will not be foiled forever; eventually it will get its revenge, and it is already proving painful all across the world. What is probably saddest about the whole sorry episode it that members of both political parties know that their regulatory fiascoes do not work, any more than high taxes bring in more revenue. The fact is, they don't care. The well-being of the country is of some interest to them; but holding onto power is the name of the game, and they will do it at all costs. Decades ago, Speaker of the House Sam Rayburn asserted that the first duty of a Congressman is to get re-elected. Are we in for a resurgence of National Socialism, piling failure upon failure? Nothing succeeds like failure in Washington. And the indifference or even contempt of the ruling class for the American people is potent if not always evident. The public is beginning to return the favor.

The Thirteenth Amendment to the Constitution expressly forbids anyone from owning slaves, but it does not forbid the Federal Government from enslaving a whole population.

Karl Marx is reported to have said that history repeats itself, first as tragedy, the second time as farce. Is the farce about to begin? And will it end in tragedy?

The signs are ominous. In *The Economist* for March 14, 2009, there were articles on policies in France and Germany dealing with the crisis. From the article on France: "In one respect, at least, the global downturn is welcome in France: it has legitimized economic interventionism in the land where Louis XIV's finance minister, Jean-Baptiste Colbert, invented it under the term *dirigisme*." In Germany the trend is much the same, although there were dissenting voices.

In the United States the Roosevelt administration that came to office in 1933 proved to be a definitive break with previous political and economic arrangements. That break would have been more severe had the Supreme Court not struck down the National Industrial Recovery Act of 1933, legislation that would have imposed full-blown National Socialism. That break was modified and softened in subsequent decades but could have become permanent with the Obama administration, had not his successor reversed some of Obama's policies. It is possible that the federal government will dig a hole with its debt burden that the country can never crawl out of and impose taxes the people cannot pay. If the government had all of our money, it would still want more.

If capitalism is at bay, as noted above, what can one say of National Socialism? Who could have imagined that so soon after the collapse of Communism, the systems inherited from World War II would find themselves in crisis. The economies based on the absurdity of John Maynard Keynes are thrashing around, hoping to find ways to save themselves from collapse. The leaders in these countries cannot admit that the principles on which they operate are wrong – perhaps they don't even know it. A century of error is hard to rectify.

Solutions, are there any? The escape from religion is into Christianity. From government there is none, except into freedom. One can hope for an informed citizenry to force responsibility and accountability in government, but from where I sit that seems unlikely to be forthcoming.

Before the end, another quotation from Ralph Gabriel's *The Course of American Democratic Thought,* p. 403. "The Constitution represents a government of law. There is only one other form of authority and that is a government of force. Americans must take their choice between the two. One signifies justice and liberty; the other tyranny and oppression. To live under the American Constitution is the greatest political privilege that was ever accorded to the human race." And from Jim Powell: "Wherever there is dictatorial power over an economy, wherever economic liberty is denied, people are sure to be suffering the agonies of the damned." (p. 266)

Finally. The untenable notion that enduring good government is possible was born here in the United States, and here it died. The constitutional republic designed by the convention of 1787 no longer exists. After the Constitutional Convention, Benjamin Franklin was asked what it had achieved. His answer: "A republic, if you can keep it." As noted above, the slide away from it was slow and incremental. The point has been made that governments exist for themselves alone. There is a cliché that experience is the best teacher. If, after 6,000 years of government failure, malevolence, and disaster, humanity has learned nothing, apparently experience isn't worth much. The historical record is clear, but who bothers with history any more? The Roman senator Cicero wrote that not to know history is to remain forever a child. Yet the conviction persists in all places that government can do good things. Barbara Tuchman's book title, *The March of Folly*, would serve as well as a description of the course (and curse) of the ruling powers from Babylonia until now.

So, where are we now? We are back where it all began in Mesopotamia with Sargon I about 1850 BC. Government is all that matters. It has always mattered to itself, but there was a brief window of opportunity for a turnaround at the end of the 18th century with ratification of the United States Constitution as a limit on the power of the state. But governments grow incrementally. And as more demands are made of it by a well-meaning public, its powers increase until it has a hand in almost every sphere of life. It is now evident that, in the view of office holders, the purpose of the citizenry is to support the government and bow to its will. The end is the destruction of civil society, when everything really does become political. What is civil society? It was defined by Tocqueville as freedom of association. It is also the freedom to think, speak, and write without being censored – or worse yet, imprisoned.

Since writing the last few paragraphs, something strange happened in the United States: Donald Trump was elected president against all expectations. A stridently pro-American president has caused outrage among members of the opposition party and a lot of Republicans.

Had a Democrat won, there would have been no protests or marches, and the media would have embraced Mrs. Clinton with nothing but positive news coverage. With Mr. Trump it has been quite the opposite: and ongoing campaign of rage and hate. And with Congress, unfortunately, it continues to be mostly business as usual. With only two years of his administration ending, how his effort will play out cannot be known. I suspect that when the Democratic Party once again gains control of the federal government, we will soon be back on the road to Utopia. And the Republicans will do their go-along to get-along dance.

The negativity of the previous paragraphs owes much to the fact that I have lived in Illinois most of my life. Back in 1952, when Adlai Stevenson was the Democratic candidate for president, he remarked that "Cleanliness is said to be next to godliness; in Springfield it is next to impossible." That grim situation has worsened a good deal in the intervening decades. The Democrats and their Republican go-along, get-along stooges have dragged the state down to the gutter. Why? Because the public employee unions are the main constituency of the Democratic Party, and it is the people who live and work in the private sector who have been made responsible for paying for the lifetime support of government employees. So, in Illinois it is the government that matters, although it is the institution that made the mess in the first place.

The public employee pension problem is a serious one, as many states have discovered. But the whole series of entitlement programs, both federal and state, pose an equally significant threat to government budgets. How did this arrangement for the government to take care of everyone originate, apart from the obvious fact that legislation such as Social Security and Medicare are primarily vote-buying schemes?

Tracing historical causes is a very uncertain procedure, but I will focus on one plausible reason for the development of the welfare state in the United States: the very badly executed free-market economy. (I prefer that term over capitalism, of which there are at least three varieties – free-market, state, and crony.) Now, the free-market economy, as it developed from the late 18th century to the present, has definitely been responsible for enormous improvements in the living conditions for millions of people. That is its virtue, and it has been so explained by authors ranging from Adam Smith, Carl Menger, Ludwig von Mises, Friedrich Hayek, Milton Friedman, and others. It is not the merits of the system that are questionable; it is the misuse by so many of its adherents over the past 200 years.

The misuse is summed up in one word – greed. The owners of factories, mines, and railroads were determined to become wealthy at the expense of their employees. Workers, some of whom were very young children, were paid barely subsistence wages. Attempts by workers to form unions were fought by the owners and assisted by governments. It is hardly any wonder that the cure for this situation became a call for socialism. In the United States, ending the exploitation of workers began early in the 20th century, during the presidency of Theodore Roosevelt and continued with his successors – primarily his cousin Franklin D. Roosevelt. There are so many histories of this era that repeating them here would be redundant, as well as lengthening this work needlessly.

The negative side of ending worker exploitation was the growth of the welfare state with its numerous entitlement programs. Accompanying this was the over-regulation of business, based largely on the very bad economics of John Maynard Keynes and the zealous New Dealers. Critiques of his theories can be found in a number of books, one of the more recent being *Where Keynes Went Wrong* by Hunter Lewis (2009). From Keynes politicians got the notion that governments can run an economy. Jane Jacobs demolished this nonsense quite effectively in her *Systems of Survival.*

The most ineffective attempts by government fall under the umbrella of socialism. Demands for it arose as early as the 1790s and continue to this day, despite the overwhelming evidence of its failure: the Soviet Union, Cuba, North Korea, Venezuela, to name a few. Great Britain came close to economic collapse, before Margaret Thatcher's policies turned the economy around. Reasons for socialism's failures are many, but one of its ironic results is that it works very well for those at the top – the politicians and their cronies; and it works badly for the citizens who have to live under it. Ironic, because this is precisely why the free-market economy was demonized.

Enough. It's time to end this thing. Genesis 1:1 states that "In the beginning God created the heavens and the earth." Verse 25 says "And God saw that it was good." The creation remained good; it was humanity that decided it would choose what was apparently good, rather than what was really good. The same can be said for the United States. Whether it was a good nation I leave for others to decide. That it was Lincoln's "last best hope of earth" there is no doubt. The history of immigration alone proves that.

Whether the country will remain the home of liberty and prosperity is very uncertain now. It can be if the citizens want it.

There's an echo of Aristotle here. But the fact persists: humanity cannot ever attain what is really good for itself any more. There will never be a perfect government, economy, or society in spite of the unwarranted romantic optimism of some politicians or their citizens at large.

In 1990 Milton Friedman published *Free to Choose,* a volume on economics that became the basis for a TV series on PBS. The title is worth considering. Christians are free to choose a separation from Christendom. Citizens are free to choose liberty over tyranny. Humanity can choose to be less optimistic about itself and its potential. But are we really free to choose? I end with four words that appeared in the Chicago Tribune on 3/10/19, "History is not inevitable."

About the author.

Mr. Moquin's first job for Encyclopaedia Britannica was as associate editor of the 20-volume set, *Annals of America.* After this he compiled and edited the materials to be included in the 10-volume *Makers of America,* documenting immigration and ethnicity in the United States from the 16th to the late 20th century. He then compiled and edited the materials for four one-volume books published by Praeger Publishers in New York. These were *Documentary History of Mexican Americans, Great Documents in American Indian History* (before they were called Native Americans), *Documentary History of Italian Americans,* and *The American Way of Crime.* In retirement he found another career as an indexer of textbooks in economics.

Index

CPSIA information can be obtained
at www.ICGtesting.com
Printed in the USA
BVHW071238220719
554055BV00004B/210/P